FROM
DARK
TO
LIGHT

FROM
DARK
TO
LIGHT

A MODERN MYSTIC'S GUIDE
TO HEALING THE SHADOW
& EMBRACING THE LIGHT

BELINDA DAVIDSON

MAYNARD BOOKS

FROM DARK TO LIGHT: A Modern Mystic's Guide to Healing the Shadow & Embracing the Light

ISBN: 978-0-6480831-0-8

Published by: Maynard Books, 2017

First edition, 2017

Cover design by: Jo Klima
Cover photos: Broderick Photography

*To Jean
and Tanya Eva*

CONTENTS

INTRODUCTION

I WAS BORN EXCEPTIONALLY psychic. For as long as I can remember, I've been able to know all about a person by looking inside them. I've also always been able to remember my life on the Other Side, as well as the experience of being born into this lifetime as Belinda.

This doesn't make me exceptional, though. Most children are born knowing things, born sensitive and intuitive, and still remembering our homes and lives on the Other Side. But what *was* exceptional about me is that, for whatever reason, my psychic and intuitive abilities didn't decrease as I grew older. Instead of beginning to *forget* about my life on the Other Side, instead of beginning to *lose* my psychic and intuitive sensitivities, they grew stronger. With every passing year I remembered more, I saw more. And I retained memories about my life *before* this life, which other children seemed to lose.

Because of this, growing up I felt like a foreigner. I felt like a stranger in this world. Feeling displaced and estranged because I'd learned that seeing inside people was bad, and that talking about what I saw inside people was even worse. I learned it wasn't right or good to know things and see things like angels, ghosts, energy, and people's thoughts and feelings; and it was frowned upon (and punishable) to be deep-feeling and aware. I didn't want to be shunned; I wanted to be loved. So I grew up pretending to be someone else. I pretended not to see and know what I did. Yet I couldn't help seeing what I did, and knowing what I knew . . .

Until, in my late teens, I discovered that my gifts could help others. I discovered that my psychic and intuitive abilities, although unusual, could bring me *closer* to others by helping them. I learned that I could connect to others through my gifts. And when others began confiding in me, telling me they were like me but were scared to come out of the (spiritual) closet, I realized I wasn't alone. There are others who are sensitive and intuitive; others who also feel estranged here on earth. Other men and women and children who feel lonely and sad and far away from where they began as light and love.

Nowadays I call the sensitives amongst us the *modern mystics*. We are the intuitives, the empaths, the mediums, and the seers; we are the healers, the shamans, the witches, and the light workers. We are the ones born with feet in both worlds, and the ones who often suffer because we don't know how to live and navigate between these worlds.

As I travel, teaching, speaking, and connecting, I meet more and more modern mystics every day. More of us are coming out of the shadows and wanting to step into the light, but we don't know how to begin. We know something isn't right—we know we need to change and heal our lives. We know we need to embrace our intuitive gifts and abilities, but we don't know how to get started.

That is why I wrote this book, the first in the Shadow Series.

You can think of *From Dark to Light* as a manual—a guide for modern mystics on how to get balanced, aligned, and in greater touch with your own psychic and intuitive capabilities, whatever form they take. Once you do that, you'll discover your soul's purpose for being here at this time, and you can start to use your mystical skills to accomplish it.

It's my sincerest wish that this book and the techniques in it bring you comfort, clarity, and purpose.

In White Light + Love,
Belinda

PART ONE

FROM DARK
TO LIGHT

CHAPTER 1

INCARNATION

MOST OF US DON'T remember our time as infants, let alone the months spent in our mothers' wombs. We don't recall our earliest days, our first joys, or our sorrows. Most of us. But for whatever reason, I do. I remember being in utero and being born, and I remember coming into this world filled with fear.

During my gestation, I felt the lightness of my spirit-form fade to dark as my vibrations were pulled down like an anchor to the earth plane. I remember dreading the heaviness of the world, its violence and aggression, and knowing that here I would feel trapped and lonely. And it was with this sadness that my soul began its incarnation as Belinda Davidson.

I came here carrying another ache, as well—one that belonged not to me, but to my mum, who was grieving the loss of her own mother.

Nine months before, I'd been hurriedly conceived in the hopes that I would meet my Grandma Jean, who was dying of cancer. She and Mum wanted the three of us to have time together before her departure, but a meeting in this place was not to be. My grandmother died five months before I was born. Instead, we bonded in another way.

In the final stages of her illness, Grandma Jean looked at my mum clutching a list of baby names and told her she only needed to consider the ones for girls. You see, Grandma Jean was a gifted psychic and intuitive. And as Jean left this life and I entered it, passing each other like shooting stars in the night, her knowing I was to be a girl, me knowing we weren't to meet in "real time," she imprinted upon me her talents—an array of otherworldly and sensitive abilities. While Jean's gifts enabled me to carry on her legacy, they would prove difficult for a child to carry.

My arrival here was unremarkable by all external accounts. I was born in Sydney, Australia, and when I was a baby, we left the city in favor of a quieter, beachside suburban area called the Central Coast. My father had just graduated from medical school and, feeling too much professional competition in Sydney, he moved us to the Central Coast.

Dad was clever and charismatic and with his movie-star looks, he was usually the center of attention. From the moment he walked into a room, he filled it up, and although Mum had looks and brains to rival his, his commanding personality far overshadowed hers.

A teacher, Mum had given up her career to support my father and care for our family. Pleasant and easygoing, she was the peacekeeper—a necessary role in our family because of Dad's white-hot temper, which we all learned to fear.

My parents moved us to the Central Coast to better Dad's work prospects, as well as to bring us closer to his parents, Grandad George and Nanna Merle.

Grandad George was a striking man of Scottish descent. He'd immigrated to Australia with his seven brothers and sisters when he was fourteen, but long after his arrival, his accent remained. He was olive-skinned and blue-eyed and had a deep love of philosophy and Christianity.

Some of my fondest memories of childhood were at my grandparents' house. I remember helping Grandad in his vegetable patch. While showing me how to pluck caterpillars from leaves or pat the earth down hard so the seeds didn't move, he'd tell me about his belief in hope and redemption.

"God loves you for who you are, Belinda. Do you know that?"

I reach for a spinach leaf, my tiny fingers wrapping around the smooth wriggling body of an earthworm. I squint at it, then up at Grandad.

"What does that mean?" I ask.

Grandad George kneels, sets down his pick and spade, and draws the back of a gloved hand across his brow.

His blue eyes sparkle and his voice is gentle, his words rich with conviction. "You don't need to do anything to be deserving of God's love. You just need to let him into your heart."

I'm unsure of how to do that—let God into my heart. All I know is I love being in the garden patch with Grandad George.

Nanna Merle was another story. A nervous person with a fragile temperament, she was plain and withdrawn, and rarely went outside. She could usually be found in the kitchen baking biscuits and cakes, tidying her already immaculate house, or in her bedroom having one of her "turns."

Her turns occurred frequently. She'd have a fizzy drink to calm her stomach, then retire to her room and draw the blinds. Our job was to be quiet and leave her in peace. But Nanna was also sweet and kind. She even smelled sweet, like she was sugar-dusted, and I loved to nestle into her, burying myself into her doughy-soft arms and breasts.

Throughout my early childhood, I adored the devoted attention of Grandad George and Nanna Merle, yet it was my mother's deep love that soothed me. We'd sit together on a large rug on the grass under the eucalyptus tree in our backyard or lie on the floor in the living room. We'd play or she would read to me. Many mornings she'd take me to the beach.

Mum plonks me down in the sand, then smiles as I start to topple over. I watch the light reflect off her big, dark sunglasses as she adjusts my chubby legs until I can sit upright. The sun bouncing off the water sends little shooting pains into the back of my eyeballs. Mum sits down next to me, shielding me. She scoops sand over my legs and tickles my tummy. Her dark hair falls down around me like a soft, airy cloak, and she laughs and tickles me some more. I hear the steady crash of waves in the background as Mum's body presses against me. I feel safe.

Outwardly safe, that is. Inside I was still frightened about being on earth. As a child, life felt narrow and restricted. I didn't like being confined to a little body that didn't move properly. It was hard not being able to express what I was thinking and feeling. It was all so alien to the clarity and expanse I knew as my *real* self.

Though challenging, these years weren't entirely bleak. In addition to the loving care of my mum and grandparents, I had a companion—one friend who understood me and kept me company: Julie.

Julie and I would be in my bedroom for hours, chatting away, playing with my dolls or at dress up.

"You can be a green princess, Julie. I'll be the red princess." I hold out a silver crown speckled with emeralds.

Julie crosses the rainbow-striped rug and sits down beside me.

I put the crown down next to her and pick up the one with bright red rubies.

"I always wanted to be a red princess." I smile, placing the crown on my head. "Red princesses are beautiful."

Julie's eyes are large and hazel. I pick up the green crown and place it on her head.

"See—you're a green princess!"

Julie laughs and we both close our eyes and travel to our secret, imagined place together where we are princesses in a castle.

Mum appears in the doorway and scans the room.

"Are you playing with Julie?" she asks.

Mum knew Julie as my imaginary friend. She'd buckle Julie in for the car ride or she'd set a place for Julie at the table. She'd read us both bedtime stories and sometimes she'd even tuck us both in at night.

Like most imaginary friends, Julie would appear whenever I was ready to play with her. But what Mum didn't know was that Julie never left my side, because she wasn't imaginary. In the nighttime or when I would play alone, caught up in my own secret child-world, Julie would simply sit in the corner of my room and wait for me to want to play with her again. She could sit like that—still as a statue—for hours. When I wanted to play with her again, she'd sort of reanimate and join in my game.

Though she talked and played like other children, even back then I knew Julie was different. She always dressed the same, wearing a long, old-fashioned lace nightgown. And she didn't look solid; she was transparent, like a watermark, and seemed hazy, as if you were looking at her through a lens that was slightly out of focus. The exception was her eyes, which were clear and sad.

Julie never opened her mouth to speak to me. Instead, she would send images and thoughts into my mind, and sometimes I would do the same with her. Because telepathic communication had been familiar to me since before my birth, before I ever met Julie: It was how we'd "spoken" on the Other Side, where we were all clairaudient and could read and hear each other's thoughts. It seemed normal that people on earth would communicate that way too. But soon, I would learn just how abnormal I was.

Inheriting Grandma Jean's psychic gifts and remembering where I'd come from made me an unusually deep-thinking toddler. I had an insatiable need to understand everything and a peculiar sort of intelligence. I could speak fluently before I was two years old and could articulate complex concepts and theories. I was always asking questions beyond my years. Adults found this equally charming and disconcerting.

When I was two years old, I waddled up to my mother, naked except for a diaper, and asked her how babies came into this world. Used to my deep and probing questions, she did her best to explain the complexities of human reproduction. When she was through, I paused, then posed another question.

"So how do you stop babies from being made?"

That night on the phone she told her sister she couldn't believe she'd had to give the contraceptive talk to a two-year-old. But my strangely philosophical questions weren't what unnerved adults most; it was the way I tried to counsel them about their problems.

Growing up, I spent lots of time in Dad's surgery. Mum worked as his receptionist and I loved to help her process people's payments, answer the phone, and tidy and stack the magazines in the waiting room. My attempts to help Dad weren't as welcome.

Ever since I can remember, I've been able to see inside a person and know all about them, including what is making them unwell. Inside and around everyone is a field of light that, when I look deep into it, shows me tiny motion pictures of their lives. While Dad's patients were waiting for their appointments, I would look in on them. Watching the little movies in their auras, I'd know why they had come and I'd try to talk to them about it.

I was completely unaware that other people didn't have the same ability. I thought everyone knew everything about each other and I was confused when adults got angry when I told them what I saw. They would deny it, even though I could see clearly that it was true. That confused and upset me; I couldn't understand why they'd lie to me.

"I'm not angry!" a young, blond-haired woman yelled at me, though her energy field was bright red and hot with rage.

"I'm not sad!" an old man shouted in my face, though his aura showed me he cried every night over the death of his wife.

"I'm not feeling sick, you little nosy parker," a woman scolded when I asked if she was feeling better after her bout with a vomiting bug.

I was called many things by angry adults: rude, nosy, too big for my boots.

I quickly learned to stop telling them what I saw.

I knew it wasn't their fault. Their lack of remembering their connection to the light caused them to both hurt inside and be hurtful to others. They were selfish and defensive because they'd forgotten where they came from. But this made me feel homesick.

It hurt to think of my soul home; about how much I missed it and how far away it was. About how loving and light and clear everything was over there, and how foggy and dark and angry everything was here.

My little heart had a gaping hole and I had no idea how to fill it.

CHAPTER 2

VISITORS

As LIFE WENT ON, I got used to being in a body again. I could control it more easily and started to feel a bit less burdened by my child status. I still knew I needed to hide parts of myself— that it wasn't safe to talk to adults about what I saw within them or how they were feeling—but I no longer felt quite so confined.

Julie continued to be my best friend and playmate, and after my mum gave birth to my sister Tanya in 1981, I came to rely on her friendship more than ever. Tanya's arrival turned my two-and-a-half-year-old world upside down.

When Mum brought Tanya home from the hospital, I blocked the entranceway screaming, *"You're not going to bring that thing into this house! Nooooo!"* Whether it was psychic know-ing or simply a toddler's natural reaction, my hunch about my sister was right. Tanya was a distressed baby. She cried almost constantly and slept and fed poorly. Because of this, all Mum's attention was now focused on Tanya, and it seemed like I'd lost the only human friend I'd had. Julie became the only one I felt connected to.

I'm unaware of having seen or communicated with other ghosts before Julie. She was an earthbound spirit—a spirit trapped on earth—so she was sad and lost, but she wasn't mean or unkind. On the contrary, she was quite gentle, but I quickly came to learn that this was not typical ghost behavior.

When I was around four years old, I started having ghosts visit me at night. As soon as Mum had tucked me in and turned out the light, they would come into my room. They would slide up underneath my bedroom door or would materialize through the walls. Others would plop down from the ceiling like fat spiders.

They looked like people, with bodies and faces that resembled those of men and women. Yet they also looked shadowy, and like Julie, they were transparent. From a few feet away they were just dark moving shapes. Up close, they were terrifying.

A ghost still has the same physical attributes they did while they were alive—the same gender, body shape, hair and eye color, and so on. But their ghost form becomes heavily imprinted with the negative emotions that prevented them from transitioning into the afterlife. The feelings the person couldn't release drench their earthbound form, making them look like a tainted version of their old self.

When ghosts began to crowd in on me at night, if I didn't close my eyes before they reached my bed, I would see in horrific detail the remnants of their negative emotions. Ghosts who were trapped in bitterness and resentment had long skeletal faces that dripped like yellow wax. Those who were full of rage or hate had large, engorged faces with flaming eyes and shark-like teeth and they would scream at me, shouting for me to listen to them. Jealous or envious ghosts had sullen and sunken faces and forms. Depressed ghosts had twisted faces and hunched bodies.

But it was the sad ghosts I feared the most, with their swollen and tear-stained faces. They weren't as menacing as the others, but they were much more frightening because they would touch me.

Their slimy, tentacle-like hands would slip in under my duvet and poke me around my ankles and legs. Then, as more and more sad ghosts arrived, jostling and fighting for a position at my bed, they would start to grab at me. Soon, their hands would be all over my body, and though I'd move and thrash about, their grips were so strong I couldn't shake them loose.

Some nights, ghosts would chase me through the house. I began to dread and hate nighttime.

My eyes are shut tight. I breathe deep, thinking maybe I can ignore it. Maybe I can fall back to sleep. But it's no use—my bladder is practically bursting. I have to go to the bathroom!

I wonder if he's still there. Slowly, I open my eyes. From the corner of the room the old man smiles at me, licking his scaly lips in anticipation. He's just sitting there, waiting for his opportunity to pounce.

I hold my breath and move slowly, shifting to place a tentative foot on the floor. He hunches forward, his eerie grin widening.

It's then I suddenly remember that Mum had left a cup of water for me which I'd drunk before bed! I snatch the empty cup from my nightstand and shove it under the covers and start to pee, my eyes fixed on the ghost. His grin fades and he slouches back into the seat, sad there will be no fun for him tonight.

I didn't turn to my parents for help with the ghost visitations. Like many parents whose children claim to see ghosts, mine thought it was "all in my head." Just a child's overactive imagination.

On the odd occasion when I did crawl out of bed and run down the hall to Mum and Dad, I was always sent back to bed and told to stop being silly. And by running to their room, I risked having a ghost chase me down the hallway. So to me, there wasn't any point in asking for their help. Even if they did believe me, they wouldn't have been able to understand what was happening to me.

My parents weren't alone—the truth is most of us don't understand the nature of ghosts. We don't understand what ghosts are and how it happens to them that they are stuck here.

When a person is unable to find the light after death and can't leave behind their connection to the earth plane and move into the afterlife, they remain bound to earth. This can happen if the natural flow of passing from earth (of leaving their human body) and returning to their spirit body on the Other Side is interrupted in some way, and there are many ways this can occur.

Some people can't transition into the light after death because they fear the wrath of God—they fear they haven't been "good" in life and that they aren't worthy to enter the kingdom of heaven. Others harbor deep secrets, guilt, shame, or anger, and can't release these emotions and move on. Some people, even after they've died and left behind their human body, feel angry and resentful because they were taken before their time. Others simply don't know they're dead because nobody is there to help them move over.

When we die, most of us find the light. We receive help and assistance from our deceased loved ones and angels and we're easily able to make the transition from our earthly life to our spirit-life. Most of us. But not all of us. Some of us, sadly, stay earthbound.

What I didn't know when I was a child is that I was born a ghost whisperer. I was born able to see and communicate with earthbound spirits. Due to the degree of my psychic and medi-umistic abilities, my astral light was shining on full wattage and this acted as a beacon to ghosts. Because of this, they flocked to me.

But I didn't know any of this when I was a child. I didn't know they were trapped, troubled, and lonely. I was scared of them the way children are scared of monsters and boogeymen and shadows. Scary dead people came to me when Mum turned out the light, and these scary dead people did unkind things to me. All I knew is that I was petrified of the night. All I knew is that I was petrified of what I could see . . .

If I had known back then that I was a ghost whisperer and that by simply "raising my vibration" I could protect myself from ghosts, as well as help them find the light, I wouldn't have lived in terror.

But it would be many more years before I'd learn this.

CHAPTER 3

EXORCISM

IN 1988, MY FAMILY—WHICH now also included my baby brother, Aaron—moved 600 kilometers north, from the Central Coast to the Gold Coast. One day, while we were still living on the Central Coast, Dad, bored with the sermon in the Salvation Army church, took a stroll and found himself at a Pentecostal church. He was so taken by the vibrancy and modernity of the church that he decided, then and there, that it would be our new spiritual home. Within a few months, Dad found a new job and we relocated to be a part of a Pentecostal church that was starting on the Gold Coast.

I hated our new rental house on the Gold Coast the moment I stepped foot inside it. Located at Worendo Place, it was a large, looming two-story dark-brick house that smelled of mold and shadows. Inside and throughout the house were cheap plastic fittings and ugly orange carpet. And it was oddly built, with each room completely boxed off from the others so that when you were by yourself, it felt as if you were in a tomb.

As much as the inside of Worendo Place was shadowy, the outside was scorching. The brick walls, veranda, and play area reflected and absorbed the sun so that when we played outside, we'd burn our eyes and feet and hands. We hated outside playtime, along with the garden and its freaky inhabitants.

15

It was at Worendo Place that we first saw a cane toad. We were petrified of the huge ugly amphibians with their bulging eyes and poisonous saliva. They were everywhere, hopping around or just sitting there like fat, brownish-green, warty-looking lumps.

There were other nasty things in the garden: huge wasps with long stinging tails; big jumping ants that would scurry up our legs and bite us all over; and patches of prickles that would sting our feet and wedge themselves between our toes. But while Worendo Place was downright hostile on the outside, it was the inside that terrified us.

Inside the house, it always felt like we were being followed. When we'd walk upstairs to our room, or go to the bathroom, or go to the garage to get ice cream from the freezer, it was as if something was after us . . . This was confirmed when that something started grabbing hold of our shoulders and jumping onto our backs.

Tanya, Aaron, and I started to move as a group, traveling together everywhere we went inside the house. After watching us do this for weeks, Mum asked what we were doing. When we told her something was following us and that it sometimes chased us, Mum was understandably concerned.

The presence would also come near us when we were going to sleep at night. Tanya and I shared a room, and when the lights went out she'd jump up onto my top bunk and we'd sleep pressed together. Aaron would often run in from his room and sleep in Tanya's empty bottom bunk. This didn't stop us seeing dark shapes moving across the room or menacing faces peering down at us, but at least none of us was alone.

Although I was scared of "the something" (along with all the scary things that showed up at night), I was also relieved. I was no longer alone in my terror. No longer the only one seeing ghosts.

But this relief was short-lived, as I was about to have one of the most terrifying experiences of all.

I'm sitting on the front step waiting for the pastor to arrive. It's hot outside and I'm shielding my eyes against the sun, watching the street for his car.

Mum told me that the pastor is going to break the curse today. He's going to pray over me and that will break the curse that's on our family. The one that's responsible for the ghosts in the house. Mum says it's because her father was a Freemason, and that's why we're cursed. That's why I'm cursed. And since I'm the firstborn, if the pastor prays over me, it will break the curse.

I don't understand what Mum means. I don't know what curses or Freemasons are, but I understand there is something "over" me and Tanya and Aaron; something around and inside us that's wrong.

"He'll just pray over you," Mum says, noticing my apprehension, "that's all. It won't take long."

When the pastor arrives, Mum scurries out of the kitchen, patting her hair and giving the house a once-over glance. She answers the door, then she and the pastor exchange a few hurried words. He's flushed and dressed as if he's on his way to preach at the church. He motions for me to follow him down the hall and when we reach the living room, he points to a white towel Mum has laid out over the orange carpet on the floor and tells me to lie down.

Though I'm afraid, I do what he says. I want to get up and run away and go back to my room, but I don't want to make the pastor mad. Once when I was at his house for a playdate with his daughter, he hit me across the face. No one else was around to see it and when Mum asked him about it later, he said I'd made it up.

He is one of those adults who pretends to like children, but really doesn't. His energy field goes red and mean around kids. I am scared of being prayed over, but I am more scared of being hit again.

"Close your eyes now," the pastor says, "and don't open them until I tell you that you can."

17

I shut my eyes.

"And lie still. Don't move at all."

I lie as still as I can, with my eyes shut tight. My heart is thumping. My legs feel shaky.

Then the pastor begins to pray. His voice is clear and loud above me.

"Dear Jesus, dear almighty Lord and Savior, may thy will be done today in the name of Jesus. Today we come before you to ask you to release this child from the curse placed upon her. The curse that her grandfather placed over his grandchildren when he was involved in the Freemasonry church. This child has been cursed—enslaved and ensnared by Lucifer, by Satan, the Devil, the king of deceit and lies and darkness. We ask today, dear Jesus, dear Lord, and our Savior, that this curse be broken and this child be freed from darkness."

I'm trying to lie still and keep my eyes closed, but my heart is pumping fast and I want to run.

"This child needs to be freed from the devil and the demons that are within her. I call upon the blood of Christ to break this curse and free her!"

The pastor places his hand on my forehead and I flinch. His hand is hot and prickly.

"I pray in God's name that this child, now, be freed from the curse! From the devil and the demons! I rebuke the devil! I rebuke the darkness! I rebuke the demons, those vile spirits of darkness that have attached themselves to the child. Demons—I rebuke you!"

Suddenly, a wave of heat rushes from my feet up to my head. At first it feels like warm water, but now it's becoming so hot that it's nearly boiling. White-hot rays of pain flash through me.

"Come forth demons, I say! Leave the body of this child!"

The pain is stronger now, and starts to collect in my chest and throat. It's pain like I've never experienced. I'm on fire. I'm boiling up!

"In the name of Jesus Christ, our Savior and Lord," yells the pastor, "I command that the demons now come forth! Come forth demons and leave the body of this child!"

The pain is unbearable and I'm choking on it and spluttering; still trying to lie still, still trying to be obedient . . .

"In the Name of Jesus, I COMMAND the demons: Leave the body of this child!"

I can no longer lie still. I begin to scream.

The pastor starts to talk in a fast, babbling language that makes no sense. The language the adults in the church call "speaking in tongues." I don't know what he is saying. All I know is I'm being boiled alive and something is pushing out of my throat.

Waves of terror crash over me. The energy that's being pulled out of me is fighting to stay in. It's holding on to my legs and abdomen. I'm being ripped apart. I can't stop screaming because it's coming out of me through my mouth!

I'm now screaming in terror. It's not only the pain. It's because, in a flash of realization, I understand what's happening.

Evil is inside me, and it's coming out!

I wake up exhausted. My throat's sore. I must have passed out.

Before the full weight of my discovery can sink in—the understanding that I am bad and dark—my Grandma Jean appears. Suddenly she materializes above me, then moves to sit next to me. I recognize her from photos that Mum has showed me. Her eyes are dark and kind and she takes my hand in hers.

"Belinda"—she looks me deep in the eyes—"right now, people don't understand you or your gifts, but when you grow up this will change. One day, many people will want to know what you see and hear. They will love you for it. And they will uphold you for it. Not hurt you for it, like they are now."

She squeezes my hand, but I'm too dazed and shocked to feel comforted.

"Ignore this silly man," she says, gesturing to the pastor, who is still kneeling next to me and speaking in tongues, "for they know not what they do."

And with that, just as suddenly as she appeared, she leaves.

I open my eyes again. The pastor is gone. I'm alone in the room and it's quiet.

I stand up. I'm shaky and weak. I walk out of the room, glancing back briefly at the tiny white towel on the mass of the orange carpet. Then I go up to my bedroom and shut the door.

Grandma Jean was right, of course—I wasn't possessed. I didn't have demons in me. And there wasn't any curse on my family because of my grandfather's involvement with the Freemasons.

When we moved into Worendo Place, unbeknownst to us, we'd moved into a haunted house. It had such bad energy that it attracted dark spirits. Years later, we found out that someone had been murdered there before we moved in. (And years after that we heard that someone was murdered there after we moved out.)

The pastor, in his Pentecostal fervor and naiveté, sincerely believed we were cursed, and he thought he could help us. But his version of help was misguided and harmful . . . What took place during the exorcism was that my soul was torn out of my body. The thing clinging to me, fighting to stay inside me, wasn't demons. It was my soul!

The physical and emotional trauma of having my soul cast out of my body created a huge tear in my aura, severely disabling my energy field. It's akin to puncturing a lung or being run over by a car—it's something one can barely survive.

My soul wasn't completely severed from my body that day. If it had been, I would have died. But the extent of the damage to my energy field was enormous. It removed any psychic protection I'd had, so I was extremely susceptible to psychic attack. Being born psychic made me sensitive. Compared to most people, I was already vulnerable. But after the exorcism, I was psychically crippled. This meant I had no protection against people's illnesses and negative thoughts and feelings. As a result, I became very unwell.

Before the exorcism, I received instant impressions about people's feelings and pain, but once I moved away from the person the impressions mostly disappeared. After the exorcism, I had no filter. No protection. As a result, once I received an impression about someone, I couldn't stop feeling how they felt. Their pain and anguish began to lodge itself in my aura—I *absorbed* their physical and mental pain.

Usually this happened in my father's surgery. When I'd look into a person's energy field, even for the briefest moment, their sickness and life problems would jump out of their energy field and into mine.

Sometimes I knew their problems had "come into me" and that it was making me feel unhappy. But many times, because it happened instantaneously, I didn't know what was taking place. I would feel these strange, strong pains in my body and not know why.

The pains were bizarre and irregular: I'd experience heaviness in my chest and torso (it felt like a large person sitting on me); deep cold pains in my back, legs, and feet (it felt like being pricked by ice needles); strange sensations of burning and pressure in my head and violent stomach cramps that would leave me retching and curled over. These pains would hit me suddenly, then leave just as quickly as they came.

These sensations were my body's way of trying to process and filter the huge amounts of negativity being dumped into my energy field each day. I was experiencing *empath syndrome*—a very real condition that happens to sensitive and deeply feeling people if they don't learn to "clear" and protect their energy field.

Of course, Dad didn't know this. He ran tests and asked his fellow doctors, but couldn't find an explanation for my pain. I was diagnosed with hypochondria and told again that it was "all in my head." So I stopped complaining to Mum and Dad about what I was feeling.

As terrible as these physical sensations were, *becoming* someone else was absolute agony. My body wasn't just experiencing pain because it was trying to process and filter out people's negativity; I was also suffering because I was absorbing other people's traumas.

One afternoon I'd sat next to one of Dad's patients in his surgery—a kind, elderly woman. She had been raped by her father when she was a teenager and the trauma of this rape was still in her energy field. Because she had never told anyone about what had happened, the pain lay there, large and wounded, in her aura. It was causing the constant stomach and blood pressure problems she was having, but she didn't know this. I knew it because I could see it in her aura, and as we talked about school and what I was learning and if I liked my grade-four teacher, her pain leapt into me. That night, I *experienced* her rape.

Another time, I vomited for hours after I sat next to a woman on a bus who was undergoing chemotherapy. On another occasion, I spent three days wanting to kill myself.

"Belinda, are you awake?" Natalie asks as she walks into my room.

She knows I'm awake, because I always wait up for her to come upstairs and say "hi." She's here every Thursday night for the Bible study group Mum and Dad run for teens from our church.

Natalie's one of those nice teenagers who likes younger kids and talks to you like you're her peer. I often sit next to her in church. I love listening to her high, clear voice as she sings the psalms.

She's usually sweet and asks me how I am or how school's going. But tonight she just walks over to my bed and sits down, and I see that her eyes are red-rimmed and swollen. She's been crying.

"Are you okay?" I ask her.

"Oh, I don't know," she says, swallowing hard. "Something strange is happening to me and I feel depressed."

I don't really know what "depressed" means, but I can feel how she feels. She's heavy and sad. All of a sudden I can hear the mean voices in her head that are saying horrible things to her.

"I don't like myself very much," she says. "I don't think I'm going to make it."

I open my mouth to respond, but a voice calls up from downstairs saying youth group is starting. Natalie jumps off the bed and scurries away.

I know she feels bad about what she told me. She thought she shouldn't be sharing these deep feelings with a child.

Even though Natalie's gone, her sadness is still here. It's clinging to me and I feel heavy and sick.

That night, the next morning, and for two days after that, I had a torrent of angry, vicious voices in my head. "You're worthless!" they screamed. "You're an idiot! You're fat, lazy, and disgusting! You'll never amount to anything!"

For three whole days I was bombarded by these vicious, cruel thoughts. I had picked up Natalie's self-hate and was under a savage attack.

On Sunday when I saw Natalie at church, I told her I knew how she was feeling. "There are voices in your head saying mean things to you. Like you're worthless and fat and lazy. And this is making you feel bad. But these voices are those of your father," I said. I knew this intuitively. "You hate yourself. You keep thinking about how much you hate yourself."

She began to splutter and cry. "Nobody knows this about me. Nobody except you. You won't tell anyone, will you, Belinda? I'm scared other people will find this out about me and think I'm bad."

I assured her I wouldn't tell anyone, then I sat with her until she finished crying. I never heard the voices after that, but the experience had been terrifying.

When I was a child I didn't know that the ability to see and heal the dark in others is a gift. I didn't know I was born an empath and a shadow hunter, and that I had the ability to "hunt" people's shadows and help them transmute their fears and negativity.

It wasn't until much later in my life, many years after I started working as a medical intuitive, that I would discover this about myself. And it took many years of struggle to learn how to work as an empath and a shadow hunter without experiencing pain because of it.

CHAPTER 4

TRUTH-TELLING

As I moved into puberty, my psychic sensitivities seemed to intensify. At the time, I didn't know that hormonal changes can bring about a spike in our extrasensory abilities. I also didn't know that it's quite common for psychics and mediums to experience an increase in intensity during the teen years.

Already struggling with the aftereffects of the exorcism, including digestive and other health problems, I also felt exhausted, stressed, and depressed. Now I was trying to cope with even stronger psychic and shadow-hunting skills. And I was still struggling to figure out what was okay to know about people, and what I could say to them without getting in trouble.

In my first year of high school I was sent out of class because of something I psychically knew. My home economics teacher, Mrs. Dawson, had been absent for several weeks. As soon as she walked into the room, I knew why—she was pregnant.

When I saw Mrs. Dawson, a strong pang of nausea leapt out of her body and into mine. The sickness landed *smack bang* in my solar plexus and I thought I was going to vomit. When I looked inside Mrs. Dawson, I saw a tiny baby growing in her tummy.

When Mum was pregnant with Rebekah, my younger sister who was born in 1989, she'd been sick in bed in the mornings.

I knew that having a tiny baby inside you could make you sick, and I knew this was called morning sickness.

I felt sorry for my teacher. She was feeling very ill and her husband had made her go back to work so they could afford everything. I liked her a lot too; she was pretty and kind. So I asked her, "Have you recovered from morning sickness now?"

Mrs. Dawson froze, her pretty face turning white with shock. She stared at me, blinking and swallowing. After the longest time, she pointed a long, shaky finger towards me and said in a low voice, "You are a gossip and a liar, Belinda Davidson, and you aren't to be trusted."

She sent me out of the classroom and I spent the morning crouched and crying against a brick wall next to the home economics room. I still felt nauseous, like she did. And I also felt sad and confused. I really liked Mrs. Dawson, but she didn't like me anymore; all because of what I shouldn't have known.

Unfortunately, there were many more incidents like that during my teen years . . .

Dad's friend, Donald, is at our house for dinner. I don't really like him much because he's one of those adults who speaks down to children, always lecturing and sermonizing at us. But he loves to tell stories. Sometimes he boasts about his new cars or motorcycles, or his latest heroic and chivalrous deeds. He speaks with his mouth full, and it's entertaining to watch the way food and spittle fly through the air and land with a plonk in a circle around him.

Tonight, though, Donald isn't his usual self. He's subdued and quiet. He's picking at his food and moving it around his plate.

I sigh and pick at my food too. I was really looking forward to being entertained by his stories. Why isn't he his usual self tonight? Maybe if I check inside his energy field, I can see what's wrong.

I look into Donald and see he's thinking about a dark-haired woman. She is petite and has curvy hips and a pert bottom. He plans to visit her after dinner, and he's wishing he could leave now to go and be with her. He's feeling uneasy about it. I can see that he's kissed and had sex with her like married people do.

I'm confused. In Sunday school, we're told that we're only supposed to kiss and love the person we are married to. But this woman isn't Donald's wife. His wife is tall and blonde and loves to laugh. Why is he loving someone else?

So I ask him, "Who is the woman with the brown hair that you're going to visit after dinner?"

Donald's head spins towards me like he's heard a gunshot. He's staring at me with his mouth hanging open.

"Wh-, wh-, what did you say?" he finally asks, his voice croaky and shaky.

I know that when adults are shocked by something, they also get angry, so I don't repeat my question. Instead, I shrink down in my seat, wishing I could disappear.

"What did you say?" he asks me again. He speaks slowly and looks me straight in the eyes.

I stay quiet.

"I said, what did you say?" His voice is louder now, and menacing.

Finally, I say softly, while keeping my eyes fixed on the table, "Who is the woman with the brown hair you're going to see after dinner?"

For a moment, it's quiet. Then he leans across the table and, sticking his big face into mine, his eyes bulging and wild, yells, "You should mind your own business, you creepy kid!"

Donald snatches his keys and wallet off the table and storms out.

No one at the dinner table says anything. I'm relieved Dad isn't home from work, otherwise he'd yell at me too.

I climb down from my chair and go off to play alone in my room.

Incidents like this were confusing. Getting into trouble for telling adults what I saw inside them was heartbreaking, but it wasn't the only thing making my life difficult. Now when I went to bed, even more ghosts were appearing, and their visitations would often last all night long.

Before, after fighting them off for some time, I could eventually fall asleep. Now their pursuit of me was relentless. This wasn't only because the exorcism had made me even more psychically vulnerable. It was also because I was now even more psychic overall, and my psychic-astral light was burning brighter than ever.

Night after night I thrashed around, fighting off the ghosts. Finally I would fall asleep, only to be jolted awake again by a ghost grabbing my ankle or fingering my hair or poking its face in mine.

Thus began a chronic pattern of night terrors and insomnia that would take me many years to overcome. In the meantime, I came up with a coping mechanism. I became two people: *Daytime Belinda* and *Nighttime Belinda.*

Daytime Belinda was the girl who woke up in the morning, brushed her teeth, went off to school, and had no knowledge of what was happening to Nighttime Belinda. Daytime Belinda knew she was unusual; she knew she could see inside people and know things about them that she sometimes got into trouble for, but she had no clue about what was happening to Nighttime Belinda—what took place when the lights went out and the ghosts came. Daytime Belinda began as soon as I woke up in the morning. With the fresh light of day, Nighttime Belinda would be erased, and Daytime Belinda would greet the dawn . . .

Many experts in child psychology say that this type of dissociation is a common way children cope with trauma—they erase certain things from their consciousness so they can get by and survive. They also say this occurs more often in cases where children don't get help, or don't feel safe talking about what's happening to them.

To deal with it all alone, I forgot. And I lived this way, split into Daytime and Nighttime Belinda, for many years.

CHAPTER 5

ANGELS

WHEN I WAS A child, I didn't know about the Law of Attraction or the importance of keeping one's vibration raised. I didn't understand that all the fear I brought into this world with me had lowered my vibration and drawn dark and scary things to me.

As my seer, empath, shadow-hunting, ghost-whispering, and truth-telling nature and abilities blossomed, and I was rebuked and silenced, I feared even more. After I was exorcised, I became even more afraid . . .

My life had become layers of compounding fears. Layers upon layers of things I was deeply afraid of—things about myself.

By the time I was a teenager, I wanted to leave this terrible life on earth behind. I wanted to return to the light-filled, joy-filled expanse and delight of my soul-self on the Other Side.

I began to think and dream about my own death. And some months later, it almost happened.

The big white church bus comes to a stop in the parking lot. It's practically rocking as all the other teens inside buzz with excitement. One of the best things about being fourteen is that I finally get to be part of the youth group. We're spending today at the water park.

The door of the bus opens and we all run off towards the wave pool.

"Let's go far out back and catch the biggest waves!" someone yells.

I stand there looking at the massive pool with its crashing waves. I'm not a strong swimmer, and I don't like going in the ocean when it's rough. I hesitate. But the other kids are already jumping in and swimming to the far end of the pool. I don't want to miss out, so I follow them.

Right away the waves come so fast and hard that I can't manage to get over them in time. I drop beneath the surface, trying to duck them, but I'm not fast enough. I start to panic.

A huge wave crashes over me and I'm pulled under. I struggle to the surface and open my mouth to gasp for air, but another wave is crashing down and my mouth fills with water. I'm pushed down again. I'm fighting to find the surface, but I can't tell which way is up. My body is flipping over and over and everything's spinning.

Finally, everything just stops. I'm floating and still near the bottom of the pool. All around me are legs and bodies— hundreds of adults and children at play. Everyone's moving in slow motion: skinny boys' legs kicking and jumping; strong men's legs, muscled and pumping powerfully; soft women's legs moving and swimming and holding chubby babies with their legs kicking like pistons.

Then I feel my body moving. A current pulls me to the right, then pushes me upwards to the edge of the pool. I realize I'm near the surface, so I try to get my head out while I reach for the side wall. The tiles are slippery and my fingers keep sliding off.

I try again, fighting to pull myself up so I can take a breath, but it's no use. I slip back into the depths of the pool, exhausted and panicked, my lungs bursting with the pressure. My strength is gone and I'm fading, falling to the bottom . . .

I surrender . . . There are those legs again, moving around me in slow motion. All those happy legs. None of them have any idea I'm at the bottom of the pool and that I'm drowning . . .

"This is it," I think. "It is now that I die."

The next thing I know, I'm being lifted from the pool. Not dragged or pulled out but lifted. Then I'm standing on the pool deck, facing away from the water.

It's impossible. There's no more water in my lungs. I'm not even panicked anymore. It's like I'm in a parallel reality where I was never in the water in the first place. Where I wasn't drowning or struggling.

There's a small boy in front of me, maybe five years old. His hair is dark and he's wearing black swimming bathers.

"Are you okay?" he asks, squinting up at me.

"Yes . . ." I say, taking a few breaths. "Did you pull me out of the water?"

"Yes," he says.

I'm about to ask him how, but suddenly he's running away. He disappears into a crowd of people, his black swimming bathers a dark flash across the horizon.

I can't explain how, but I know my life was saved that day. Even back then, I knew something miraculous had taken place, that my life had been spared.

I believe an angel saved me. Either an angel had given the small boy superhuman strength to pull me out of the pool, or the angel had disguised itself as a small boy to save my life. Either way, something *otherworldly* had taken place which saved my life.

Back then I didn't know much about angels. They weren't something the Pentecostal church often spoke about. Yet somehow I knew one had just saved me, and that it had done so because God wanted me to live. I knew there must be a purpose to my life.

In bed that night I thanked God for saving my life. I thanked Jesus and the angels for letting me live. I didn't know what my future held or what my purpose was, but I knew that what Grandma Jean had told me was true . . . That it would be okay and things would turn out in the end.

As I lay in bed, peaceful for the first time ever, not fearing the descent of ghosts or the nighttime, I heard God speak to me. In a quiet, calm voice—a voice very different to that of people or ghosts—God said, "The one who fears deeply, can love deeply. This is your purpose. This is what you chose."

And with that—with a heart and soul at peace—I fell asleep.

CHAPTER 6

INTEGRATION

A FEW WEEKS AFTER my miraculous experience at the pool, my family left the Gold Coast. We moved back to the Central Coast, which was a homecoming in more ways than one; we were able to move back into our old house at Forresters Beach, which my family had built.

It was also a move back to Grandad George and Nanna Merle. I was so glad to be near them again. Their house had always been a refuge for me, and when we returned to Forresters Beach, I started spending several nights a week there. Strangely, I never remember seeing ghosts or anything else scary at Grandad George and Nanna Merle's house. They were always so kind and caring that I sometimes wonder if their loving energy raised the vibration in their entire house, blocking anything negative from entering.

I felt safer being close to my grandparents again. I also felt safer because when we moved, we left behind the Pentecostal church. Its fanatical nature and extreme beliefs had become too much for us, especially for Mum. All the talk of demons and curses and "fighting against the dark" in the name of Jesus was overwhelming. It was full of fear and negativity. Our experiences with the Pentecostal church tainted Christianity for us. After that, Mum and Dad didn't want us going to church at all, so returning to the Central Coast meant we also stopped being Christians.

In my life outside of the church, I had a very different impression of God. I'd had the beautiful experience of hearing God's voice after being saved at the pool, and it did not match at all what we were being taught on Sundays. So while I was sad to leave my friends behind, I was relieved we no longer had to go to church.

In many ways, normalcy returned to our lives. I don't know why, but for a time the weird psychic stuff didn't happen as much. I began to think I'd let go of my dark past. I thought I *could* leave it behind. But you can't let go of your past if you don't heal it—if you don't accept, integrate, and move beyond it. And it would take years before I could truly do that . . .

At the time, I felt that the move was a chance at a new start. It felt like being lifted out from underneath a dark gray cloud. Some afternoons I'd be doing my homework or writing short stories or reading a book, and the breeze of the ocean would find its way into our backyard and up into my bedroom window. Its coolness and freshness gave me hope for a new life.

Still, it was difficult making the adjustment to this new life. For years, I'd had only minimal contact with people who weren't involved in the church. We'd attended Pentecostal church twice each Sunday and we socialized only with people from church. Because I attended a Pentecostal school, most of my friends and peers were Pentecostal, and we shared the same views. We all understood why it was important to talk in tongues or why we needed to be saved and to save others before the end of the world came.

To suddenly need to make friends with "normal teenagers" and their "normal issues" was challenging. I was a fish out of water, and for all of the ninth grade I felt lonely.

Much of my loneliness was also because I was hiding. I was working hard to make sure my new peers didn't discover the truth about me—about my abilities or my Pentecostal past. I was scared it would somehow slip out and I'd be rejected. I wanted to be normal and I wanted my peers to like me; I wanted to make friends. For a while, it seemed to work. I could pretend I was someone else and they didn't seem to suspect anything.

Slowly . . . slowly, I started to find friends. I started to be accepted within certain circles and be invited out. Then, when people found out I was smoking weed, I quickly gained more friends.

My neighborhood was a small, seaside community. There, marijuana was easy to come by. All my neighbors and most of the kids on my street smoked weed, and grew it, too. For many people, rolling a joint or smoking a few bongs was like having a beer. It was no big deal.

But at the grammar school I attended, some of my friends hadn't smoked weed yet. They didn't have the same access or exposure I did. I had a friend who lived in a similar neighborhood as mine and we'd smoke in her basement.

I didn't start smoking marijuana to be popular, though. I did it because I was curious and I loved the way it made me feel. Weed seemed to make my brain slower in a fuzzy, lovely kind of way. It made me chilled and relaxed. I was never a serious marijuana smoker, but smoking before I went to bed helped me sleep. It would lull me into a deep rest and would stop me from experiencing (or remembering) my ghostly nighttime visitations. It seemed to take the edge off my psychic sensitivities.

Weed was great, but things came to a crashing halt when, at sixteen, I tried acid. I'd overheard one of my girlfriends at school talking about it at lunch. She said acid was just like weed, only much better because it made the world sparkly and cosmic. She was going out with a guy whose dad sold drugs, so she could easily get me some. She said she'd drop it off at my place, and my friend Susie and I could get high on the weekend.

It's Saturday night and I'm sitting on my bed. Susie's here too. I can hear the faint sound of the TV from the front of the house, where my family is.

Susie and I are looking at my hand. I'm holding two tiny pieces of something that looks like thin cardboard. They have Bart Simpson's face on them. He's smiling up at us, as if cheering us on.

We were told to take only half of each tab. I tear one in half and stick a piece under my tongue. It doesn't just look like cardboard, it tastes like it too. Susie does the same.

We wait . . . And wait . . . Nothing's happening. Where are the sparkles and cosmic visions? Maybe it's not working.

We decide to take the other half too.

Still nothing's happening.

And then . . .

Suddenly I'm in a parallel universe. The world is a kaleidoscope of shifting colors! There's the sparkly, cosmic experience our friend promised!

Susie and I are sitting opposite one another, peering into each other's eyes. It's like a slideshow; I see different people inhabiting Susie and expressing themselves through her. Then her face transforms into the faces of my friends and family.

We spend hours exploring this magical new world. A spider in the corner spins a web that grows large and turns purple. There's a fireworks display on my wall that explodes into a million colors. Susie and I make up a private language that only we can understand; and we marvel at all the secrets the universe is now revealing to us. We understand the reason for our existence, and for the existence of all life forms on earth.

But now something's shifting. The sparkle's fading and my visions are changing. They're becoming dark and scary—visions of demons and violence. They're getting worse and worse, and I can't make them stop!

A psychic bleed-through had started. All the terrors that Nighttime Belinda had experienced began to seep into the consciousness of Daytime Belinda. Visions of demons, possessions, psychic rape, and violence began to rise up and seep into my psyche, like dark-red blood spreading out on a white handkerchief.

I had no idea what was happening and was completely unprepared for this purging. It was like Pandora's box had been opened and I was helpless as the full weight of my traumas came bearing down on me.

While psychedelic and hallucinogenic drugs have long been used to help people confront their inner demons, for me it was too much, too fast. Under the right circumstances, taking drugs can be mind-opening. It's why people took LSD in the sixties and why people go into ceremony and take ayahuasca. When used carefully and with proper support, these drugs can be life-altering and provide a spiritual and liberating experience; they can show you what needs to be purged and help you do it.

In reality I had never healed from the exorcism done to me years before, and I still carried multitudes of suppressed traumas. Though I thought things were finally beginning to improve, my darkness was just lingering below the surface. The acid trip broke through that barrier and the trauma of the exorcism came racing back into my awareness. It was too much for me to handle at once.

After my experience with acid, I became plagued by disturbing images. At random times during the day or night, I'd suddenly see a flash of a girl lying on the carpet with demons coming out of her mouth. Or I'd see a skeletal face peering over me, or feel a ghost grabbing me by the throat and trying to choke me.

The image that came to me most often was among the most disturbing: that of a young red-haired girl, bound and chained. She'd be falling towards me, down from the sky, reaching out to me with her bruised and bound hands. She'd be speaking to me, trying to tell me something. But her words were garbled and I couldn't understand her.

At the time I didn't realize that taking acid had forced the sudden integration of Daytime and Nighttime Belinda . . .

There were thousands of such pieces of myself scattered within me, floating in the abyss of my subconscious mind. I didn't know I needed to retrieve these long-lost parts of my soul and piece them together so I could heal. What happened instead was that I developed panic disorder.

Although I never did acid again—and after this incident I rarely smoked weed—the visions and the panic I started to experience after that acid trip became even more acute. From out of nowhere I'd be hit by one of those frightening images, and it would often quickly bring on an anxiety attack. Sometimes this would escalate to a full-blown panic attack.

When a panic attack came on, I'd be left fighting for breath, and for my life. At times I hyperventilated so badly that I would turn pink and blue. I'd dig my fingernails into my hands, making them bleed. I started carrying around Rescue Remedy and a paper bag.

Mum sent me to a therapist, but it didn't help. I didn't tell the therapist about the visions that were triggering the panic attacks because I was scared she would send me to an institution. I was so afraid of being institutionalized, of being locked up in a crazy house, that I pretended I was scared of other things instead. I made up stories about how I was struggling at school and with my friends. For better or worse, my therapist seemed to believe me. On the one hand, I wasn't going to be institutionalized. But on the other, the therapy did nothing to solve what was really happening with me.

In addition to the panic attacks, I was still experiencing other people's pain and suffering. I had grown accustomed to my empath nature; I was now used to constantly feeling some pain or malady in my body which had come from someone else. But after taking acid, I began to experience much more sickness. I'd spend hours in the bathroom with severe stomach pains and cramps. Or sometimes my blood-sugar levels would suddenly drop and I'd faint.

Dad couldn't find a cause for my low blood pressure or my stomach ailments, so again, I was diagnosed as being a hypochondriac. I once again started to hide my pain and discomfort because I didn't want Dad's disapproval or to be his "weakling" daughter. And I still feared being labeled as crazy and being put in an institution.

Maybe people didn't think of me as crazy, but anyone who knew me back in high school would have known I was troubled. I wasn't behaviorally out of control. I wasn't in trouble with the police or addicted to drugs; I was always too cautious and sensible for that. But I was emotionally troubled; pensive, melancholic, and depressed. I hated my body and face. When I looked at myself in the mirror, and into my own eyes, I saw evil staring back at me. I felt I *was* evil and ugly.

Everything once again seemed desperate and dark. The radiant love and beauty I'd experienced after nearly drowning at the water park was a distant memory, and I had no idea how to find my way back.

CHAPTER 7

THE TOP HOUSE

AS TIME WENT ON, I was also faced with Grandad George and Nanna Merle's declining health. He'd had a stroke, and she was diagnosed with Alzheimer's, so it was decided that my grandparents would move in with us so Mum could care for them. That meant some rearrangements in our living situation.

Our house at Forresters Beach had a "top house"—an older, smaller house in front of it. It used to be Dad's surgery before he moved his practice down the street. When Grandad George and Nanna Merle moved into the main house, Tanya and I were asked to move to the top house.

At first we were thrilled. We would have our own house and could do what we liked. We envisioned staying up all night, sleeping all day, and getting up to all sorts of shenanigans. We planned a massive neighborhood party!

But right away, it was apparent something was wrong. The first night we stayed in the top house we took my cat Charlotte up with us. Mum had already moved our belongings and had set up our new bedrooms. Mine was the larger one adjacent to the kitchen, and Tanya's was a smaller one at the front of the house.

As I carried Charlotte through the back entrance of the house, Tanya followed behind me up the small rickety wooden steps. Suddenly, Charlotte leapt out of my arms and raced back to the main house. Tanya ran after her. After much coaxing and prying, we finally caught Charlotte. Holding her extra tight this time, we walked back up the stairs into the top house.

As soon as we walked through the back door, Charlotte started to squirm. She wriggled this way and that, trying her hardest to get out of my arms. I'd never seen Charlotte do that. She was usually docile and placid—a cat who didn't mind being picked up and carried around. But now she was squirming fiercely, scratching me to get out of my arms.

I dropped Charlotte on the floor and she ran to the back door to escape, but Tanya had already closed it. Charlotte then turned around to face the wall. The hair on the back of her neck slowly rose and she began to hiss and spit at the walls as if she were cornered. Her body was coiled tight like a rope and her teeth were bared.

Tanya and I watched in horror as Charlotte then started swiping at the walls. It was as if she were attacking *invisible people*. We had never seen her hiss or snarl before, but now she was in the midst of a vicious fight, jumping at things we couldn't hear or see; things that seemed to either be in the walls or just in front of them.

I screamed and Tanya ran out of the top house to get Mum. When Mum walked in and saw Charlotte hissing and attacking the walls, she said, "Let the poor cat out!" I opened the back door and Charlotte took off. She never came to the top house again. Her animal instincts told her that something dark resided there, but it would take months before we'd flee too.

Tanya and I began to experience hauntings and supernatural occurrences that were even more disturbing than those we'd experienced at Worendo Place. We witnessed doors opening and closing by themselves, loud footsteps stomping through the house at night when we were trying to sleep, and eerie black shapes hanging around and moving about the house. We also experienced physical attacks and being pushed by invisible forces.

Every night, Tanya would sleep on a mattress on my floor because if she slept in her room, she'd be woken by loud clanging noises next to her head. A presence would also push down on her and then try to lift her out of bed.

One night, though, Tanya tried to sleep in her own room. It was a huge mistake.

On Friday she'd had a girlfriend stay over. They were up late and had crashed out in Tanya's room. I was working as a receptionist at Dad's surgery every Saturday morning and was just getting home from work when I heard screams coming from the top house.

I raced inside and found Tanya, along with my mum and my aunt, in Tanya's room. Tanya was screaming hysterically, "Where did it come from? Why in my room? *Why has this happened to me!*"

I stepped inside and it was ice cold, like I'd stepped into a refrigerator. Then I saw what the commotion was about. Tanya's entire room was covered in black dust.

It was everywhere. It was all over her bed, her books and clothes, as well as the ceiling, the walls, and the windows. Absolutely everything was covered in a thin layer of black dust—her desk and schoolbooks and bags and cosmetics. It looked like an explosion had left an aftermath of black soot. I looked up at the ceiling. The dark powder had settled on the large cobwebs up there, making her room look like a scene from a horror movie.

Mum was trying to calm Tanya down. "There's an explanation for all this. Don't worry. We'll find out why it happened. We will," Mum said. But I could tell by Mum's voice that she was shaken too. She didn't know what had happened, and she was scared.

My aunt was hurriedly trying to clean up the mess, but she was white in the face and clearly upset. She was a high school teacher who prided herself on her intelligence and rationality. For her there was a logical explanation for everything, but even she knew there was no natural explanation for this, only a dark and unnatural one.

Whatever it was, whatever had caused the black dust in Tanya's room, it didn't want us living in the top house. We could all feel it, and right away Tanya and I were moved back down into the main house.

Afterwards, none of us talked about what had happened. Like the black dust, it was swept away.

CHAPTER 8

NEW ZEALAND

IN 1996, I GRADUATED from high school. Three months later, I left behind the house at Forresters Beach and the terrifying incidents that had happened there.

By the time I finished school, I'd begun to feel a deep rift between myself and my friends, and I wanted to get away from the Central Coast. I'd always felt different from other people there—more deep-thinking and sensitive—but now that I was done with school, I didn't want to bother trying to fit in anymore. I wanted to leave. I was tired of pretending. I was also starting to dislike the person I was becoming—increasingly unkind, sneaky, and mean. And I didn't like the friend I was becoming to my friends.

I wanted a new life, and I wanted to "discover me." So a few months after leaving school, I moved to New Zealand. I ended up staying in New Zealand for ten months and it was the most empowering experience I'd had in my life to that point.

I lived on a farm, and spending hours walking by myself in the green fields, riding my motorbike out on the plains, and tending to the animals and gardens was deeply healing. It was the first time I'd spent so much time alone in nature, and also the first time I realized that living on the land and being connected to nature could heal you. There's something incredibly comforting about the steadiness of the natural world—how the cycles of life keep moving and the seasons keep changing no matter what else is happening. I felt like I finally had a space where I could reflect upon my childhood and life and gain some perspective.

In New Zealand, I experienced the freedom of not having a past. No one knew me. Apart from the constant snide jokes about me being Australian (Australia and New Zealand have a rivalry; it's mostly to do with football) I felt like I could be anybody. I was eighteen, and I felt like I could change my life for good, so I began to think about who I wanted to be and what type of life I wanted to live.

It was also in New Zealand that I discovered Tori Amos's music. I had first heard of Tori Amos in Australia, a couple of weeks before I graduated, when a girlfriend at school sang one of her popular songs—"Winter"—at assembly. I loved the song so much I went out and bought all her albums, and in New Zealand I spent many hours on the couch in the living room listening to her. With a headset on, drinking Baileys, I'd lose myself to her music. Something about the rawness and passion of her sound and lyrics connected with me and I felt understood; it changed and healed me, motivating me to want to create a new life.

I felt energized. New Zealand and all it gave me was the beginning of my path to deep, lasting healing. When I returned to Australia, I was a different person.

I returned to Sydney in December 1997, enrolling in university and beginning a course of study in Media and Communications the following year. I hadn't yet properly dealt with my past or learned how to cope with my psychic abilities, but I felt hope. I was motivated and ambitious. I was the captain of my own ship; the creator of my destiny. I would grab life with both hands and mold and shape it to *my own* design.

And then I met a woman who had a slightly different forecast for me.

I'm sitting across the table from an astrologer. She's nice enough—polite and well spoken. Her house is cozy and charming. I've come to her for an Aura-Soma reading, but she's asked if she can look at my astrological chart.

I don't really believe in astrology, so as she goes on, reading my birth chart to me and telling me about my life and childhood, I'm skeptical.

You'd think that with all the things I've experienced in my life, all the strange and psychic and supernatural things, that I would believe in astrology, but truth be told I'm a pragmatist. Until I get proof, tangible, evidence-based proof, until it happens to me or someone I know and trust, I don't believe it. Until then it's all theory and fluff and woo-woo.

So far, what she's said about my childhood sounds accurate but also generic. Yes, my childhood years were hard. Yes, I had a difficult relationship with my father. Yes, I felt lonely and isolated in my teens. And yes, I'm trying to figure out who I am and what I want to do with my life. But don't all teenagers feel that way? Who didn't feel lonely in their childhood, at least sometimes?

"See here," she says, pointing to a line on my birth chart—there are so many lines running up and down the page I don't know which line she means—"this line indicates the near future, around the year 2000, and this shows me that in this year you'll experience a rebirth. In this year your old life will completely dissolve and a new life will begin."

I stifle a sigh.

"In this year," she continues, pointing to the line on the page again, "a fire will sweep through your life, burning up everything that is old and outdated and needs to die. Then, like a phoenix rising from the ashes, you will be transformed."

It was 1998, and supposedly in eighteen months' time, my new life was to start—after a massive fire. I didn't love the outlook, but I wasn't particularly worried; after all, I didn't put much stock in astrology in general, or in her psychic talents in particular.

But although I was doubtful, her prediction about the year 2000 proved to be accurate.

CHAPTER 9

THE FIRE

WHEN THE ASTROLOGER PREDICTED that a fire would sweep through my life, I didn't know she meant it literally. (Perhaps she didn't either.) But in July 2000, the main house at Forresters Beach burned to the ground.

My brother Aaron was minding the house while my parents were on vacation with Tanya and Rebekah. Aaron and his friends were cooking french fries on the stove, and the oil ignited with the gas. Within minutes, the entire kitchen was alight. The Forresters Beach house was made entirely of timber, so the fire spread quickly. Within the hour, the whole house was burning.

Years before—prior to moving to Sydney—I'd seen visions of the house burning down and had told Mum about them. They'd started as soon as we moved back into the house, after we returned from the Gold Coast. I'd be walking through the house and suddenly I'd have a flash of it on fire, or when I'd fall asleep at night, I'd see myself surrounded by a wall of red and yellow flames.

I knew it was a premonition—a vision that would happen one day—but I would brush it away or try to push down what I saw. I was frightened of my abilities and my inner visions; I never wanted to see future events, like how my primary school friend would die young (she died in her early twenties), or how another friend would contract a terminal illness (which happened when

49

she was nineteen). I was terrified of what I saw because I still believed, although it was years after we'd left the Pentecostal church, that I was bad and cursed.

But I wasn't the only one who had a feeling that something was very wrong with the house.

I'm lying on my futon reading through lecture notes from one of my classes at university. The phone rings; it's Mum. Her voice is edgy and strained.

"What's happened?" I ask her, feeling my own chest constrict with tension.

"Nothing," she says, ". . . yet. But I'm worried about the house. I think the ghosts from the top house have come down to the main house. The house feels dark and creepy. Something isn't right."

I pause, taking it in. This is the first time she's talked like this about the house. I'd also never heard her say the word "ghost."

"I feel like the house is growing darkness," she continues, ". . . spreading it. Something evil is living in our house and I don't know what to do. It feels like bad spirits are trying to make the house dark in an attempt to push us out!"

I want to comfort her, tell her it wasn't true; but I can't, because I agree with her. The last few times I'd stayed there the energy in the house was so heavy and dark that I'd gone to my boyfriend's parents' place for the night.

"Rebekah is having terrible nightmares and seeing scary shapes and shadows on the walls in her room," Mum goes on. "I keep trimming back the garden and the plants to let more light into the house but it isn't working. I've been burning candles and praying, but that isn't working either! The house just seems to be getting darker! The bad energy is getting stronger and it feels like I'm in some spiritual battle, in spiritual warfare with the dark spirits. I'm scared something bad will happen if we don't leave! What should I do, Belinda?"

"I don't know, Mum." I wish I can say something to help, to comfort her, but I'm at a loss.

I didn't yet know how to raise the vibration of a house and cleanse it of bad spirits. If I had, maybe the house, and everything else we lost, could have been saved . . .

I will never forget the day it happened. It was a Sunday afternoon, and I was at my boyfriend's house. A neighbor phoned us with the news that the Forresters Beach house was burning to the ground, and that Aaron had been in the house with his friends.

"He's in really bad shape," my boyfriend said to me, relaying the news. "He almost didn't get out in time. He made it just before the house exploded."

When I finally reached Aaron on his mobile phone, he was crying so hard I couldn't understand what he was saying. Eventually I could make out that he was trying to tell me he hadn't been able to rescue our little cocker spaniel, Sam, from the house before the explosion. I later learned that none of our pets—our dog or two cats—had survived.

It was almost too much for me to take. Plus my dad and mum and Tanya and Rebekah were away and I didn't know what to do; I couldn't get hold of them to tell them what had happened. I started crying uncontrollably.

My boyfriend drove me to Forresters Beach. From the top of the drive, as we made our way towards the house, we saw big, thick tendrils of black smoke rising from the ground and reaching far and wide into the sky. Crowds of people and police and firemen stood around and I frantically scanned the crowd to try to find Aaron. Someone finally pointed him out to me and I ran to him and hugged him.

Standing with Aaron were two firemen and a police officer, along with the friends who'd been in the house with Aaron when the fire started. He told me they were giving a statement. I left them to walk to the end of the driveway and look at the burnt, wet mass that used to be our family home.

All that was left was the blackened and scorched frame of where our house once stood. The fire had incinerated almost all the walls as well as our furniture and belongings, and everything was scattered because of the explosion. I couldn't even tell which room was the one that used to be my bedroom until I noticed the stinking, smoldering remains of my bed.

Together, my boyfriend and I walked down the side of the house to see if we could salvage anything from the charred wreckage. As we reached the end of the house, where Rebekah's bedroom used to be, suddenly a dark energy came rushing at me, almost shoving me over backwards. It felt like a punch in the solar plexus, like the wind had been knocked out of me. Then something huge began bearing down upon me, pressing against me and pushing me away.

Looking over at my boyfriend, I could tell by the shocked expression on his face that he had felt something too. We fled back to his car, and as we ran, I could hear the voices of the bad spirits. They were calling out to me, following me, their chanting mocking and menacing:

Ashes to ashes, dust to dust. Never come back . . .
Ashes to ashes, dust to dust. Never come back . . .
Ashes to ashes, dust to dust. Never come back . . .

I never did.

It turned out that the house was only the first of our losses that year. Shortly after the house fire, Nanna Merle passed away. Then in October, Dad left Mum, ending their twenty-four-year marriage. Grandad George had passed away the year before. Even my relationship with my boyfriend ended.

Like the astrologer predicted, my life completely dissolved.

On top of it I suddenly became very unwell. I was vomiting all the time and couldn't work out why. There was a terrible burning feeling in the pit of my stomach; I was constantly nause-ated and often couldn't sleep because of the pain. Months later, I had a gastroscopy and the doctor told me I had an acute gastric ulcer—one of the worst he'd ever seen. I felt like the fire that had burned through my life, dissolving everything in its path, now also was burning me up from the inside, too.

Unbelievably, it even seemed that my psychic, empath, and shadow-hunter gifts had become *stronger* again because now I was receiving so many impressions and taking on so many peo-ple's pains and illnesses that it was making me feel like I was crazy. There seemed to be no protection anymore, somehow *even less* than before. My panic attacks became so bad that there were days I couldn't leave my apartment.

I didn't feel safe *anywhere*. Not out in public, not in my apart-ment. Not even in my own body.

I'd come into this life with fear, and every time I felt that things were getting better—that I'd turned a corner—everything fell apart again. I was trying so hard to have a life that was hap-pier, but all my fears just kept compounding. I became utterly discouraged and began to fantasize about how I might end my life. I'd imagine tying rocks to my feet and walking into the ocean or taking a handful of pills and falling into a deep, dark sleep from which I'd never wake up.

Finally, I confessed to Mum what was going on. I told her about my physical sickness, panic, and despair, and also about the things I was seeing.

"When I close my eyes," I told her, "I have this recurring vision. I see a red-haired girl with blue and black bruises, bound in chains, and she's falling down out of the sky towards me. I don't know what it means. I haven't only been having this vision lately. I've had it for years; and when I see this, when I see her falling towards me, I'm frightened, but I also feel like she is trying to tell me something."

"Find a therapist," Mum urged. "Find someone you can talk to about it. I think the red-haired girl is trying to tell you something, and you need help!"

I contacted a mental health professional, hoping this therapist would be far more successful in helping me than the last one.

CHAPTER 10

THE DARK NIGHT

I TOOK MY MUM'S advice and found a therapist; I even committed to seeing her twice a week. Right away, however, it was evident she wasn't going to be able to help me.

I'm sitting in the therapist's office. It's our first visit, and she's introducing herself and telling me a bit about her approach. I'm listening, but something just next to her catches my eye. It's an older woman. A spirit. She's standing there waving to me and saying hi.

"What are you looking at?"

I turn back to the therapist, who is looking at me expectantly.

"I can see your deceased grandmother," I say.

The therapist frowns and takes a deep breath. I recognize the disapproval in her manner, but she doesn't say anything. She's waiting to see if I have anything else to say.

I'm silent.

She shifts in her chair, then sighs again. There's pity in that sigh. Or perhaps exasperation. At this point in my life, I'm accustomed to both.

"Belinda, in the course of this therapy you will come to realize that spirits aren't real and that they are inner-personalities—fictitious entities—that you have created in order to survive a difficult childhood . . ."

Now I'm watching her lips move without sound. My heart drops with a thud—she doesn't believe me. She can't help me. Still, I try to focus back in on what she's saying.

". . . so that you could cope with the trauma you've experienced. You've made them up," she's saying. "Spirits aren't real; neither are ghosts. It's all in your imagination."

She takes a deep breath and looks at me solidly as if she's just made a profound declaration that she's prepared to defend. My eyes fall to the floor and all I can think is, "I wonder how many sessions I'll have to have with this person to keep Mum from worrying about me?"

I'd been hopeful that these sessions would provide at least some relief from what I was experiencing, but it wasn't to be. Instead, the therapist's reaction just made me feel even more isolated. My last vestiges of hope—the feeling that my life would change for the better—had disappeared.

This time was truly the darkest in my life. These years were the years in which I experienced what many refer to as a "dark night of the soul."

The fire that swept through my life—through my house, through my family, through my solar plexus, through my psyche—burned up and dissolved everything I'd known and loved. It felt like I was experiencing the wrath of purgatory—*ashes to ashes, dust to dust*—and a new life, the new life the astrologer had promised me, was nowhere on the horizon. I was gazing into the abyss . . .

A dark night of the soul is beyond depression. It feels like the pain of it will never end; that the darkness will never lift. It's as if you've been cast out, thrown away, or tossed aside with no way back. It can feel as though you're being punished for something, or that the entire purpose of your life is to suffer. The pain feels never-ending, and you become the *walking dead*.

There I was walking, searching, clutching, trying to find solace and comfort and stability . . . Every time I reached for something, it dissolved like dust in my hands. Everything around me was gray and withering and dying . . .

It was earthbound hell.

But like all cycles of life, like all deaths, rebirth *does* follow. Just like the astrologer had predicted for me. Although I doubted it and thought I was never to be released from my inner darkness, the dark night of the soul does, inevitably, lead to release. We do come out of the pain and the darkness to find the light.

At first, it's hard to see the brightness amidst all the dark; there are only the smallest, faintest splinters of light, like a tiny window atop a prison wall. But if we focus upon these light-splinters, however small and faint, eventually they grow into shafts of light, then the shafts become streams of light . . . And before you know it, the light is cracking through and pouring down on you. You're bathed in light, and you can see the new path ahead.

You've moved from dark to light.

The lessons of the dark night of the soul are among the hardest to learn because they are lessons of faith. In that space, the sense of despair is so heavy, the feeling of abandonment so great that it's nearly impossible to imagine having faith in anything again. And yet that is what ultimately pulls you through. Those little shafts of light are messengers—reminders that you are not alone. That you can never be truly alone, because you can never be separated from God. You can never be separated from the Source, or Love, or Light; that from which we all come.

It seems backwards, finding love and connection in the midst of such darkness. But somehow, when all else is gone, it becomes undeniable that the only thing left is that which can never be destroyed—your divinity.

As you begin to know this, not just with your mind but also with your body and soul, your vibration starts to rise. And once you begin to embrace your own sacredness, real healing begins.

My life fell apart in the year 2000, in some respects literally. After that, my hope was gone, and I was ready to give up. But as it happened, when I finally stopped trying, when I finally stopped pushing for an answer to the question of why all this had happened to me, an answer came.

My dark night of the soul had begun with the dissolution of my family, but it came full circle and ended with a healing of my family—a message from my Grandma Jean.

I'm sitting on my bed trying to study for an anthropology exam, but I'm distracted. I'd rather be heading into town and meeting up with a girlfriend for lunch, but I need to cram because the exam is on Monday.

I glance out the window and see my neighbor across the road trimming her rose bush. She looks lovely in her white cotton dress and gloves, with her long, white-gray hair tied back.

She sees me and waves from across the street. I wave back, wanting to jump off the bed and go out and chat with her— anything other than having to learn about the symbolism of ancient Australian Aboriginal cave paintings—but I make myself stay.

I turn the page and begin reading, when suddenly a voice speaks to me. Clear and loud it says, "Put down that book and listen to me!"

I freeze. I know it's the voice of a spirit because it says things I wouldn't say or know, but I've never heard a spirit voice come through so audibly. Usually when spirits speak to me, I hear them inside my head; they sound like my own internal voice talking to me. I know though that it's not my voice. But this spirit speaking to me now is audible and loud, which makes me fearful.

"Belinda, don't be afraid. It's your Grandma Jean, and I need to talk to you!"

I sit bolt upright. I'm still afraid, but I know this must be important.

Grandma Jean had seven children—five sons and two daughters—and she begins to tell me about one of her sons.

She's telling me private and intimate things about him, secret things too—things I didn't know about him that had happened before I was born. I don't understand why she's telling me any of this or what I'm supposed to do with this information.

But then Grandma Jean urges me to contact my uncle and tell him what she's told me. He needs to know she loves him and that she is worried about him. It is urgent that I contact him today.

Clearly Grandma is very worried, but I don't want to contact my uncle. I hardly know him, and I'm scared he'll think I'm crazy. Also, I'd promised my therapist I wouldn't listen to the voices anymore. I need to learn to ignore them, to push them away and quiet them, and listening to Grandma Jean's voice may make them all start to come flooding back in. I want to be normal, not crazy.

I decide I won't contact him.

But then her voice booms so loud that my head shakes. "BELINDA! YOU WILL CONTACT HIM!"

Two hours later I was speaking to my uncle on the phone. He wasn't scared about what I told him, nor did he think I was crazy. He was understandably shocked but also deeply moved.

Unbeknownst to me and my family, he had been struggling with depression for years. He was deeply unhappy, and had been thinking about ending his life. Grandma Jean had known that, and through getting me to reach out to him and relay her message, she had saved his life.

My uncle had never been able to share the pain of his depression with another person, but now there was hope. I understood him. His mother understood him. Somebody cared. He didn't want to end his life anymore, and in the years after my phone call to him, he, with the help of a beautiful woman (who would later become his wife), was able to heal from his depression and live a happy life.

I cannot overstate the impact of that day—the day Grandma Jean contacted me about my uncle. It changed *everything* for me, forever. It was the first time something good had come from my abilities. I'd thought I was cursed and needed to hide myself. But, for the first time, I had brought light into someone's life through *sharing* myself.

When I ended the phone call with my uncle, Grandma Jean patted me on the shoulder and said, "Remember, dear child, I told you that when you'd grow up it would be different. See— there is a reason you have these gifts. You can help others. It's time to begin!"

And I did.

CHAPTER 11

GERMANY

FINALLY, I HAD BEEN released from the dark night of my soul. I realized that the psychic and empathic abilities that had burdened me for so long were gifts; now I needed to learn how to use them. But life needed to take me away from the country of my birth for this to happen.

The year before, I'd been visiting my father at a remote Aboriginal community where he'd been working as a Flying Doctor. On the red-eye flight from Darwin to Sydney I sat next to a tanned, attractive man from Germany. Nine months later I immigrated to Germany to be with him, and it's there that my career as a psychic would begin.

I fell in love with Germany the moment I laid eyes on it. As we made our descent into Frankfurt Airport, flying low over the countryside, I just adored its green fields and forests and quaint villages and churches with their sloping roofs and medieval architecture. There was something so mystical about Germany, so Gothic and fairytale-like. I was smitten.

But there was also something deeper than that. When I stepped off the plane and onto German soil, I was hit by the strongest sense that I was home again. That I had *returned*. That I had come back to where I belonged.

Yet this feeling of deep connection and homecoming was also tinged with angst. I couldn't help feeling like something bad and old had happened to me here, too. As I walked through Frankfurt Airport, then went through passport control and waited for my luggage, my heart was beating fast and I was sweating. I knew life had brought me here to blossom, to throw off the shackles of my past and create a new life, but I was now filled with trepidation . . . This likely meant further and deeper (and probably more painful) healing.

In the following months, this proved to be true . . . Something bad and old *had* happened to me in Germany: my past lives.

I'm standing in the queue at the supermarket, waiting to check out.

Abruptly, everything around me disappears. I'm no longer at the store, I'm in the past. In another era. When I go to move, I feel the bindings—I can't move my body or my hands. I'm tied to a post!

Suddenly I'm surrounded by a circle of fire. I scream and struggle, trying desperately to free myself, but the fire's moving too quickly. It's closing in on me! I can feel the heat on my body. Now my flesh is starting to scorch and burn. It's melting off me like wax!

I blink my eyes and I'm back in the store, clutching my groceries and breathing hard. I drop everything and run out of the store, leaving everyone staring after me.

I race to my apartment. It's only minutes away and thank goodness, because I make it only just in time before the vision returns and overtakes me. I'm on the ground sobbing. I'm burning! They're killing me because I'm a witch!

I'm shaking, feeling shocked and overwhelmed. Yet at the same time, I have a sense that this vision is trying to tell me something.

Days after the first vision, I was out walking along the Rhine River when another struck me. This time in the vision, I was dragged out of bed in the middle of the night by a group of men, jailed, tortured, and hanged. Another time, I was renounced by my entire family at a public hearing and was tortured and drowned for being a witch.

Over the course of several months, I relived roughly twenty of my past lives. They would appear suddenly, out of nowhere, and overtake me, and I'd find myself re-experiencing another trauma—another death, murder, beating, or hanging.

It took me some time to realize that these visions I was having were of past lives. I'd heard about reincarnation, but I didn't know if I believed in the notion of past lives. I'd also never heard of anyone spontaneously re-experiencing their own.

Even though I'd begun to understand what I was seeing, it was incredibly stressful never knowing when a vision would hit. Eventually I learned how I could hold them off. When I would feel a vision coming on, I would block it as much as I could until I made it home, where I would relive it entirely. Many times I had to flee the language school where I was learning German so I could get home, crawl under my duvet, and be in a safe space for a vision to come through.

I didn't know *why* I was reliving my past lives, but somehow I intuitively knew I needed to let them come forth and show me what had happened to me.

Before long, it started to become clear—the lives I was being shown all had a central theme. Over and over I had been persecuted for my psychic abilities and talents. Sometimes I was called a "witch" or a "heretic" and was tried and murdered for my gifts. Other times it happened in less traumatic and public ways. For example, I was abandoned, or punished by one of my parents, or cast out of my village, or was rejected by my parents and family because I was "different."

I didn't always die painfully because of what I could see or do, but I was *never safe to be myself*. And I came to realize that in my present life I was suffering this again because I was still carrying the *unhealed* energy of these past-life persecutions.

But while the experiences of reliving the traumas of my past lives were unpleasant and at times frightening, they were also liberating. For the first time ever, my childhood made sense! I now understood how the Law of Attraction works: *Your past will become your future unless you heal it.* In my childhood I had unconsciously attracted persecution and pain because I hadn't healed the persecution and pain from my past lives. My present life was a reflection of my past lives.

I also understood why I'd been led to immigrate (return) to Germany. Europe was not only my long-lost love, it was my long-lost pain. I had returned to the core of my pain for it to be purged and healed.

All this inspired me to want to heal my old wounds and dissolve the pain and persecution so I wouldn't have to deal with its lingering effects anymore. It urged me on to heal *whatever* was holding me back from accepting my abilities.

For the first time ever, I was ready to embrace my psychic and mystic abilities fully. But I still needed to learn how to use them.

CHAPTER 12

FORTUNE-TELLING

BEFORE I'D MOVED TO Germany, I had done a little exploring of my talents. For a few months, I worked in a psychic café
on the Central Coast where I was paid to read people's fortunes.
It certainly wasn't my dream job, but after what had happened
with Grandma Jean and my uncle, I decided I needed to begin
somewhere.

To apply for the job, I was to bring my own tarot deck and
give the owner of the café a reading. I had a pack of tarot, but I
didn't know how to read them; there had never been any point—
I didn't need cards to read someone. I figured I'd just shuffle the
cards, place them on the table, and make it look like I knew how
to read them, but instead I'd just look inside her and read her
energy. No problem.

When I arrived for the interview, my heart sank. Covering
the walls and windowsills were pictures and figurines of fairies,
elves, ascended masters, and Native Americans, all jammed in
amongst crystals, wands, runes, and silver pentagrams. I had
arrived on Planet Woo-Woo. I thought, *If I get this job, apart from
Mum, I won't tell anyone ever that I'm working here!*

The owner of the café came gliding out to meet me. She was a
woman in her late fifties, dressed in a long, emerald-green, Egyptian-
style robe with a matching silver headpiece and necklace. Her

badly dyed black hair was pulled back in a tight bun and her eyes were heavily made up with black and blue eye shadow as if she believed herself to be the reincarnation of Cleopatra.

But it wasn't so much her looks as her air of spiritual arrogance that made me dislike her instantly. Holding out a bejeweled hand, she ushered me over to one of the small tables at the front of the café and told me to hurry along and get started with my reading. She sat herself down across from me and looked at me expectantly.

"Okay," I think, trying to remember what that book on tarot that I'd borrowed from the library had said. Right—I'm supposed to shuffle the deck.

I shuffle the cards around in my hands for a few moments, then cut the deck, then . . .

Wait, what's next? Do I tap the cards to infuse them with our energies, or do I lay the spread first?

My heart's beating faster.

I think I need to tap the cards, but was it supposed to be with my left hand or right? The book was really specific, but I can't remember! And hold on—does she lay the cards or do I?

This is a disaster. I'm sure at this point she can tell I have no idea what I'm doing.

I glance up. The reincarnation of Cleopatra is staring at me, eyebrow raised, clearly unimpressed. I start to shuffle again, but she places a hand on the table, signaling me to stop.

"Do you know how to read tarot, Belinda?" she says.

My shoulders drop. "No," I sigh. "I don't know how to read tarot. But I do know how to read people. Here—give me your hand and I'll show you."

She's wary, but slowly she offers her hand. I take it in mine, close my eyes, and just like that, the tiny movies start flashing and I can feel what she's feeling. For the next half hour, I tell her all about herself.

When I'm finished, I open my eyes and see that she's crying. Her face is blotchy and her entire demeanor has changed; she's now meek and soft. Slowly she slips her hand from mine, reaches into her bra, and pulls out a sparkly purple handkerchief.

"My dear," she sniffs, "you don't need tarot cards to read people. I don't know how you knew all that about me, but you have a gift. I've never seen that type of talent before." She takes a moment to dab at her smudged eyes, then continues. "But in this café, people don't want to hear about the troubles in their lives. They come here because they want relief from them. You can't tell people all about themselves and their problems. If you work here, you will need to read people's fortunes because that is what they pay for. Do you understand? You have to read their futures and give them hope."

Right from the start, I hated telling people their futures. I wasn't telling them everything I could see about them, but instead sharing only what would *probably* happen in their lives.

At any moment in time, stretched out in front of us are many paths, many probabilities of how our futures *could* unfold. Whatever choices we make in the present moment influence our futures; we can shape and choose our destinies. But I wasn't supposed to tell people this; I was paid to predict only one future.

I did my best to find the most *probable* path in a person's future and talk about that. People seemed pleased with the futures I predicted for them, most likely because I was telling them what they wanted to hear.

I became very popular at the café, but inside I was ashamed. I tried to ease my guilt by reminding myself that most psychics simply told people what they wanted to hear. But even so, I felt like a fake. When I left Australia to live in Germany, I decided I would never work as a fortune-teller again . . .

I was also having doubts about whether I wanted to work as a psychic; I didn't really fit into the "psychic scene." Most readers were at least thirty years older than me, and somehow seemed to have attractive, younger Native American spirit guides. And by some coincidence, happened to be famous people, queens, or goddesses in their past lives as well! At that time in my life, it seemed to me that spirituality largely boiled down to the fantasies of bored middle-aged women.

But I was a realist and a critical thinker, and that all felt like fantasy to me, far removed from people's *real* life issues. I couldn't help but think: What is the point of having psychic gifts if you can't use them in a *real* way to help people with their real-life issues? I kept searching, thinking there must be another way to use my abilities.

CHAPTER 13

MEDIUMSHIP
TRAINING

I DIDN'T WANT TO be a fortune-teller and I didn't fit into the psychic scene—that much was certain. But I still felt guided to pursue the path of developing my psychic abilities.

I had always seen spirits, and I thought perhaps I could try working as a medium. All my life I'd been talking to the dead, to spirits (who, as it happens, are a lot more alive than most humans), so I knew I could do it. I'd just had the experience of talking to a spirit—my deceased grandmother—and it transformed her son's life. Perhaps relaying messages from the afterlife could bring other people peace and comfort too?

So in 2002, I flew from Germany to England to attend a six-day mediumship course. I was unsure what to expect—whether we'd be communicating with spirits who had returned home, or with ghosts who hadn't found the light and made the transition to the afterlife.

Truth be told, I was just as interested in learning how to help ghosts as living people. Ever since moving to Germany and reliving my past lives, my experiences with ghosts had started to change. I was still seeing them most nights and they would still crowd in on me and want to talk with me, but somehow it wasn't as scary as before. They would no longer touch me or fight each other to try to get my attention. I was starting to realize they didn't want to harm me. They weren't scary or menacing, just desperate for help.

What I didn't know at the time was that I was changing my energy. My vibration was rising and because of this, my energy field was becoming more luminous and ghosts were no longer able to energetically pull my vibration down.

There were other positive effects from my rising vibration too. I was still a shadow hunter—I was still attuned to see people's darkness and to know what was wrong with them—and I was still a ghost whisperer, but I was no longer experiencing the suffering these abilities had caused me in the past. I was less fearful, more resilient, and better protected. This in turn made me much less afraid of my abilities and much more motivated to get started using them.

As I set out for England, I hoped this course would finally be the beginning of a career where I could use my abilities. And that is exactly what happened, just not in the way I'd thought . . .

I arrived at the course full of excitement, expecting to acquire the practical skills I'd need to work as a medium. But by the close of the first day I had learned one thing—that mediumship was not for me.

I was disappointed to learn that mediumship did not involve helping ghosts (we were told *not* to connect with or communicate with ghosts). But I was even more disappointed (and shocked) by the state of health of the mediums running the course.

The five mediums who taught and tutored us were all in very poor health. This wasn't something only I could see with my psychic sight, it was apparent to everyone. All three of the female tutors were so overweight that they struggled to walk across the room and to get into and out of chairs. Both of the male tutors, although only in their fifties, already used crutches.

One of them could barely talk, and he could do little more than hobble because he'd been struck down with an unknown virus that had paralyzed his face and body.

On the first day of the course we were told that he'd contracted the disease because mediumship work is taxing on the body, and makes you weak and vulnerable. And because this could also happen to us, the way to protect ourselves against it was to "ground" ourselves by being overweight.

The tutors told us that the *very* best and most gifted mediums were *very* overweight, and I watched in shock as my fellow course participants nodded and accepted this. I couldn't help but wonder if they could look inside their tutors and see their liver problems, their developing diabetes and osteoporosis, their fatigue and mental fogginess and exhaustion, as I could, if they'd still have been as excited to work as mediums.

So when we were told that this state is a necessary by-product of being a medium I immediately thought, "No thanks!" But also, I just wasn't vibing with the course and what we were learning.

I could easily see, communicate with, and pass on messages from the Other Side, but somehow it didn't feel right. Many of my fellow students were loving the course. They quickly developed their abilities and thrived in their newfound roles as mediums. But for some reason, I didn't share their passion for passing on messages from the Other Side.

The morning session is packed. Fifty or more people are in the meeting room, humming with excitement as we prepare to take our turns giving live demonstrations.

One by one, people get up in front of the group and start relaying messages from our dead relatives. Everyone's so happy to be doing this . . . except me.

I can't help it. I'm trying to get into it. I have no trouble seeing spirits or hearing their messages, but it just doesn't feel right. It's not me.

I'm starting to fidget. What am I doing here? And if this doesn't work, what will I do? I already know I don't want to be a fortune-teller. So what's left?

Forget it. This really isn't for me. I slip out the rear door unnoticed and head upstairs to my room, where I throw myself down on the bed. The tears come quickly.

The course is over tomorrow and then what? I can't stop being psychic. I can't make it all go away, so why is this happening? I was sure I'd been guided here, to this course, but it's so clearly not for me.

Finally I sit up and take a deep breath. That's it—I'm done with the course. I'll skip the evening session and catch a taxi to the airport in the morning.

No sooner do I decide this than I hear a familiar voice, loud and clear.

"Go downstairs and attend the evening session, Belinda. It will all work out. I promise."

It's my Grandma Jean, and by now I know better than to ignore what she's telling me. I drag myself off the bed and leave my room.

I didn't understand why Grandma Jean had urged me to continue, why she'd sent me downstairs, but I went. During the evening session, I was partnered up with an elderly man with a lovely open face and green eyes. We were to work as pairs, connecting to the Other Side and communicating with any deceased loved ones of our partner who would come through and speak to us.

My partner, who could tell that I had been crying, gently walked me out of the room and down the hall, looking for a quiet place for us to work. He found a comfy old couch and sat me down opposite him. I started to cry again and he handed me a tissue, then I poured out my heart to him.

When I finished, he said, "So, if you don't want to be a medium and relay messages from the afterlife, and if you don't know what you want to do, what *can* you do? How do you read people?" Like I did with the owner of the psychic café, I reached over and took his hand. The images began and I started telling him all about himself . . .

I told him everything about his life and struggles and dreams. Then, starting at his feet and working my way up his body, I looked inside him and told him every health problem that was ailing him.

He was dumbfounded. He couldn't believe I knew these things. As it turned out, he was a medical doctor and a doctor of osteopathy. Not only was I completely accurate in my diagnosis, the information I gave him was specific, detailed, and as he said, "Simply incredible!"

He told me I didn't need to worry about not wanting to work as a medium because I was a "medical intuitive." I'd never heard the term before. He asked me if I'd heard of Caroline Myss and her work and I told him I hadn't.

"They sell her books here, Belinda. Right here in the college!" he said. So as soon as they opened the following day, I bought two of her books—*Anatomy of the Spirit* and *Why People Don't Heal and How They Can*. Starting on the plane ride home and continuing in the following weeks, back in my small apartment in Düsseldorf, I read them both cover to cover.

Finally, I had discovered that I was a medical intuitive. Not only was there a term to describe what I could do—perceiving what was wrong with people—but I could also make a career from it.

Caroline Myss didn't read people's futures or talk to dead people; she told people what was wrong with them. *She used her gifts to help people in a real way with their real-life issues!* This was the piece of my life-puzzle I'd been looking for.

CHAPTER 14

MEDICAL INTUITION

AFTER I RETURNED TO Germany, I told a few people at the language school where I was studying German about my ability to "see inside" people. They asked if I would do sessions for them, and I did. Afterwards, they told their friends about me, and things just grew from there. Within three years I had a solid reputation as a medical intuitive.

People from countries all around the world started to consult me about all kinds of problems: why they were unwell or depressed; why they were struggling in their marriage or with their children; why they were tired or lacking passion; or why they couldn't find the right career or figure out their life purpose.

In time, doctors and other professionals within the medical community heard about my abilities and they started to come to me for sessions too. After I proved myself to them, they started consulting me for help with their patients.

I would conduct these sessions in my apartment in Germany, or via the telephone. (I don't have to be in the same room with someone to read them—I can see and feel people's energy from thousands of miles away.) At the start of every session, I'd relay to people their past-life histories and problems. I didn't know if other psychics or medical intuitives worked this way, but I found it incredibly helpful. After all, I'd learned through my own experiences that past-life issues can become present-life challenges.

Offering past-life readings to my clients not only showed me *exactly* what negative subconscious patterns they brought into this life, it also showed me *how* these negative subconscious patterns were causing a person's struggles and conflicts. The past lives would give me volumes of information about a person's current life—about their health, relationships, creative ventures, family life, and career.

After I'd read someone's past lives, I'd scan their body, reading their health and illnesses, getting even more detailed information. I would always start at the feet and work my way up because it simply felt "right" to work like this.

Though Caroline Myss's books had introduced me to the concept of chakras, it didn't seem important to me at the time. I was deriving so much accurate and detailed information from people's past lives that I had all the information I needed. Of course, I was reading people's energy fields and the chakras within them, but at the time I didn't know them as such.

After I'd scan the body, people could ask me questions. This was their first opportunity to do so because at the start of every session, I asked clients *not* to tell me about themselves or what had caused them to seek my help. I wanted it to be clear that all the information I received was through my psychic and intuitive channels.

After I completed the reading, my clients would ask me about their relationships, their career choices, their purpose in life, or about their finances. Often people would ask me about a deceased loved one, and I'd be able to make contact and speak to their family or friends on the Other Side. Though they'd often ask, I always tried to avoid answering people's questions about the future.

Initially, my sessions would last roughly two hours. Eventually, they started to become shorter as I started to find the core reason (or reasons) for a person's ill health or life problems more quickly. But I always worked in the same order, starting with a past-life reading, then scanning their energy field and chakras, and finally answering their questions.

A woman named Monika is on the telephone. She's sixty years old and lives in Switzerland. I'm struggling to understand her. Though I now speak German fluently, her Swiss German is difficult for me to understand easily. It's no matter, though—I can see her energy field perfectly, and anyway, it's my job to do the talking.

I start the session by explaining to Monika how I work, and just as importantly, how I don't work.

"I don't work as a doctor and I'm not a healthcare practitioner, so I don't diagnose people's physical or mental conditions. It's important that you understand that what I'm about to tell you about yourself and your energy field is based upon the impressions I receive by working as an intuitive and spiritual coach. While I'm not a doctor, I do work together with many doctors, and if I feel you have a healthcare concern that needs medical attention, I will happily refer you to one of them."

I continue. "What I also don't do is work as a fortune-teller. I do not believe in fortune-telling or future-predicting. I believe we create our own destinies, and it is my job as an intuitive to help you create the destiny you want by pointing out to you what isn't working in your life."

"It's important that you understand my role." I pause again, wanting to emphasize this point. "My job is to show you, to highlight to you, to talk to you about what isn't working in your life so that you can get it working."

I realize Monika will likely be more receptive to this idea than many of my native English–speaking clients. I've found that Europeans and German-speaking people want to hear about what isn't working in their lives, but if I don't stress this point to native English speakers—to Australians, Americans, and the British—they can become disappointed with the session because they think I've only focused on the negative.

I explain to Monika that I will look at her past-life history, which will help to reveal what past-life patterns and subconscious belief systems are affecting her present life.

"It isn't important who you were or what you did in your past lives," I say, "but it is important to know what happened to you and how this made you believe what you do about your life. I need to find those negative, limiting, and life-depleting subconscious belief systems within your past. I need to go to the root of them, so that we can find them, dig them up, and throw them away and replace them with positive, limitless, and life-affirming belief systems. Because what you believe about life, consciously or subconsciously, creates your reality."

I explain that I will then look at her energy field, working my way from her feet up, and that I'll be looking for blockages, stagnations, and pockets of disruptions in the flow of energy—or chi—in her energy field. I will also be looking for health problems, I say, and that then she may ask me questions.

Monika says she understands this, and the session begins.

I take a deep breath and open my channels. It's like opening the floodgates. All my senses—sight, taste, touch, hearing, smell—are simultaneously bombarded with feelings and visions and impressions, and I let it come towards me. I let it wash over me in large waves of energy and information, which then begins to sort itself into a type of map or plan. In my mind's eye I see it all moving around putting itself into order; the problems and issues and shadows are lining up for me to understand what they are and how to get started.

I see Monika as a young man on a ship bound for England. She's wearing a small, dark-colored cap and trousers and she's clutching onto the side of the ship, white-faced and looking out at the treacherous sea. The waves are huge and black and rolling, and the captain is calling out and commanding his crew and the passengers on board to hold on so they can make it through the storm, but Monika knows—the boy she was in that past life knows—that her life will most likely end here tonight.

And it does. A crack of lightning lights up the sea for a terrible second and she sees a huge dark wall of a wave moving towards the boat. It crashes against the boat and capsizes it. Monika is thrown into the freezing water and drowns, amidst the confusion and terror of the other passengers and the wild sea.

"The first thing I see is that you have a fear of the ocean and of swimming," I say. "You think this is an irrational fear because you don't know why you are so afraid of the sea."

"Oh my goodness," she gasps. "This is true. I've always been scared of the ocean and when I was a small child and my family took me to the sea, I wouldn't go in. I wouldn't even put my toe in and my sisters would tease me about it."

I explain her past-life experience to her. "Now you know where this fear comes from," I say, "and now you also know it isn't irrational. You have drowned before and your body—the cells of your body—remember this. But now that you know this, you can let it go. It happened then, but you can release yourself from it now."

"I'm so relieved to find out that I'm not crazy!" Monika cries. "There is a reason why I'm scared of water!"

I laugh, understanding very well what it feels like to be afraid you're crazy.

"But this isn't the most important thing I want to tell you about this past life," I continue. "The main problem you have in your life is that you are terrified to step out of your comfort zone and take any risks. You've had the experience that adventure and trying something new leads to failure and pain. This has happened in many of your past lives.

"In this past life where you drowned, you had taken a shot at a new life. Everyone had warned you that it wouldn't work out, but you felt it was the right thing, regardless. You were yearning for a new life; you needed change. But it went wrong for you, so now you fear your pioneering spirit and are afraid of change because you don't trust your own judgment."

I then relay to Monika how she was once imprisoned for marrying the man she loved, that she was rejected by her family for moving to another town, that she died of hunger and starvation on a trip to the desert, that she was robbed and beaten when walking alone into town at night. I continue, listing experience after experience that has contributed to her present fears.

I then explained to Monika that her past-life history of being punished for trying something new had led her subconscious mind to try to protect her from further hurts by leading her to avoid change. However, this was making her bitterly unhappy. Monika's fear of change had caused her to marry her first boyfriend, stay in the village in which she'd grown up, take up the same profession as her mother (teacher), and not travel as much as she wanted. Monika was still a pioneer at heart, someone who needed to expand her horizons and explore new things, so she was suffering. Deeply. And I could see that she felt she was *drying up* and *dying* inside . . .

As soon as I began Monika's body scan, I saw a dullness in her second chakra—the chakra responsible for passion and joy. Monika had no passion, and because of this, she had an array of gynecological issues. Working my way up from her feet to her legs to her lower abdomen, I saw that she had recurring bladder infections and had had a partial hysterectomy. I also saw she had constant pain and discomfort in her vagina and pelvic area, and that when she was younger she'd had two abortions.

Monika had the abortions because of her husband. He had told her to terminate the pregnancies because he was worried they "couldn't afford" a child. I also saw that her recurring bladder problems were because she was having intercourse with her husband when she didn't want to.

Further, it was apparent to me that Monika didn't like where she lived in Switzerland. Her secret fantasy was to live in the tropics. On one of the rare holidays she'd taken, she'd fallen in love with the sun and the warmth and the humidity. She'd never felt so good, and with her teacher's pension she could now afford to buy a small holiday house. But her husband didn't like her being away, and she didn't like displeasing him. It was clear to me that Monika felt trapped in her life because she felt trapped in her marriage.

As I moved further up her body to her stomach and digestive areas, I saw that she often had an upset stomach and felt nauseous. This wasn't only because she was afraid of her husband, it was also because she hated him. I could see anger and rage trapped in her stomach, and this anger and rage was giving her heartburn and indigestion.

But there was more: Monika also hated herself. Some of that anger and rage she was feeling was directed at herself. She felt she was weak and "without any backbone." She detested her own fear and passivity, and this self-hate was making her digestive issues worse.

"Yes, this is true," Monika told me when I relayed my impressions to her. "I hate this about myself and I wish I could change it. I don't want to be this way."

"You are this way because you subconsciously fear change," I said, trying to console her. "In your past lives you've experienced suffering and tragedy when you dared to make a change or be different. Your subconscious mind remembers this, and those memories are keeping you small and afraid. So don't be too hard on yourself and add more hate to the hate you are already experiencing. Let me look further at your body to see what else I can find and then we can talk about what you can do."

When I moved up into Monika's heart and chest region, I saw a heart murmur, as well as sadness and grief. Monika had been attending therapy for many years and had been taking antidepressants. I also saw that she felt very lonely during the day, so she asked her husband for a pet, a dog or cat to care for, but he said no. I saw that her husband was very traditional in his thinking. He could go to work and do as he pleased in the evenings, attending his clubs and social events, but she was supposed to be at home and wait for him, giving him her full attention (and body) whenever he wanted. It was easy to understand why Monika was so unhappy.

When I moved up into her throat, I saw Monika often lost her voice because she was afraid to speak out against her husband, and when I looked at her brain, I saw it was underused. Monika was a witty and intelligent woman, a natural academic, but she did nothing to feed her quick and eager mind.

I told Monika all these things and we discussed how she could become more aware of the past-life patterns keeping her stuck so that she could overcome them. As the session ended, Monika seemed uplifted and determined to change. I felt confident she would set out to become more mindful of how her past was affecting her present, and to step away from her attitudes of scarcity and "small-ness."

Sessions like Monika's were typical; I could see an incredible level of detail regarding people's past lives and how they were creating present physical and emotional challenges. Working with people in this way—helping them to understand what forces were at play in their lives—was very fulfilling.

Up until the year 2007, when I was twenty-eight years old, I worked full-time as a medical intuitive. I had a booming practice, and enjoyed wonderful relationships with doctors and health-care practitioners.

I loved the connection with people and the way I could shed light on their life troubles, and I felt honored and blessed to be able to do this work . . . yet I was harboring a secret—I didn't feel that being a medical intuitive was my *soul purpose*. I *did* want to help people, but I still felt there was something else out there for me.

CHAPTER 15

THE VIBRATIONAL
SPECTRUM

AS THE YEARS WENT on, I enjoyed my work as a medical intuitive less and less. The sessions had become increasingly draining and I was losing my passion for it. I felt guilty about feeling this way; I'd been given these abilities to help people and should feel honored and grateful. Still, as the days went by, it became more and more apparent to me that medical intuition was only a stepping stone in the direction of my life purpose, and I was ready to find the next step.

Not only was I losing my passion for my work as a medical intuitive, I was also becoming disillusioned by my profession. I could see the root cause of my clients' problems, but I didn't know how to help them bring about a permanent change that would give them relief. I knew *what* needed to be healed, but not *how*.

The excellent medical professionals, therapists, and alternative practitioners I was surrounded by—people at the top of their game in the healing profession—were struggling with this too. Our clients would consult us repeatedly with the same health or emotional problems; we didn't know how to help them resolve these issues.

And I didn't know how to heal myself, either. Like many of my clients and colleagues, I didn't have excellent health and wasn't feeling much joy in life. I also wasn't experiencing abundance, and I felt creatively blocked and unhappy.

I was in a funk, and although the acute ill health and torment of my childhood and teen years had abated somewhat, I found myself lacking passion and purpose. I still had constant digestive problems, to some extent I still took on my clients' and other people's negative feelings and emotions, and I was dragging myself through each day. I just didn't feel *alive*.

During my years as a medical intuitive, as dedicated as I was to my work, a niggling feeling stayed with me. It sat small in the pit of my stomach and whispered: *Medical intuition isn't your life purpose. Something else awaits.* And in August 2007, after many months of declining health and giving session after session, I decided I had to listen to that niggling voice. I had to discover what else was out there for me, and I had an idea of where to start.

A friend had recently told me about Eckhart Tolle's book *The Power of Now.* I'd read a passage where Tolle says that if we are confused and lost and seeking life direction, we can find it by accessing the power of the present moment. Reading this, I knew instantly that was what I needed to do—to find direction and purpose by getting quiet and listening to my inner self. I decided to sit and wait until I discovered my life purpose.

So I took a month off, canceling or postponing my sessions, and spent almost all day every day for weeks sitting in my white chair in my white office being "present." And it was while I was meditating that it happened . . .

I was sitting there, still, my mind restful, when suddenly I found myself outside of myself, standing and watching my "other" self meditating. It was as if someone had picked me up and placed me directly opposite myself.

It was shocking, yet strangely, it wasn't an unnerving experience. I didn't feel scared or unsettled; in fact, I felt marvelous.

I suddenly felt completely relieved of any burden of thought or ailment!

Around me and within me was only a pervasive sense of stillness and peace. There were no thoughts in my mind and there were no emotions in my body; I felt completely free, and for the first time ever, I felt completely alive—radiant, vibrant, and expansive.

While I stood there, in bliss, watching myself meditate in my white chair, I noticed that I was comprised of two parts, or two selves: *a dark-self and a light-self.* My dark- and light-selves were polar opposites of one another.

My dark-self (my egoic self, which is fearful, anxious, and insecure) existed right alongside my light-self (my soul, which is loving, brave, and wise). I'm unsure of *how* I suddenly knew these things, but somehow I did.

And in the moment that I understood this, in the moment that I understood I consisted of *equal parts* dark and light, I began to experience the dark, as well as the light, within me . . .

It started as an experience of the vibration of *pure dark.* Suddenly I was plummeting down, down, down, headfirst into the deep dark depths of low vibration. Somehow I knew I was headed into the bowels of the human experience—into the lowest of the low and the darkest of dark, to the lowest end of the spectrum—but strangely, I didn't feel afraid. I knew I was learning an important life lesson and that I needed to experience the feelings of the vibration of pure dark. So I allowed myself to plummet.

When I landed at the bottom of this spectrum, when I arrived at the complete and total suffocating blackness of the vibration of *pure dark,* I felt only dread. This was a feeling of hopelessness and desperation; a dark and grasping fear of annihilation, pain, and despair . . . times one million.

It was suffocating, engulfing, debilitating. Malignant, woeful, doomful, it was utter despair and utter depression.

It was non-life.

Yet these dreadful feelings didn't overwhelm me. I felt them around me. They were *external* to me—I didn't feel them as my own emotions.

Before I had time to process all this, I found myself moving upwards. I was being gently lifted and pulled up and beyond the vibration of pure dark. I was moving above it.

Finally, I came to rest. Here in this new, higher place, there wasn't the same blackness or feeling of complete doom. This vibration also felt dark and suffocating, but it wasn't as dark. From the teeny, tiny sliver of light here, I knew I'd moved up a level.

In this place I felt the emotions of depression and grief and self-hate. It wasn't utter despair and desperation like before—it wasn't complete *non-life*—but the vibration of this place was still deeply negative and fearful.

This was the vibration of deep depression and suicidal feelings. But once again, before I had time to think or experience more about this vibration, I found myself being lifted up . . .

When I arrived at the next vibration, I instantly experienced the emotion of unworthiness. The vibration of this place seemed to be of a deep lack of self-esteem and self-worth. Here were feelings of lowliness, shame, and degradation. Here were also feelings of self-reproach.

Suddenly, in a flash, I received an insight. I saw that many people get trapped at this low level of vibration—that many people experience this dark negative vibration—because they dislike themselves. I saw that disliking ourselves is a dangerous thing to do, and that all the violence in the world, all the atrocities and sufferings in the world stem from our inability to love ourselves.

It was a massive revelation, but once again, before I could think further about it, I found myself being lifted higher . . .

As things shifted yet again, I started to understand that I was being moved up a spectrum of sorts, from the darkest of the dark, to the lighter shades of the dark. I had experienced the vibration of pure dark, of pure fear and dread, and I was now moving up the scale. With every rise, I saw and experienced more light; I had started in blackness, but now was experiencing shades of gray. I had also moved further away from negative emotions and closer to positive ones.

The next vibration I was lifted to was of anger, bitterness, and remorse. I also sensed guilt, jealousy, and revenge. This vibration didn't feel completely hopeless and desolate like the lower vibrations I'd just experienced, but it was still deeply negative, violent, and harmful. It was *anti-life.*

Then again the energy lifted me up higher . . . At the next level I felt doubt, worry, concern, stress, and pessimism. This vibration, this *shade of gray,* was slightly lighter.

The next highest vibration was one of lethargy and stagnation. Here the vibration felt tired, drained, passive, complacent, and discouraged. The emotions here weren't as negative as those at the lower levels, but they weren't positive either. The feeling here was of flatness. It was a dull place; a place of apathy, void of energy, vitality, and color. The life force here was that of a wilted flower, or a dying person.

When I was pulled up to the next vibration, something different occurred. I wasn't just lifted, I was also pushed through a threshold . . .

It was as if I'd been raised up through a large gray cloud, like an airplane gaining altitude. Suddenly I found myself on the other side of the cloud in a vast blue expanse, and here everything felt lighter and clearer. There was far more space and room compared with the lower vibrations, which had felt cramped and dark. Quite literally, I felt *uplifted.*

I realized then that I had transitioned from the darker to the lighter shades of gray. This vibration felt peaceful, contented, hopeful, and happy. All around me was lightness and space.

Then once again, as soon as I'd understood the vibration of the place, I was moved upwards . . .

The next vibration I came to was of even more lightness. I was surrounded by a white light, and all around me I felt hope. This was a place of optimism, of deep peace, and positivity. The positive emotions here were more potent than on the previous level, and they had more energy—more life force. There was more vibrancy here; more radiance and joy.

Then I started to travel up the light-gray spectrum more quickly. At each new vibrational level, I experienced more light, greater expanse, and more life force. I experienced the vibration of enthusiasm and motivation. After that, the vibration of inspiration and passion. Then there was wonder, exhilaration, and joy, followed by radiance and splendor.

These higher vibrational states were so light-infused, so *ethereal,* that I was beginning to struggle to be able to know what they were. The feelings seemed to exist beyond the range of emotions we know on earth. They felt transcendental or God-like; they were blissful beyond human comprehension. Yet somehow there was still more to experience.

Up again I traveled until I was brought to my final destination—the highest level of the vibrational spectrum—which is the most difficult of all the levels to describe. No words can adequately convey what happened next—to encompass the ecstasy that awaited me there. I had arrived at the place of pure positivity—the place of pure light. *Of light without any dark.*

When I arrived there, the light emanating from the vibration was so strong that instantly I was blinded. The light didn't hurt my eyes, yet I couldn't see anything around me. The sensation in my body was like millions of tiny needles of light were penetrating me, but there was no pain. It was quite the opposite; it was as if countless little firecrackers of love and light were exploding inside me.

The light frequency here was so pure that absolutely everything was illuminated. Nothing could escape the strength and reach of this light, and everything dark and hidden was transformed. The pervading sense was: *All will be illuminated.*

In that space I was being metamorphosed, alchemized by love and light. I was being fully held, understood, and seen. I was experiencing deep unconditional love.

The experience was ecstasy. It was an experience of pure bliss, joy, radiance, and peace. This was pure love—the absolute euphoria of the sum total of all positive emotions. It was the highest denominator; the highest vibration on the spectrum: elation. This coming into the light was a homecoming, to myself and to God.

I had never felt so alive.
I had never felt so loved.
I had never felt so understood.
I had never felt so at home.
I had never felt so free.
I had never been so close to God.
I had never been so close to myself.

I was in the vibration of unconditional love, and for the first time since I was born, I was experiencing the bliss of my soulself. *I was home.*

I'm not sure how long I was in this space—in the vibration of pure light. It may have been ten minutes in earth time; it may have been more. But it felt like forever. It felt as though time was stretching out before me for eternity, and I was lost in the light.

I had traveled all the way up the vibrational spectrum from darkest dark to lightest light and here I was, held in rapture. And yet, incredibly, that was only the start of what I was to experience that day. For I was about to have my first encounter with time *beyond* the earth plane . . . I was about to experience circular time.

CHAPTER 16

THE CAVE

BEFORE I GO ON, I want to note that I understand my experiences could seem as though they would be overwhelming. After it happened, it took me months to process everything I'd witnessed and learned.

I'm often asked if in their own spiritual work, others should expect or need to go through something similar to what I experienced, and the answer is "no." Each of us learns things—each of us is *shown* things—in a way that makes it most accessible to us. I share what happened to me not to indicate that it is *the* way to understand one's soul purpose, but rather to relay that it was *my* way of learning it. Everyone travels a unique path, and while someone else may have experiences similar to mine, it's more than likely that theirs will be different, at least in some ways.

I believe one of the reasons I was shown all these things was so that I could relay what I learned to others. As I will discuss later, the methods I recommend (and practice myself) for attaining balance and insight are actually quite simple; they are distillations of what I learned during these meditative experiences.

All that said, I continue my narrative . . .

In my meditation, I had just traveled the entire vibratory spectrum from darkest dark to lightest light. What happened next was perhaps even more mind-blowing, in part because it didn't so much happen *next*, as at the *same time* I had my vibrational experience.

Having multiple concurrent experiences is difficult for our rational minds to comprehend, yet when you are in the midst of it, somehow it makes perfect sense. You can easily feel and understand that the experiences are occurring in multiple dimensions. And that's what happened to me.

I was still resting in the highest vibration, experiencing the love and bliss of pure light, when another of my "selves" began walking towards a door. There were now three of me: my first self meditating in my white chair in my white office, my second self standing and experiencing the vibration of pure light, and my third self walking away from the vibration of pure light towards a door. Some degree of my consciousness remained with each self, yet at this point my focus shifted primarily to the self walking towards the door.

It was a large glass door with a turquoise-colored handle. As I came closer to it, I noticed it was covered with a beautiful gold-and-silver-patterned mosaic. There was also a brilliant white light shining from behind the door, illuminating the mosaic.

I reached for the handle and opened the door, and as I walked through it, I found myself standing on a path. Everything before me was misty and white, making it difficult to see too far ahead. I looked down at my feet; the marble stones beneath me were large and shiny and covered in the same gold and silver mosaic as the door.

I started walking. The path was long and sweeping, and the weather was quite windy at times; I kept having to change directions and re-orientate myself to stay on it. Even so, as I walked along, I felt clear and hopeful and full of joy.

Suddenly, the path ended and I found myself standing outside a cave. It was large and brown and jutted out from the earth. It reminded me of the large ant nests in the central desert of

Australia, which are so tall and round you can mistake them for small boulders.

At the entranceway of the cave was a little door. It was dark and I was apprehensive about trying to squeeze myself through it, yet I found myself moving forward anyway. Before I knew it, I was inside the cave.

It took a few moments for my eyes to adjust to the darkness, which painted the cave a deep indigo color like the rich blues and violets of the sky at dusk. The vibration of the cave also felt darker than outside, almost *shadowy*, and my body tensed as I sensed that I was about to do *shadow work*—to confront some of my deepest fears.

The room I was standing in was completely round and I found myself in the very center of it. On the floor were drawings and lines etched in the dirt. They looked somewhat like compass points, but instead of the eight traditional directional markings, there were twelve. I bent down to take a closer look and saw that the directions were each marked by a small stone with a number painted in gold.

The line marked "1" was closest to me, just to the left of where I was standing. Without thinking I walked over and stood upon it, and as soon as I did, I found myself falling through the floor . . .

I land on my feet and as I look around, I see I'm standing in the middle of a large, square-shaped room. Though it's dark, I can make out the gray stone walls and the cobblestone floor. In front of me is a narrow spiral staircase lit by a few small torches whose faint light casts an eerie glow.

I'm overcome by the room's stifling energy. I search for a way out, but suddenly am aware that nothing bad could happen to me here and that I've been sent here for an important reason, so I begin to relax.

I look around and my eyes fall on an iron cage in the corner of the room; it's tall and narrow, and inside it is a woman. The cage is barely big enough to hold her. Her back is to me and she's sitting on the floor, facing the wall. Her head is in her hands and she's sobbing. Her long hair is matted and filthy, and she's wearing a dress that's been badly ripped. Most of her back is exposed, and I can see that it's covered with lash marks and bruises.

I take a step towards her and she quickly stands up and turns to face me. Her eyes are blue and wild, her face pale and swollen with a deep red gash running across her left cheek. I know somehow that she'd once been a beautiful woman, a woman of culture and class and nobility, but now she is a prisoner.

The woman and I lock eyes and immediately I understand— her soul is trapped. Though she had died many years before, she still believes she is trapped in this dungeon, in this place and time in history. She is an earthbound ghost.

"This woman is you in a past life," my inner voice says to me. "It is a fragment of your soul that is lost and stuck. You need to free both of you from her pain and put her soul to rest."

I walk towards the woman in the cage, my arms open and outstretched. When I reach her, I put both my hands through the bars and touch her head. Then I look into her eyes and words appear in my mind, then just as quickly come out of my mouth: "I see your pain. I know your pain. I feel your pain. Let me help you heal your pain."

The woman shudders and seems to relax. I repeat the words and again she shudders, then softens.

All at once, my head is filled with a story—her story. She had loved a married man and been imprisoned for adultery. She hadn't known he was married; she'd believed him when he'd told her he wasn't. But at the trial he had denounced her, calling her a liar and a seductress and a witch. She was sentenced to life imprisonment. This is why she's still trapped in this dungeon—she has a broken heart, and a broken belief in truth and love.

Then I say the words to her again. In a flash, a powerful White Light appears from above the ceiling of the dungeon and floods the room, drenching us in its magnificent glow.

Before my eyes, the woman begins to transform. It starts at the top of her head—her dirty and matted hair untangles and becomes clean and shiny and blonde. Then all the bruises and the gash across her face disappear and the color returns to her cheeks. Her bodice is suddenly mended, her white satin skirts crisp and clean. Finally, her pearls and jewels are made sparkling and beautiful.

Before me, the woman now stands tall, beautiful, and regal, and her pain and suffering are gone. The cage door bursts open and she walks out.

In a flash she transforms again, this time morphing into a bright ball of light. The ball spins and hovers over me momentarily, then shoots upwards out of the dungeon.

I stand there in awe, knowing that now she is free. We are free. A fragment of my soul has just returned to me.

Suddenly the dungeon dematerializes and I'm back in the cave, standing on the line of the number 1. Automatically, I walk over to the line marked "2" and as soon as I do, I'm falling through the floor again . . .

I land, and this time I'm not in a dungeon, but a tower of sorts. Somehow I've "moved up" into this tower, which is high and round, with walls made of pale-colored stone and large round windows that overlook fields of green and brown.

The air feels old and trapped; the room reeks of death. To my right is a large wooden door, and when I turn to look at it, I see her—a woman in chains. Her dress is dirty and ripped, and she's crouched down and crying, her hands covering her face.

She is painfully thin, and her arms and legs are covered in black bruises and welts. Her dark hair has been roughly shaved—there are patches of blood and scabs on her scalp.

She too is trapped in her despair. I walk towards her, saying the words I know will free her. "I see your pain. I feel your pain. I know your pain. Let me help you heal your pain." Instantly, she stops crying and looks up at me. There is hope in her eyes, amongst all her pain and fear. I reach out to her and touch her on the head and say the words again. And in that moment, I receive a flash of her tragedy.

I see that this woman is a psychic and healer who had been captured and tortured. She'd once been a respected woman, but now is labeled a "witch." Many of the people in the village who she'd helped with her knowledge and predictions had denounced her. She is awaiting her death.

When I say the words, the White Light begins to beam down onto both of us. I watch as her dark hair grows back long and full, her face is healed of its bruises and scars, and her dress is cleaned and repaired. The chains and bindings fall from her wrists and ankles . . . The transformation is complete, and before me stands a magnificent and powerful woman with raven hair and glistening eyes.

Then, as with the woman in the dungeon, her form dissolves into a ball of light. It shoots upwards and out of the tower. She transitions, and I'm returned again to the cave . . .

As I made my way through lines 3 to 7, I discovered that some of these past lives—those containing my soul fragments—were ancient, dating back to prehistory. None of them matched the past-life recollections that had come to me when I'd first moved to Germany, though many had the same recurring themes: being persecuted for seeing and telling the truth, and for having psychic and mediumistic abilities. But there were other themes, as well.

On line 8, I experienced how I was unable to fulfill my dreams as a performer because I was afflicted with an illness in my teenage years. I had been a talented dancer and singer, but I'd been crippled by a strange sickness that damaged my legs. When I freed that teenage girl, I saw that the part of my soul that was a *repressed performer* was also freed.

On line 9, I saw an elderly gentleman dressed in his night-robe, hunched over a desk and scribbling furiously. I saw he'd written a series of revolutionary books that he'd been beaten and imprisoned for. All the books, his entire life's work, had been burned or destroyed and he was desperately trying to rewrite them. When I freed him, I released a *repressed author and visionary* portion of myself.

On line 10, I was in a temple—a huge, cathedral-like building with massive stained-glass windows and hundreds of white marble pews. There was a teacher—a priestess of sorts, wearing a long white robe and gold headdress. When everyone fell silent, she tried to speak . . . but no sound came from her mouth. She'd lost the power of speech. She was devastated that she could no longer conduct her services because speaking and lecturing was her life's passion, and she felt like a charlatan because she didn't know what was wrong with her or how she could heal it. In this soul retrieval, I saw that I had been a *repressed teacher and healer.*

On line 11, I saw a painter, a young boy of eleven. This child had painted canvases of immense proportions—magnificent majestic paintings of angels and saints—but he was sitting with his head bowed, despondent, in a room full of half-finished canvases. He was grieving because his mother had forbidden him to paint. Fearful of his prodigious talent, she had given away his paintbrushes and paints and had sent him to a monastery. The pain of not being able to paint was so great that within the year, he ended his life by hanging himself from a tree. In this soul retrieval, I freed my *repressed artist* from his pain and anguish.

In each of these first eleven experiences, I had identified and retrieved pieces of my soul that, having been imprisoned, were still affecting me in this lifetime. This had kept me from living my soul purpose. When I stepped on the line marked "12," a different experience awaited me . . .

CHAPTER 17

FROM DARK TO LIGHT

AT EACH OF THE previous numbers, I was taken to a place where I encountered a single, tangible past life where a piece of my soul had been trapped. When I stepped onto line 12, I felt myself being swept upwards; it was like I was flying straight up into the sky.

When I landed, I found myself on what seemed at first to be the peak of a mountain, but as my senses adjusted, I realized that what I was standing on was the highest point of some kind of glass dome. I looked down at my feet and saw that the glass was emitting a brilliant white light: *the* White Light, the *pure light*. The energy emanating from it was amazing and I was overtaken by euphoria.

Then I noticed a group of tall slender beings dressed in long white robes walking towards me. As they came closer, I could also see that they had long, straight white hair and beautiful faces with large, pale-blue eyes the color of glacier lakes. There were about twenty or so of these beings, and I wasn't sure if they were male or female—they seemed to be both.

When they reached me, these *White Light Angels* looked at me lovingly as they formed a circle around me. I saw that their robes were tied with either a gold-, violet-, or turquoise-colored sash; as though to indicate a sort of hierarchy or order among them. As they closed the circle, I was asked telepathically to move to the center of it.

As soon as I did, a sensation like a wave engulfed me, lifting me up and propelling me as if I was riding the crest of the wave. Back it took me through time and space until just as suddenly, I was once again standing still. The wave had brought me back in time to my very first incarnation on earth.

I saw that I'd been born a male child and had lived only a few weeks due to a heart condition. This life wasn't influential or eventful, but it was my soul's *very first* incarnation.

As soon as I'd seen and understood this, the wave moved me once more, to my second incarnation on earth. I was again born a male child, and had lived that life as a slave who died from heat stroke.

One by one, I was taken through all my past lives. I discovered that my past-life history had spanned thousands of years and that I'd chosen to incarnate hundreds and hundreds of times, many times on earth, but also on planets in other galaxies. Between incarnations, I would return to my life on the Other Side. There I would rest and resume my life, and when I was ready, I would begin to plan and map out my next incarnation.

I saw that many other souls, including myself, were eager to incarnate into another life, because doing this granted us the opportunity to deepen our experience of love. On the Other Side, we know ourselves to be "one with all that is," but by forsaking the light of our true home and entering into the darkness of the earth plane, we can experience greater love. By experiencing polarity—light and dark, love and fear—which doesn't exist in our true home, we're able to arrive at higher insights and understandings. *We can only truly know ourselves to be the light when we are confronted with the dark.*

Through this experience, I also learned that the ultimate spiritual goal is to rediscover that you are love and light and one with the entire universe while you are *away* from your soul home and in one of your incarnations. In other words, our primary goal in coming to earth is to awaken to our own divine inner light here, amongst the fear and darkness around us.

As I experienced my past lives, I also discovered that although each soul creates a life-map, planning out its next incarnation, there is no guarantee that these goals and visions will be fulfilled. The Law of Free Will operates on the earth plane, so once a soul enters the womb and then is born, anything can happen. That's why, when I worked briefly as a fortune-teller, it was impossible for me to tell people their futures—because they are not set in stone. Our choices matter; what we do in life shapes our paths and futures.

Once I saw and understood all these things, the wave transported me one last time, and I saw myself being born into this lifetime. I saw myself inside my mother's womb; I saw my vibrations lowering so that I could adjust to the earth plane; I saw myself being born; and I saw how the silver cord attaching me to my soul home on the Other Side was cut.

During my meditation, as I watched my incarnation as Belinda, I saw myself falling down into the vibration of the earth plane, my once-radiant, White-Light-filled self quickly becoming fearful and dark. The moment my cord was cut, I was born, and I took my first breath as Belinda.

I then saw everything that had taken place in my life—every experience, every decision, every realization up until this point, these moments in August 2007, when I was sitting in my white chair in my white office meditating. In painstaking detail I saw everything about my life.

Some of the things I saw I can't explain—they are too complex to put into words. But during this life review I saw many things that I had mapped out before I came to earth, such as being my grandmother, Jean's, granddaughter and being my mother, Rhondda's, daughter. I also saw I had planned to incarnate into Australia, but would return to Europe early in my lifetime, and that I'd chosen to be born with red hair and green eyes—the traditional markings of a witch.

I also saw that I had planned to be born *too* psychic. I actually wanted to have scary and unsettling experiences with people's negative emotions, sicknesses, ghosts, the church, and the shadow aspects of the psychic and spirit realms because I knew these experiences would help me acquire certain skills—*shadow-hunting skills*. These skills would be among the spiritual gifts that would help me fulfill my soul's purpose.

I saw too that the veil between the worlds of spirit and earth were being lifted, and that earth's frequency was rising rapidly. It was clear that the new breed of mystic and light worker that was now incarnating on earth would need these shadow-hunting skills—the ability to clearly see and navigate through the realms of shadows and darkness—to help people heal themselves and find their way back to the light. I saw too that I had chosen to experience as much of the dark and shadow of the spirit realms as possible, so I could teach other shadow-hunting mystics and light workers how to heal their shadows and rise up. I saw I'd chosen to know the dark of my gifts in my childhood and early twenties because it would enable me to help others.

What was also clear to me was that we have all made this journey, traveling from light to dark, experiencing our vibrations lowering as we incarnate on earth. We've all done this many times, but most of us don't remember it. Though, for some of us, as part of our spiritual work, these memories can return . . . I remembered the pain and fear of my vibrations lowering as I incarnated, but this was intentional, so that I could someday help others learn how to move from the darkness back to the light . . . *Remembering* was key to my purpose in coming here.

During this experience, I also came to understand what soul purpose really means—that it consists of those things that we love best and do best. I was shown that our soul purpose is the *fusion of our talents and passions*, and that when we are living out and expressing our talents and passions, we are on fire with life. In this state we are powerful, luminous, and strong, and from this place we become spiritual change agents and miracle workers, spreading beauty and light wherever we go.

By embracing our talents and passions, we raise our vibration and heal our shadow. This is our *collective* soul purpose—to heal ourselves so we can *heal the world*.

Then, as suddenly as the whole experience had begun, it ended. I opened my eyes and found myself back in my white office sitting in my white chair. In earth time, one hour had passed.

CHAPTER 18

REVELATIONS

THE DAYS FOLLOWING MY enlightened moment were spent in meditation, and resting, recuperating, and writing down everything I'd experienced. I knew something profound had happened—the universe had revealed its secrets to me—but I was also perplexed by all of it.

As grateful as I was for these experiences, I couldn't stop wondering how this had happened to me. How had I traveled the spectrum from dark to light? How had I done the "shadow work" of retrieving my soul fragments? How had I come to know these things about my soul and my soul purpose and the journey that all souls take?

Was it only spontaneous—a once-in-a-lifetime experience? Or could it be brought about or triggered somehow? I wanted to be able to consciously access these vibrations and dimensions; to journey there again. And most importantly, I wanted other people to be able to have these experiences too. But how?

Fortunately, I didn't need to wait long for the answer.

Three days after the initial meditation, I was again sitting in my white chair in my white office, meditating and practicing presence, when suddenly I found myself being pulled upwards into the high, blissful vibration of pure light.

Again I was immediately engulfed by feelings of love and lightness, and again, as with my other experiences, I found myself outside myself, looking at myself. There were two of me, and I somehow knew I was about to witness powerful and marvelous things.

Suddenly from above me appeared the White Light—the beautiful, exquisite light of *pure light* from before. In a flash, I saw a large, round, luminous column of White Light stream down from the heavens. The light was coming towards me, then it was pouring down from the heavens into my body . . . The feeling was incredible.

Watching the White Light pour down from the heavens into me, in that moment, I saw my real self; my true, essential, and light-filled self. I saw my full energy field and my chakras.

My energy field was a vast field of light, radiant and magnificently designed. Within the field were twelve chakras—twelve powerful centers that looked like vortexes or spinning wheels of light.

I saw that seven of my chakras—my lower ones—were located within my body and head, and that five of my chakras—the higher ones—were located above my head. My highest chakra, my chakra 12, was receiving the White Light energy and was acting as a sort of funnel for it, pushing it into my lower chakras all the way down to chakra 1 and into the earth.

Pure light was streaming into me, and I was *embodying* heaven on earth . . .

And in that moment, I also learned something else of great importance: that the chakras play a crucial role in my life. As I looked upon my energy field and the way in which the White Light was streaming into my chakras, I saw that each chakra had a different geometric and energetic structure. I saw that each chakra was designed slightly differently; each chakra has a unique purpose, with the job of looking after individual and important parts of my life.

I then realized something of monumental importance (which has become the foundation of my entire life's work): If certain areas of our lives aren't working properly, it's because our chakras aren't working properly!

At the same time, I also knew that the chakras not only fulfill their own unique purpose and destiny, but also work together to serve our *soul purpose.* I knew that if we can't discover and live our purpose, it's because our chakras aren't working properly.

The chakras are essential to our soul purpose.

As the White Light streamed into me, I witnessed it repairing the blockages in my energy field and chakras. I saw that my life problems—ill health, exhaustion, money issues—were a result of blockages in my chakras, and that these blockages manifested themselves as patches of gray and black, or rips, tears, distortions, or stagnations in my energy.

I understood that blockages cause the chakras to work sluggishly or otherwise improperly. They cause negative and self-depleting belief systems, which in turn cause negative and self-sabotaging life experiences.

As the White Light poured into my energy field, it instantly moved into these blockages and healed them, allowing chi—life force—to once again flow through me without interruption. I observed with exhilaration how the White Light healed my *shadowy parts* and instantly transmuted them into light, creating health, happiness, and abundance within me!

Witnessing this led to a further revelation: that there is a difference between the lower and higher chakras. I saw that my seven lower chakras look after my present life—my health, my relationships, my career, my creativity, and so on—whereas my five higher chakras look after my soul—my talents, passions, and spiritual gifts. I then understood that until we heal our lower chakras, we can't effectively access our higher ones.

The key to being able to access the higher chakras is cleansing and healing the blockages in our lower chakras, and working with the White Light is the way to do this.

But this was not all I was to experience . . .

As the White Light continued to stream into my energy field, coming down from the heavens into me through my higher chakras, I felt myself being lifted up. Again, like in my previous experience a few days before, another "me" appeared.

There was the me that was sitting in my white chair in my white office having the White Light pour into my energy field. There was the me observing this taking place, understanding and assimilating all that was being revealed about the chakras, healing, and the White Light. And now, again, there was also another me; a third me that was being lifted up higher, higher, and higher, into another vibration and dimension . . .

When I came to rest, I found myself standing in front of a door. It was a large glass door with a turquoise-colored handle—the same door from a few days before!

Again, there was the beautiful gold-and-silver-patterned mosaic and the brilliant white light shining from behind it. I went to grasp the handle and open the door, and with striking clarity and illumination I knew:

The journey into the five higher cosmic chakras is the path of the modern mystic and spiritual seeker . . . But to discover your true soul purpose, you need to undertake the shadow work journey and heal your soul fragments.

Healing the shadow is the way to the light.

And with that, the meditation ended, and my life was changed forever.

CHAPTER 19

GETTING STARTED

I NOW REFER TO the experiences and revelations I had during that meditation and the one that followed as my "enlightened moment." In those remarkable sessions, not only had I healed my own past-life wounds, changed my energy, and discovered my soul purpose, I was also shown how to help others do the same. Since August 2007, that is what I've spent my life doing—teaching others how to change their energy and change their lives.

Since my enlightened moment, I have worked with my chakras and the White Light every single day (and almost every day I've journeyed to the door and into my five higher cosmic chakras). And I can attest that each of those revelations I had has held true. Since then, I've helped thousands of people apply what I learned to heal myself and change my life, and it has transformed their lives as well.

When your energy shifts as much and as quickly as mine did during those days in August 2007, it turns your life upside down and inside out. Within only a few months, my relationship ended and I left Germany and moved back to Australia. My friends and clients in Germany fell away, and all that was left from my old life were the small suitcases of clothes and belongings I took back to Australia with me. It was as if my entire life before my enlightened moment simply dissolved.

This wasn't an easy time; it required a lot of faith. But I knew I'd had a huge vibrational shift and that my life just needed to vibrationally catch up. And I trusted I was being led to much higher shores, which of course I was.

During this time of huge shifting and change, the White Light became like a friend to me—a steady companion. Every day I would sit in meditation and allow the White Light to come into my energy field and work on my chakras. And every day the White Light would lovingly hold me and heal me and support me and take me places . . .

We often want things to come quickly, but patience is an important tool—one enabled by the practice of presence. I gave myself time to just sit and be, to assimilate all my new insights and knowledge. I sat with the White Light and allowed it to work on me and heal my life.

In that time, my lifelong stomach and digestive problems were healed. My oversensitive and empath nature came into balance, and I no longer energetically took on others' pain and negativity. My panic disorder disappeared. The headaches, migraines, and constant back pain that had plagued me were resolved. And I no longer felt burdened by my psychic gifts and abilities.

Working with the White Light also gave me much more energy and drive. I was used to feeling lethargic most of the time, drained and dragging, but suddenly I felt clear and invigorated. My work with the White Light also healed my low self-worth issues, and I grew much more confident and outgoing. Instead of wanting to change myself, I started to embrace those parts of me that were uniquely me; and through this I began to surround myself with people who were lifting me up instead of holding me down.

I also became much more prosperous and could easily attract money, as well as support and care, into my life. I became much more self-empowered and learned to intuitively know and speak out about what I did and didn't want.

Thanks to my new connection with myself, I knew I no longer wanted to work strictly as a medical intuitive, and so over the course of many years I shifted my focus away from medical intuition and began to work more as a mentor, coach, and teacher. But in those intervening years, I shared with my clients what I'd learned from the White Light. I showed them how to heal their lives by working with the White Light, and by cleansing and balancing their chakras.

This was when I started to include a chakra diagnosis in my sessions. Once I knew how important the chakras were and how it was through the chakras that we heal our life and discover our purpose, I made them a major focus of my work. Over the years, I've consistently watched this method—chakra balancing and White Light healing, combined with a daily practice of mindfulness—transform people's lives.

I've watched my clients quickly heal their health problems. I've watched them quit jobs they no longer wanted and easily manifest new ones. They've been able to heal their marriages and family hurts, and overcome insecurities and self-doubt. They discovered their passion and soul purpose; and bravely began to live the life of their dreams. I've witnessed huge breakthroughs, and seen people transition to a much *higher* life.

And now it's time to help you do the same.

PART TWO

CHANGE YOUR ENERGY, CHANGE YOUR LIFE

INTRODUCTION
TO PART TWO

WELCOME TO THE "HOW to" portion of this book. Here I will explain how I took the experiences I had during my enlightened moment and translated them into a set of spiritual practices that thousands of people have now used to heal their energy systems. And this is where I teach these practices to you.

In today's world of noise, distraction, and darkness, we need practices that keep our chakras strong, our vibration positive, and our minds calm. We must stay aligned with the light, while staying grounded here on earth. These practices will help you do that.

At the core of these practices is balancing your chakras. A good understanding of the chakras and how they work is helpful to "diagnosing" any problems you're having in your energy anatomy. So in the chapters to come, I will discuss each of the chakras and the areas they govern, and how imbalances or blockages in a specific chakra could impact your life.

I want to take a moment here to acknowledge that there is a lot of information out there about the chakras—some texts go back centuries—that describe these centers or wheels of light in our bodies. I don't discuss these other texts, writings, or theories here because the truth is that I haven't read many of them (apart from Caroline Myss). My understanding of the chakras and how they work, along with the methods I'll discuss for strengthening and supporting them, comes from my own direct experience as a medical intuitive and through working with my own chakras.

Through my work, along with my own meditative and mindfulness practices, I've grown to understand more deeply what the chakras are, how they function, and how we can best support them. In this book I only describe the practices I know will help you balance and strengthen your chakras and raise your vibration. And with a raised vibration, you'll be able to easily and joyfully walk between the worlds, embodying your true nature as a modern mystic!

CHAPTER 20

THE CHAKRAS

WE CURRENTLY LIVE IN a unique time in history. The vibration of our world is rising rapidly, prompting a sudden and great cosmic transformation. As the veil between earth and the spirit realms is being lifted, it is ushering us into a spiritual revolution.

Previously, many of us were happy going about our lives paying more attention to earthly concerns (the realm of the lower chakras) than spiritual ones (the realm of the higher chakras). But the massive energetic shift toward spirituality that's now taking place is causing us to move very quickly from our lower chakras up into our higher and more spiritual and cosmic chakras. This is prompting many people to focus on becoming more conscious and living a more spiritual and soulful life.

However, because the majority of us have weak lower chakras, this shift from lower to higher is challenging. When the lower chakras, focused as they are on more earthly concerns, are weak or blocked, it's difficult for energy (or chi) to rise into our higher, spiritual chakras. This inability of energy to move easily through our chakras creates physical and emotional problems in our lives. Because the energetic shift propelling us into our higher chakras is meeting blockages, a sense of discord or struggle is also created. (Think of driving your car and trying to accelerate on a road dotted with speed bumps.)

Understanding how we can support the rising vibration in our own bodies and energy systems is critical to living a more awakened, balanced, joyful, and fulfilled life. And learning how to navigate this shift starts with understanding how to raise your vibration.

Raising Your Vibration: What Does It *Mean?*

Raising your vibration is an idea that many spiritual seekers struggle to understand. The concept is often vague in its implications: What is a "vibe" and why does it need to be raised? Or sometimes we talk about the concept in a way that comes across as spiritually elitist: Of course you need to raise your vibe—*didn't you know that?*

Let's take a moment to get clear about what it actually means to raise your vibration.

During my enlightened moment, I learned that the universe is a place of vibration. I also learned that when we incarnate on earth we consciously choose to move to the lower vibration of earth, so that we can then undertake the journey of moving from dark to light on the vibratory spectrum. By doing so we open ourselves to all the incredible lessons and experiences available to us on this earth plane.

This means that our ultimate goal here is to relearn that we are the light, even in the face of the dark—the lower vibration and shadow—of the earth plane. But it's painful for the soul to experience shadow; it's abnormal and unnatural. When this pain becomes significant enough, the soul seeks answers. It seeks to understand and awaken, and in this way we begin to explore why we are here and what the purpose of our life is.

The experience of *our own shadow* causes us to awaken and begin to raise our vibration. This is why, as the spiritual teachers and sages of the world say, to truly awaken we must go within ourselves.

Unfortunately though, much of the spiritual mainstream has adopted an idea that the goal is to ascend *out* of ourselves—that spiritual awakening means leaving the body and our "lower nature" behind. Sadly, many religious traditions teach that being in the body is a barrier to true enlightenment. But the reverse is true. It is being *embodied* that allows us to have an earthly experience of consciousness. Raising our vibration from an embodied, grounded space allows us to experience true awakening. Enlightenment is not something that can be discovered outside of ourselves; it can only be achieved by traveling inward. Ascension is not a linear concept, as in going from down to up or low to high, it's about *going deeper.*

When we go within, we discover and free ourselves from the sources of our pain, and in the process we discover that the light and joy we were seeking was already *within* us. We were never truly separated from the light! And there is no experience more moving or miraculous. Indeed, it is why we came to the earth plane.

Discovering we are the light while we're embodied here on earth is what the soul longs for. The soul's journey—our journey—is to move up through the vibrational spectrum, consciously choosing to become more light and less dark . . .

The choice to reach a higher vibration—to strive for a more positive, elevated, and light-filled emotional state—is what it truly means to raise one's vibration.

How to Raise Your Vibration

Simply put, the state of your chakras determines the state of your vibration. And the state of your vibration determines the state of your life. *As within, so without.* To change your vibration, you need to change your *energy.* This means making your chakras healthy, powerful, and strong so your energy can flow freely from the lower chakras to the higher ones.

Raising your vibe probably sounds like an arduous process, but it's as easy as doing the short daily meditation that cleanses and balances your chakras and brings the White into them. It is really that simple! The people who have a difficult time with these practices struggle because they have a hard time making them routine, not because the practices are difficult.

Many people say to me, "I know I need to work on my chakras, but I can't find the time for it!" Others do make the time, but when they sit down to meditate, they are disrupted by distracting thoughts and give up. (In Chapter 32, I will discuss how to deal with distracting thoughts, but just know that nearly all of us, myself included, experience them.)

For others, they begin to do the practices, but don't stick with them long enough for things to change. It can take weeks to see the changes, but if you are consistent in your practice, your life *will* improve!

But before you get going on your vibrational upgrade, it's important to understand what the chakras are and how they function.

Your Chakras

Within you is a complete and highly intelligent energy system that governs your entire life. It is comprised of twelve chakras, which are energy vortexes that govern specific areas of your life ranging from your physical and emotional well-being to your spiritual health. These energy centers make up your energy field, and your energy field and chakras together make up your energy anatomy.

Put simply, the state of your chakras and energy field determine the state of your life—your health, wealth, love life, career, success, and joy. Your inner world creates your outer world. Get your chakras working and your life will follow!

As for the location of your chakras, seven of your twelve chakras have their focal point in your physical body, and five of them exist above your physical body. (Technically, chakra 7 exists above the body, but the focal point for working with it is the top of the head.) Together the chakras create a large and luminous field of light.

Each of these chakras fuels and sustains certain aspects of your life. They do this by receiving energy from the universe, then transporting this energy to the areas of your life and physical body where they are focused.

In this way, your chakras look after every aspect of your life and health. You have a chakra that looks after your creativity, and one that is responsible for creating abundance. You have a chakra dedicated to making your life joyful and fun, one that is responsible for helping you discover your soul purpose, and so on.

Your twelve chakras have individual tasks, but they also function as a whole, with each chakra influencing and working together with the others. In this way, the health and functionality of each chakra affects the health and functionality of all your chakras. For example, a weak chakra 1 can block the flow of energy to chakra 2.

When your chakras receive energy from the universe, they either pull the energy up from the ground (the earth-to-heaven energy flow system), or they pull it down from the heavens (the heaven-to-earth energy flow system). When your energy field pulls energy up from the earth, it starts by pulling it into chakra 1, then the energy moves its way up to chakra 2, and so on until it reaches chakra 12. Similarly, when you receive energy from the heavens, this energy-flow current travels down from chakra 12 into chakra 11, and all the way down to chakra 1. (When you learn about the Chakra Cleanse Meditation and channeling White Light in Chapter 30, you'll see the meditation works with both ascending and descending energy flow systems.)

If there are blockages in *any* of the chakras—if they aren't working properly—your energy-flow current will be compromised. And if your energy flow is compromised, you'll experience recurring problems, which stops you from having an amazing life!

Also, to be clear, while the lower chakras carry a *lower vibration* than the higher ones, that doesn't mean the lower chakras are in any way *negative*. The lower chakras are simply more embodied—they govern what is more to do with this earth plane—than the higher chakras. Each chakra, whether lower or higher, is beautiful and powerful and equally important in supporting you.

Why Chakras Don't Work Properly

Your chakras are funnels for energy, as well as energy generators and distributors. If their ability to receive, generate, and distribute energy is compromised, they can't do their jobs properly.

Think of the chakras as eager, diligent workers. If they are tired, unwell, and underfed, they can't work productively; and, if they can't work productively, they become blocked, stagnant, and weak.

But how do our chakras become weak or blocked in the first place? The answer—pain and darkness we take on when we incarnate on earth. Each time we return here, we also return to the negative conditionings of our past lives. And throughout life, we pick up on and absorb the negative subconscious beliefs of others. All of this *taints* our chakras.

Think about it: You are who you are and you believe what you do about life due to many different influences. These include your country of birth, your culture, your race, your language, how you were raised, the genes you inherited from your parents, your parents' personalities, in what city you spent your childhood, where you went to school, who your first best friend was, and so on.

There are also other more esoteric influences on each of us. The placement of the moon, sun, and the planets at the time of your birth; your mother's experience at your birth; your experience in the womb; your past lives; your life on the Other Side; and so on. These all have a bearing on our attitudes and beliefs.

In other words, you are the sum total of many beliefs and opinions about life, as well as a variety of circumstances over which you have no control. You didn't consciously choose most of these things, and some of them you didn't even directly experience! Yet they have the effect of weakening your chakras.

To heal ourselves and our lives, we need to counteract the negative influences that are working on us and our chakras. We need to change our belief systems from negative life-depleting ones to positive life-affirming ones.

But this requires something other than repeating positive affirmations or mantras. Doing these things and changing our thought patterns *is* powerful, but I call it "taking the long way 'round." It will have an effect eventually, but the problems in our lives are there because of problems in our energy systems. That's why changing our thoughts has limited impact. But when we heal our energy systems, a new, more positive way of thinking naturally emerges, and our life circumstances change (not the other way around).

Before we talk about *how* to work with your chakras to change your energy and change your life, let's look at each of the chakras and the aspects of your life they govern. (You will also find a chart summarizing basic information about each chakra in Appendix A.)

CHAPTER 21

CHAKRA 1: GROUNDING

CHAKRA 1 IS THE first level of your energy anatomy. It's also called the root chakra or base chakra, not only because of its location (at the perineum and between the feet), but also because chakra 1 is the beginning of our journey here on earth, and is the chakra that "roots" and "grounds" us.

At your essence, you are a *spiritual being without form*. All of us exist as spirit on the Other Side until we choose to incarnate again. When we return to earth, we go through a process of lowering our vibration to accommodate the lower vibration on earth (as compared to the very high vibration of the Other Side) and to take on an earthly body. So as you grew in the womb of your mother and were then born, you slowly began to adjust to the physical world of matter and form. To protect your new physical body, you need basic survival instincts. You also need to accept earth as your home away from home for the duration of your stay here. Chakra 1 oversees these instincts.

You can think of your chakra 1 as your energetic foundation; it governs your survival needs, driving you to obtain that which you need to exist here in physical form. If your first chakra is functioning properly, you seek out food, water, and shelter, and will defend your body—as well as the things necessary to your survival—if they are threatened. If your first chakra is balanced, you can readily manifest that which you *need* to survive this journey on earth.

To live a healthy life, your physical body also needs stamina and strength. A balanced first chakra provides these and helps you connect with and draw energy from the earth and nature. This link helps you feel supported, nourished, and cared for.

As humans are designed to connect with nature, we also are designed to connect with one another. We are "herd animals"— being part of a group or tribe makes it easier for us to survive and thrive. Therefore, chakra 1 also oversees your drive to seek out a tribe (community) to which you belong, and feel loved and accepted by. A sense of connection is essential to developing healthy self-esteem; without this, life is full of struggle.

A sense of disconnection from your surroundings can also cause you to struggle; you need to be where you can thrive. Your first chakra drives you to find that place or environment in the world in which you are truly at home. If chakra 1 is balanced, you not only feel loved and accepted in your family and community, but you'll also love the place where you live.

Chakra 1 Basics

Names

This chakra is also called the first chakra, base chakra, or root chakra.

Location

Chakra 1 is the only chakra for which there are two points—the perineum *and* between the feet.

Areas of Body Governed

This chakra oversees the physical areas of the spinal column, legs, feet, hips, and the lower part of the large intestine (colon).

Drive and Issues

Chakra 1 governs our drive to survive as well as seek out a tribe and environment in which we feel at home. This is the chakra that grounds us and gives us a sense of belonging in the world.

Let's look at some clients I've worked with and see how a chakra 1 imbalance affected their lives. Then we'll explore this chakra in more detail.

Note: In my eighteen years of working as a medical intuitive, I gave hundreds of sessions, conducting them all in the same way: I started each ninety-minute session by giving a cold read of my clients' energy fields without knowing what had caused them to seek my help (I asked them not to tell me anything about themselves before I began). I then told them about their past lives and how these were affecting their present-day life; once the reading was complete, they could ask me their questions. After my enlightened moment, I added a chakra diagnosis, which I would do after reading their past lives. In a few instances, when clients were referred to me by healthcare providers, I did have some basic medical information from the provider at the start of the session. But in most cases, I simply started with a cold read before we discussed anything.

Most case studies presented in this book are from individual client sessions. In a few cases, I have combined pieces from several different clients to present a broader view of different issues that can occur when the chakras are out of balance. In all cases, names have been changed to protect the identities of the clients.

Case Studies

Pauline

> *Pauline is at the end of her rope. She arrives several minutes late for her session looking exhausted; she's got dark circles under her eyes, her skin is pale, and when she takes a seat, she shrinks into the armchair.*
>
> *Though the session hasn't even started, right away I can see that Pauline is in her mid-thirties and has been diagnosed with chronic fatigue syndrome. For the last eight years, she has "tried everything," but nothing seems to help. She also suffers from chronic lower back pain, constipation, and iron deficiency.*
>
> *After I tell Pauline how the session will run, I give her my initial impressions. "Yes, that's correct, but I don't know what to do," she says, nearly in tears. "And then there's my love life."*
>
> *"Your relationships often end up in codependent or otherwise unhappy spaces," I say as impressions keep coming to me.*
>
> *"That's right," she sighs. "Part of the problem is I just never feel good."*
>
> *When I ask Pauline about her living situation, she says she rents a place in a noisy building in the city, and it's difficult for her to sleep well at night because of the sounds from the street and adjacent flats. She says she'd love to live out in the country, or at least go there on weekends, but she can never seem to get off the couch and get moving.*
>
> *I scan Pauline's energy as she's talking, and I'm not surprised to see that her first chakra is severely weakened. "Your base chakra is in such an underactive state that it's incapable of drawing up energy," I tell her. "And when your first chakra can't draw up energy, your body and your entire energy field become depleted." I explain that although the two don't always go hand in hand, in my practice I've seen many people with a diagnosis of chronic fatigue also having a very weak first chakra.*

"But there's hope. If you work with your first chakra to strengthen it, this should significantly improve your physical symptoms, along with the rest of your life."

"Really?" she asks. It's the first spark of life I've seen in her all session.

"Absolutely," I say, and I encourage her to follow her desire to spend more time in the country. "Your connection with the earth and nature is a critical component of supporting your first chakra. That's why you're getting that urge to get out of town. Follow it!"

David

"I'm trying not to move around anymore," David tells me, "but it's just not happening." David is in his early fifties and for most of his life, every eighteen months or so, he has felt the need to move house. As I listen to him, I see images of homes in Italy, Sweden, Germany, Canada, Holland, England, and New Zealand. The worn leather shoulder bag at his feet clearly has some miles on it, and as I watch David in the chair across from me, he's even having trouble sitting still.

"It's been an adventure," he tells me, "but by my late thirties, I got tired of moving all the time. The trouble is, I just can't stop. It's gotten exhausting, and the expense of so much moving has badly impacted my financial situation."

"Yes, like I said when I first scanned your energy field, my attention is pulled to your first chakra. Every time you try to settle down, something happens. Either your work sends you away again, you can't tolerate your disruptive neighbors, the apartment just isn't right, the relationship ends, or something else goes wrong."

"Yes!" David says. "I don't know what to do. I just want to settle down and stay put."

"Do you really?" I ask.

"What do you mean?" he asks, eyebrows raised.

"Well, your first chakra is showing me that you equate 'settling down' with boredom and a loss of youth and fun. You

believe that if you stop moving, your life will end. The fun will stop and you'll be confined."

David goes to say something, then closes his mouth. He sits back and rubs his mustache. "My first instinct was to say that wasn't true," he says, "that you were wrong. But you know, now that I think about it, my father feels this way. I think it's something I inherited from him."

"Come to think of it," he says, "when we were kids, my sisters and I were moved around all the time—every eighteen months to two years, in fact. Dad would get restless and he'd sell the house and build or buy another one. We were always 'in transit.' He'd say to us that we need to get out and live life and keep moving; otherwise, our lives would be over."

David sits quietly for another minute, then shakes his head and offers a wry smile. "I can see now that my dad's behavior and beliefs have affected my life. What can I do to stop it, though?"

"We've got to get your first chakra working properly," I tell him, "because it's the job of your base chakra to help you find your true 'home' in the world. When you do this, your life will work and you'll find both your metaphoric and real-world homes!"

Katja

I'm speaking to Katja on the phone, and the first thing I notice about her voice is its lackluster tone. It sounds flat and lifeless, as if she's watching her life go by instead of living it.

When I begin to scan her energy field, I find that it too is lacking luster. Most of the colors of her chakras are washed out and pale, and I receive the image of her being like a wilting plant that isn't getting enough water and sunshine. Unfortunately, many of Katja's chakras are weak and blocked, but her first chakra is particularly so.

"Katja," I say, "I see that you're struggling to make ends meet. You're feeling lonely, living on welfare, and estranged from your only daughter."

"Yes," Katja says without a trace of emotion or self-pity as I relay the impressions of her energy field to her. "Everything you've said is true. I'm poor and alone."

I see no fire in Katja's energy field—no sense of engagement in life. What I do see in her first chakra is that most of the time she feels "out of it."

"Your energy is very ungrounded," I say.

"I'm not surprised," she says. "All my life I felt sort of dizzy; not quite here. Most of the time I find myself mentally drifting away." She also tells me she's constantly fatigued and has lived with depression for as long as she can remember.

There's something else I can see in Katja's first chakra: In a past life she was accused of stealing money from a rich family and as a result had been imprisoned and hanged. She had not committed the crime and had proclaimed her innocence even while being tortured, but she was convicted and murdered anyway. The trauma and betrayal in this past life was causing Katja to fear being back on earth again.

"Katja," I say, "do you think of earth as a dark and cruel place?"

She shudders and whispers, "Yes, I don't like it here at all."

I tell Katja that she's being affected by a past-life memory. "These memories run deep within us, especially those in which we have experienced trauma. Even if we can't consciously remember them," I say, "they still exist in our chakras, where they can hinder the flow of energy throughout our energy field. That's why cleansing and looking after our chakras is so important. Otherwise we can still be living out past-life struggles, as you are. But I can help you clear this trauma from your first chakra, and if you commit to a regular meditation practice, I'm confident things will improve for you."

"Well, I'm willing to try it," Katja says, and though I still don't hear any real conviction in her voice, for her sake I hope she will.

These examples from my practice as a medical intuitive show some of the many issues and challenges that can stem from a weak or imbalanced chakra 1. Let's look at your first chakra and see how fit and healthy it is.

Chakra 1 Self-Assessment

To get an idea of how fit and healthy your first chakra is, ask yourself the following questions:

- Am I grounded in my physical body and in my life?
- Do I have and seek out a connection to nature?
- Do I look after my physical body through a good diet, relaxation, adequate rest, and exercise?
- Do I feel that I belong to a community or tribe?
- Do I live in an environment I love where I feel safe, secure, and at home?
- Can I easily manifest and create what I need to live in this world?
- Am I free of problems with my lower spine, legs, feet, hips, and/or large intestine?

If you answered "no" to one or two of these questions, you have some challenges with your first chakra. If you answered "no" to many of them, you probably have a significant blockage.

Chakra 1 Out of Balance

If your first chakra is not working properly, you may have challenges with your physical or emotional health, finances, love life, relationships with family and friends, or your career and creativity, such as the following.

Physical Health

- Weakness or other issues in your legs (such as varicose veins), hips, back, or knees
- Lower back pain, sciatica

127

- Chronic constipation or sluggish bowel
- Chronic fatigue
- Iron deficiency
- Autoimmune disease or low immunity
- Being overweight or obese
- Feeling disconnected from your body

Emotional Health

- Feeling scattered, forgetful, or tired
- Feeling ungrounded, dizzy, or floaty
- Stuck in a struggle cycle, which causes a feeling of burnout
- Wanting to "check out," frequently wishing you were someplace else
- Attracting dramas that create more drama and stress
- Feeling lazy, fatigued, or depressed
- Feeling chronically tired and stressed

Finances

- Stuck in poverty or a struggle cycle
- Living from paycheck to paycheck
- Struggling with greed and hoarding
- Overly focused on material possessions

Love Life

- Driven by the need to feel secure
- Inability to feel safe, secure, and trust yourself, others, and life
- Don't have time for a relationship
- Low libido

Relationships with Friends and Family

- Driven by the need to feel secure
- Inability to feel safe, secure, and trust yourself, others, and life

- Inability to feel settled and connected to home and your family members
- Inability to provide for yourself and others
- Struggling because you don't have time for others

Career and Creativity

- No time and space to work on your career or be creative
- Can't see what you need to do to further your career
- Believe that you have to do it all alone
- Exhausted and depleted because you don't have time for creative pursuits

Nourishing Chakra 1

There are a variety of ways to get each of our chakras working properly. In addition to the Chakra Cleanse Meditation (see Chapter 30), which strengthens and balances *all* our chakras, each lower chakra has "special likes"—things that "feed" it. Engaging in these activities or indulging these likes can help to enliven these chakras.

Among the things your first chakra likes are:

- The color red. Wear red, paint or draw with it, visualize it, add more red to your décor . . . Be creative!
- Nature
- All forms of movement (especially wild, crazy dancing)
- Anything that grounds you. You can go for long walks or hikes, spend time gardening, even hug a tree!
- Spending time in places and environments where you feel good or at home
- Spending time with people who love and support you

Remember Pauline, David, and Katja? I'm happy to report that once they began to work on their base chakras, things started to shift in their lives.

Pauline's turnaround was one of the more dramatic I've seen. It didn't happen overnight, but with regular meditation and chakra balancing, and more trips to the country where she could connect with nature, Pauline saw drastic improvements in her health. She had more energy and more vitality, her lower back pain and bowel issues resolved, and she began finding more satisfaction and enjoyment in her relationships.

When David began to work on his first chakra, his urge to stay "on the move" disappeared. Realizing he felt most at home in Amsterdam, he settled there. He married a Dutch woman and they had a child, and he retired!

As for Katja, when her base chakra began to improve, so did her ability to attract more money and abundance into her life. Her ex-husband suddenly decided to buy her an apartment. Clients she hadn't spoken to for a long time began contacting her again and her daughter phoned her out of the blue and wanted to rebuild their relationship.

Remember, chakra 1 is the keystone chakra. If it is impaired— a common issue in today's world—you cannot effectively draw energy up into the rest of your chakras. You also won't feel grounded, supported, or at home.

Now, let's look at chakra 2.

CHAPTER 22

CHAKRA 2: INDIVIDUATION

CHAKRA 2 IS THE second level of your energy anatomy. Also called the sacral chakra, it's located in the area of your sacrum just below your navel. While chakra 1 governs your drive to seek out that which you need to survive, chakra 2 oversees your ability to draw to yourself that which you *desire.*

Your second chakra is like a powerful magnet; when it is balanced and energized, you can easily recognize that which you desire and draw it into your life. In other words, chakra 2 magnetizes your personal power so you can learn how to get what you want.

Chakra 2 is concerned with other aspects of desire as well: It oversees our sensuality, sexuality, abundance, and creativity. A strong second chakra allows you to take delight in this life, but helps you remain balanced in the process; you can experience joy in the sensory world without getting lost in it.

Your second chakra also helps you determine how to express yourself creatively and sexually. When chakra 2 is healthy, you regularly undertake creative activities that help you nourish your soul and express yourself as an individual. You also feel comfortable expressing yourself as a sensual and sexual being.

Considering that chakra 2 oversees sexual expression, it's not surprising that it's also the energy center that drives you to seek out intimate relationships. These can be romantic relationships or friendships. These relationships provide the polarizing forces necessary to help you learn about yourself and discover key aspects of who you are.

As you can see, chakra 2 oversees quite a lot, and it may not surprise you to learn that we live in a time of massive chakra 2 imbalance. We yearn to have what we desire and what makes us feel good; our entire lives revolve around wanting and striving for more. We want to enjoy our lives and experience pleasure; we crave it. But when the second chakra is out of balance, we feel guilt and shame about wanting to feel good! And then we become trapped in cycles of addiction, yearning, and striving for pleasure and what we desire. To be healthy, we need to be able to seek out and experience joy without feeling bad about it.

Chakra 2 Basics

Names
Chakra 2 is also called the sacral chakra.

Location
It is located in the area of the sacrum, just below the level of the navel.

Areas of Body Governed
This chakra oversees the physical areas of the lower abdomen, pelvis, reproductive system, kidneys, bladder, and the upper part of the large intestine (colon).

Drive and Issues
Chakra 2 governs our drives to pursue individuation and plea-sure. It is the chakra that oversees our sexuality and sensuality. It rules the pursuit of intimate relationships, and governs our

ability to feel comfortable with having incarnated in our body as a man or a woman in this lifetime. Chakra 2 drives us to engage in creative pursuits that nourish our soul, and to experience delight. It also magnetizes our personal power so we can easily attract what we want.

Most people have at least some degree of imbalance in their second chakra; so let's look at some clients I've worked with who experienced chakra 2 imbalances. Then we'll explore this fiery power center further, so you can get yours fit and healthy!

Case Studies

Peter

In my work as a medical intuitive, I've always taken pride in being objective; I see inside people and do my best to tell them what I see without judgment or imposing my own beliefs. Though I usually succeed, with some clients it's more difficult, and this is the case with Peter. When I hear his voice over the phone, I take an instant dislike to him. It's not just his voice; I also recoil at the psychic and physical impression that appears to me. With his large eyes, black hair, and darkly tanned skin, he probably has no trouble attracting women, but to me he comes across as creepy.

Peter begins to speak, but my attention quickly strays from his words to his energy field. As I begin to scan it, the image of a huge black spider rises in my mind's eye. I see that Peter creates giant webs around people to trap, then devour them. No wonder I have such a strong reaction to his voice!

"I'm incredibly successful," Peter boasts. "Money is definitely not an issue for me," he oozes, and as he talks, I see that he's a master manipulator who can get people to do whatever he wants. He uses and goes through people to fulfill his own needs. I also see that he is very skeptical about my psychic and intuitive abilities.

I stop Peter, explaining that I like to do the energy reading first, without hearing anything about his life.

"Go for it," he says, and in my vision of him I can see his bright white teeth and Cheshire cat-like grin.

I focus on his energy and tell him exactly what I see, leaving nothing out.

After I'm done sharing my impressions, Peter takes a few moments before responding. "I, uh . . ." he stammers, then clears his throat and tries again. "Like I said, I've got lots of money," he says, his voice now meek and shaky, "but the truth is, it's a problem for me. I can't stop amassing wealth . . . But somehow it seems like there's never enough."

I tell him that it's his imbalanced first and second chakras—especially the second—that are causing him to feel that way. "Your fear of scarcity is driving your need to accumulate wealth at all costs. Your second chakra is severely imbalanced. I can see that you're just as driven to acquire pleasure, and that these drives and fears are ruining your life."

Peter is quiet for a minute, then says, "It's true; I spend just about all day every day working." He tells me he's also left behind him a trail of angry and bitter men and women who he's used to acquire power and wealth, or for sex. "I've just gotten out of another relationship. Well, an affair, really. It never got beyond that. I'm also in the middle of another lawsuit with a former business partner." Then he laughs. "You know, it seems strange, but I'm actually happy that you can see all this about me. I feel relieved."

"Because you're not honest with anyone," I say. "You don't have authentic relationships in your life. And on top of it, you're struggling with prostate, bladder problems, and back problems."

"Yes," he says, agreeing with me once again. Peter's master manipulator mask is now completely removed, and behind it is a frightened little boy.

"The truth is, you have a lot of money in the bank, but you are deeply afraid of life. You don't have true wealth because you have no support system—no friends or family."

"Yes," he says, "that's all true."

"You can change all this, Peter," I tell him, "but you've got a lot of work ahead of you."

Nancy

Nancy comes to me via a referral from her doctor, so I am already aware that she has ongoing issues with her reproductive system, and that for decades she has been plagued with ovarian cysts, as well as chronic urinary tract infections.

"You know what my doctor told me to try for the infections?" she says. "Drink cranberry juice. That was easy. Just add a little vodka and we're off to the races!" She throws her head back and laughs, showing off the studded leather choker that encircles her neck.

Nancy is in her late thirties. Deeply tanned, she's got long, bleached-blond hair and is wearing a black Bon Jovi tank top, tight jeans, and high leather boots with stiletto heels.

Nancy tells me she also has problems with relationships. "All the good ones are taken! Every time I think I might have found one, he up and leaves. Oh well!" she laughs. "Nothing a little retail therapy won't cure. Men aren't worth all the fuss, anyway."

I don't have to scan Nancy's energy field to know what's happening—her second chakra is virtually leaping out at me, begging for help. "You're swinging back and forth between a very undernourished and a hugely engorged second chakra," I tell her. "That's what's causing your child-like behavior."

The smile disappears from Nancy's face briefly, then returns. "Getting old is overrated," she fires back.

"Your issues with your second chakra are causing you to engage in some dangerous behavior, bingeing on drugs and alcohol and engaging in unprotected sex with virtual strangers. You're searching for a high, for acceptance, or for a way to feel alive," I say without judgment.

"Well, who doesn't want to feel alive?" she counters.

I don't respond. Nancy goes to say something else, then closes her mouth, her smile eventually fading. When she speaks again, her voice is completely different, almost like a little girl's. "What do I do?" she asks.

"Well, we need to get your second chakra in balance," I say. "That should help with your physical and financial problems, as well." Nancy looks at me, clearly surprised I can see that she's got money problems. "You're always in debt because of your shopping habit. It's another addiction—another way to get that high."

Nancy nods but says nothing. She looks like a child who's been called to the principal's office.

"It doesn't mean you're a bad person," I reassure her. "You're just engaging in some very unhealthy behavior, and that's affecting your relationships, too. You're trying to have relationships with grown men while acting like a teenager. There's nothing wrong with the men you're attracting into your life, you're just afraid that when they get to know you, they won't like what they see, so you start to 'act up,' and that drives them away."

"Wow, you really nailed it. You must see a lot of women like me," she says.

"Actually, I more often see women with an underactive second chakra—women who are scared of their sexuality, afraid to open themselves up and make mistakes, unwilling to be spontaneous, free, creative, and impulsive . . ."

"Oh, yeah, that's definitely not me!" Nancy declares.

"No, it's not," I say, "but in both cases—overactive and underactive—when people get their chakras aligned and healthy, things start to make a dramatic turnaround. And that's the only 'drama' you're allowed to create now, Nancy," I tell her. She laughs, and this time I join her.

John

John is a perfect example of how diagnosing the true source of a chakric imbalance can be a bit tricky at times. In many ways, his life seems perfectly in order. He owns a popular franchise chain, and as he sits in front of me in his perfectly pressed tan trousers and jacket, he looks like the picture of success.

But John's energy field shows me something different. All his working life, John has been able to land the job he wants, and he has the resume to prove it. He also works as a life coach and runs successful inspirational seminars. However, he's having trouble with money.

John nods as I tell him what I see. "I don't get it," John says, shrugging. "I'm great at what I do, but"—he leans forward and lowers his voice, clearly embarrassed—"there just never seems to be enough. I don't want people to know that I'm struggling," he says. "Who would want a coach who has trouble making money?"

"Let's take a deeper look," I say, and when I begin to scan, I see a rather significant blockage in John's second chakra. When I home in on this blockage, I see that John has an ambivalent attitude towards money, which he's inherited from his father. John's father believed "rich people are bad and the poor are good," so John has subconscious guilt and feels bad about his desire for money.

I tell John what I see. "Yes," he sighs, "my dad always told me that an honest man works hard for his money and has just enough to get by. I know rationally that it's okay to desire money and enjoy it, but obviously subconsciously, I must still feel bad about it."

John sits thinking for a few moments, crossing and uncrossing his legs, scratching his head. Finally he shrugs and says, "Belinda, you're telling me what I already know. This is not really news to me. I've known for years that this has been holding me back, and I've been trying so hard to overcome it, but I can't see why it's not working. What am I doing wrong?"

"The answer to your question is twofold," I reply. "First, your ambivalent feeling about money is certainly one of the reasons you're struggling financially, but it isn't the only one. And second, although you've been trying to change your thoughts, it hasn't yet changed your energy. I'll teach you how to clear out these blockages and change your energy."

"So what's my real problem, then?" he says, leaning forward.

"Unrequited love," I say. John's mouth opens slightly in surprise. "In a past life," I continue, "you deeply desired a woman who didn't desire you. Although you tried for many years to win her affections, she chose another man, married him, and they moved away. Yet you still believed that the two of you were destined to be together, so you began to pray vigilantly every night for God to bring her back to you. This began a recurring dream; a dream in which your beloved showed up at your house one day, asking for forgiveness for her misguided action of marrying another and asking you to accept her as your bride."

John sits spellbound as I continue. I tell him that, convinced his visions predicted the future, he anxiously awaited her return. And it happened soon enough.

John opened the door of his house one day to find her on his doorstep, pale-faced and crying. Her husband and child had just been badly injured in an accident with their cart and wagon nearby, and she begged John to come with her to help them.

John was convinced that his beloved was only making up this tale so she could get him away from the prying eyes and wagging tongues of his neighbors; that she would lead him down into the village where she could profess her love and dedication to him privately. Eagerly, he followed her out of the village gate and onto the road.

When he stepped out of the village gate he saw that, indeed, a wagon lay overturned on the street and a man and small boy lay on the ground unconscious. John was confused. Suddenly, *he realized his beloved was telling the truth, and that she was not his beloved after all.*

John fell to his knees wailing, feeling tricked and betrayed by love and hope and God. He then suffered a severe stroke and spent the rest of that life alone and isolated.

When I finish, John is holding back tears. "I can't believe what you're telling me," he whispers. "This is exactly what's happening in my life right now! My girlfriend has left me for another man and although she's told me it's over and that she wants to be with him and not me, I can't give up on her because I love her and believe we're destined to be together. I dream every night that she comes back to me, professing her love and apologizing for her mistake."

"But that's not all," he continues, "this has also happened to me in my previous relationships. My girlfriends have all ended the relationship with me, and each time I hoped and believed they would come back because we were destined to be together. But they never did come back, no matter how much I believed they would, and I've felt betrayed by my own hope and faith. Now I realize that all this time, I've been living out a wound from a past life!"

He sits there, arms crossed, processing what he's just learned. "So," he says, after a long pause, "I understand how this past-life wound has affected my relationships, but what does this have to do with my money problems?"

"The job of your second chakra is to make sure you can attract into your life that which you desire," I say, "and money is a part of that. Because you deeply desired this woman and thought that God would give her to you, and God didn't, you've internalized a message that says your deepest desires will not be fulfilled. Your father's negative beliefs about money only served to cement this belief in your energy field."

John is awestruck. "Who would have thought that unrequited love in a past life could stop the flow of money into my life in this life? I never would have made that connection, but now that you say it, it makes perfect sense!"

It's obvious that John needs to clear out the pain of this past life, as well as work on his chakras, and I teach him how to do this, advising him to pay particular attention to his second chakra. He promises to stick with the practices.

As you can see, chakric imbalances can present in many ways. John's example in particular illustrates that what at first may seem to be the problem (in his case, money) could be the result of another issue entirely.

Don't worry—you don't have to be psychic to figure these things out (though over time, your work with the Chakra Cleanse Meditation can help to enhance your intuitive abilities). Once you develop a thorough understanding of the various aspects of each chakra and start working with them regularly yourself, getting to the bottom of these issues gets easier.

Now let's look at chakra 2 in detail.

Chakra 2 Self-Assessment

To get an idea of how fit and healthy your second chakra is, ask yourself the following questions:

- Can I easily manifest that which I desire in life?
- Do I have a sense of my individual identity and what I want?
- Am I willing to explore life and find out more about myself?
- Do I enjoy my life, and can I take pleasure in the small things?
- Do I feel good about myself as a woman/man?
- Can I express myself sexually? Am I sexually fulfilled?
- Can I express myself creatively? Am I creatively fulfilled?
- Do I honor my creativity by making time for play?
- Can I let go and simply enjoy life?
- Am I free from problems with my reproductive system, kidneys, bladder, and colon?

If you answered "no" to a few of these questions, you have some challenges with your second chakra. If you answered "no" to many of them, you probably have a significant blockage.

Chakra 2 Out of Balance

If your second chakra is not working properly, you may have challenges with your physical or emotional health, finances, love life, relationships with family and friends, or your career and creativity. It's important to note that an imbalance in one chakra will likely affect the energy flow to the chakras above and below it. So if you have a weak or blocked chakra 2, you may experience one or more of the chakra 1 problems as well.

The following are some challenges you could experience if your second chakra is imbalanced.

Physical Health

- Gynecological issues, such as ovarian cysts or endometriosis
- Fertility and sexual issues, sexually transmitted diseases, low libido, menstrual problems, pain, or PMS
- Bladder, kidney, or pelvis issues
- Chronic lower back pain, including sciatica

Emotional Health

- Excessive feelings of shame or guilt
- Feeling alienated or cut off from others
- Mood swings
- Addictive behaviors
- Unhealthy promiscuity or frigidity
- Envy
- Denial and judgment
- Issues with boundaries, such as having no or ill-defined boundaries, or intruding on others' boundaries

Finances

- Feel bad about wanting money
- Obsessively attached to money
- Don't have enough money to enjoy life's pleasures

- Frugality
- Spending binges

Love Life

- Intimacy and sexual issues, such as frigidity, promiscuity, or being sexually demanding
- Untrusting, feeling like the other person is after something
- Inability to feel safe, secure, and trust yourself, others, and life
- Looking for a partner to make you feel better
- Choosing partners for selfish or immature reasons, such as someone who makes you look good
- Libido that is too low or too high

Relationships with Friends and Family

- Can't be open or honest
- Can't give physical affection
- Withdrawn, shy, untrusting
- Selfish or demanding
- Irresponsible or emotionally unstable
- Manipulative

Career and Creativity

- Lack of creativity
- Can't feel and express joy
- Lack of ability to stop and smell the roses
- Excessive creativity to the extent that you are not functioning in the real world and meeting your daily needs
- Self-absorbed
- Climbing the career ladder to get ahead and "be someone or something," or great aspirations to be a celebrity or otherwise well-known

Nourishing Chakra 2

In addition to doing the Chakra Cleanse Meditation (see Chapter 30), engaging in these activities or indulging these "likes" can help enliven your second chakra:

- The color orange
- Beautiful environments, such as art galleries, botanical gardens, and old Gothic churches
- Massage, hugs, and lovemaking
- Romance
- Gorgeous, breathtaking sunsets
- Losing yourself in the fullness and beauty of the present moment
- Dancing naked
- Anything that you find delightful

Remember Peter, Nancy, and John? With some diligent work, including an extra focus on their second chakras, beautiful changes started happening in their lives.

I told Peter that he had a lot of work to do on himself, and I'm happy to report that he did it. The next time I spoke with him, he told me he was changing his life by changing his chakras, and I knew he was telling me the truth because when I heard his voice, I no longer had the instinct to run and hide!

Nancy too had a long road ahead of her. She had a few stops and starts but finally was able to make a routine of working with her chakras. When I spoke with her a year after her session, she had been alcohol- and drug-free for three months, and was working on repairing several of her friendships. She was dating a new man, and though it was challenging at times, she was sticking to her new mantra: "No drama!"

When I last spoke with John, he was experiencing much more financial abundance, and he was happily single. He'd decided to stop pining for love and he would no longer allow himself to think about the past or miss his ex-girlfriends. He had started anew and was enjoying his time as a bachelor.

Now let's turn our attention to chakra 3.

CHAPTER 23

CHAKRA 3: STRENGTH

CHAKRA 3 IS THE third level of your energy anatomy. Also called the solar plexus chakra, it is located in the area of your stomach. Where chakra 1 governs your drive to meet your survival needs and chakra 2 oversees your ability to manifest that which you desire, chakra 3 governs your ability to make your way in the world and to stand up for what you want. It helps you know what is right for you, and to live it.

Your third chakra is the energy center that generates self-esteem and self-empowerment. When you have a healthy sense of self-esteem, you recognize what empowers you, and make choices that are in your best interests. Your third chakra enables you to set healthy boundaries and to protect yourself by saying "no" to unhealthy people and situations.

You can think of chakra 3 as your "bodyguard." It helps you detect unhealthy people and situations, and sense when a person's energy is negative or encroaching on yours. That gut feeling that someone or something isn't good for you or that someone is draining your energy is your third chakra talking.

In addition to alerting us to negative and potentially dangerous situations and people, chakra 3 is also where you create your personal honor code, and generate the willpower to stick by it. If you lack self-esteem, you tend to let others dictate what happens to you. A powerful third chakra enables you to stand up for what you want and what you believe in, but still be able to compromise from a place of self-empowerment.

Chakra 3 Basics

Names
Chakra 3 is also called the solar plexus chakra.

Location
It is located in the area of the stomach.

Areas of Body Governed
This chakra oversees the physical areas of the stomach, liver, gallbladder, digestive system, and spleen.

Drive and Issues
Chakra 3 generates your personal power and helps you maintain strong, healthy boundaries. This chakra also oversees your self-esteem and sense of self-empowerment. Chakra 3 is where you set your moral code, and generate the resolve to stick to it by standing up for yourself and what you believe in.

Like chakra 2, chakra 3 is another area where weaknesses are common; many people struggle with their third chakra. (Think of how many people you know who have solid, healthy boundaries versus those who don't.) To get an idea of how a chakra 3 imbalance can affect your life, let's look at a few of my past clients.

Case Studies

Laura

Laura is a quiet woman with a shy demeanor. As she sits before me, she looks as if she'd like nothing more than to disappear into the pattern of the chair. She's slouched forward, arms crossed, and everything about her seems drab and downcast, even the beige tones of her sweater and leggings.

When I look at Laura's energy field, I can see she is suffering badly from a recent breakup. She routinely gives all of herself in relationships, but always ends up broken-hearted. She's not only sad, she's confused about why this keeps happening.

With Laura in so much pain I take extra care with how I talk to her about it; instead of telling her everything I see, I start slowly. "Laura, I see you're in a difficult spot because of a recent breakup."

"Yes," she says and winces, then takes a deep breath. "I don't know what's wrong with me. I'm such a loving person. I take such good care of my partners, but it never seems to work out. All I want to do is find someone who can receive what I have to give."

Laura works as an acupuncturist, running a busy community clinic where people can receive treatments on a discounted basis. She gives her all to her clients as well, often working overtime.

"When's the last time you said 'no' to someone, Laura?" I ask her.

"What?" she says and straightens a little, clearly caught off guard. "What do you mean?"

"I mean you're severely lacking boundaries," I say. "I can hear it in your words, but your energy field also shows me that you have almost no willpower. And your self-esteem is weak. Laura, do you know who you are?"

"I don't know what you . . ." she starts to say, but trails off. She reaches up and rubs her necklace. It's a gesture I've

seen her do several times since arriving for her session. "I guess you're right," she finally says.

"Your third chakra is extremely weak," I continue. "You need to learn to create boundaries in your relationships and stop letting people—especially men—walk all over you. You've got to learn to stand up for yourself and say what you want."

"But I gave him everything he wanted," she sobs. "I gave everything and even that wasn't enough!"

"Maybe that was the problem," I say. "Perhaps he stopped respecting you." She looks at me, but says nothing. "You've got 'empath syndrome,'" I continue. "You have a big heart and are sensitive to others' feelings so you want to help everyone. But you haven't got the boundaries or discernment necessary to make wise choices about who to help and how. And worst of all, you're not caring for yourself. That's why you're tired all the time. You've got adrenal fatigue from working so hard, and you're letting others steal your energy. We have got to get you grounded and in a space where you can be more discerning with your heart and your healing talents, and where you can declare who you are and what you need."

"But . . ." she starts to say, then trails off again. Finally, she nods. "Okay," she says. "Show me how."

"You're going to start by turning that love you have inward and focus on yourself," I tell her. "We're going to get your third chakra nice and fit so you have greater self-esteem, along with better judgment about where to spend your precious heart energy."

Barbara

The first thing that strikes me about Barbara is her grouchy mood. I'm speaking to her on the phone, and as she says "Hello," I instantly receive the visual impression of a woman who is overweight, tired, and grumpy. Normally, I have a more formal way of starting my sessions, but I can sense that Barbara is someone who likes people to give it to her straight, so I say, "Barbara, you're tired of being cranky and overweight. You want to know how to change."

Through the earpiece I hear an outburst of sharp laughter followed by Barbara's voice. "Too right!" she declares.

"You also feel like people take advantage of you, but you have a hard time telling them so, so instead you just find ways to shut them out and use food to comfort you."

"I know I don't eat well," Barbara counters. "Plenty of doctors have told me that. What else can you tell me?"

"You're stuffing yourself with these foods because your fourth chakra is being starved of love. You need to feel that love energy in your heart chakra.

"You need healthy relationships in your life. You need love and companionship. We all do. I can see that your true nature is very warm, but your experiences have made you hard and mean. You take your frustration out on others, and I can see that you don't like this about yourself."

"Okay," Barbara says, "you're right again, about all of it. What else?"

"I can see as I scan your energy field that in addition to not having healthy relationships, you're having some problems with your physical health that are contributing to you being overweight," I continue. "Your third, fourth, and fifth chakras are weak and blocked, particularly your third chakra. In fact, they're so blocked that it would be almost impossible for you to not feel angry and frustrated. But beyond that, I can see in your third chakra that your liver is exhausted; it's desperately trying to do its job, and so is your pancreas, but both these organs are struggling with all the sugary and fatty foods you're consuming. It's too much for them to process."

"Wow," she says.

"Plus I'm seeing in your fifth chakra—in the area of your throat—that your thyroid and hormonal levels are very imbalanced. You really need to go to an endocrinologist to help you get that sorted."

"Great," she grumbles, "another doctor."

"Look, Barbara, I know you've had some bad experiences with doctors, but this really will help. We've got to get those hormones balanced, plus get these blockages cleared from your chakras so the energy can flow and you can release this anger."

"Fine," she sighs.

"Barbara, I mean it," I say.

"Okay, okay," she laughs. "What do I do?"

I explain the chakra system to Barbara and instruct her how to start cleansing her chakras. I tell her it's going to take some faith on her part to keep with it because she's got a lot of healing to do. As we end the session, Barbara also promises to see an endocrinologist straight away.

Simone

"I can't stand my boss," Simone says the moment she sits down. "She's ruining my life and I hate my work." She sits rigid and upright, clutching her purse in her lap. Everything about her looks tight. Her lips are pursed, her knees and ankles are clamped together, and her blouse is buttoned all the way to the top of her neck.

"Okay," I say. "I can tell you're anxious to get going, but let me start by telling you what I tell all my clients—it's better for you not to give me any information yet. I like to get a clean impression from your energy field without being influenced by anything you might say. How about if you get comfortable and I'll look at your energy field and see what's happening?"

"She's terrible," Simone continues, her features pinched so tight her eyes are squinting. "It's like she—"

I hold up a hand. "Let me just take a look first, and see what your energy field is showing me. Then we can talk about your boss."

Simone goes quiet, then leans back in the chair slightly, her spine still straight as a rod.

When I look at Simone's energy field, I certainly see what she's talking about—she really can't stand her boss. She thinks almost nonstop about how mean her boss is, how unfairly her boss treats her, how demanding her boss is, and how her boss fails to recognize all that Simone does.

Simone's third chakra is heavily depleted, not only because she focuses incessantly on how much she dislikes her boss, but also because she feels powerless to change her work situation.

"You think too much about your boss," I tell her. "This is making you tired and sick. It's giving you an upset stomach, and it's making you irritable, which you often take out on your children."

"Of course I think too much about my boss," she says, sitting upright again. "You would too, if you had to work with her!"

"Here's the thing," I explain. "I can also see that your boss is the type of person who respects people who stand up for themselves. You need to show her that you're strong. The problem is that you're so stressed about your boss, you feel weak and depleted, and that's encouraging your boss to be even more dominant. You've got to show her some backbone."

Simone thinks for a minute. When she speaks again, her voice has lost some of its edge. "She's just so pushy and forceful."

"I know," I say, "but you've got to learn to hold your own."

Simone offers a little more resistance. "But she deserves it that I think badly of her!" she says. Then I point out that this attitude is only serving to deplete Simone and lessen her power in her boss's eyes.

"Spending all this time thinking bad thoughts about someone else wastes your own precious energy. It's wearing you out!" I say.

Finally, something clicks. "Yes," she nods. "That does make sense. I think I can feel what you're talking about. It's tiring. Exhausting, in fact."

I take Simone through an exercise on holding her center—called "shielding"—which is designed to energize the third chakra. "This, along with the chakra cleansing and strengthening I described, will help you hold a firm line with her."

"Let's hope," Simone says, and for the first time, she seems to relax a bit, even offering a hint of a smile.

"Keep me posted," I say. "I definitely want to hear how this works out."

Chakra 3 Self-Assessment

To get an idea of how fit and healthy your third chakra is, ask yourself the following questions:

- Can I say "no" and stand up for what I believe in?
- Do I have healthy self-esteem? Am I self-confident?
- Can I "hold my center," feeling balanced and sure of myself in spite of other people's thoughts and emotions?
- Can I put my mind to something and follow it through?
- Do I have a sense of what is good for me?
- Do I have a moral code, and do I live by it?
- Can I set boundaries emotionally?
- Can I protect myself from taking on other people's lower energies?
- Can I protect myself from feeling overly responsible for other pcople's lives/emotions?
- Am I motivated, and do I feel empowered?
- Can I hold my ground instead of giving away power to avoid confrontation?
- Am I free from digestive problems and anxiety attacks?

If you answered "no" to a few of these questions, you have some challenges with your third chakra. If you answered "no" to many of them, you probably have a significant blockage.

Chakra 3 Out of Balance

If your third chakra is not working properly, you may have challenges with your physical or emotional health, finances, love life, relationships with family and friends, or your career and creativity. Remember, an imbalance in one chakra will likely affect the energy flow to the chakras above and below it. So if you have a weak or blocked chakra 3, you may experience one or more of the problems related to chakras 1 and 2 as well.

The following are some challenges you could experience if your third chakra is imbalanced.

Physical Health

- Stomach ulcer
- Liver problems
- Diabetes, pancreatitis, or hypoglycemia
- Gallstones
- Irritable bowel syndrome, frequent vomiting, or a "nervous stomach"
- Anorexia/bulimia
- Colon and intestinal problems
- Adrenal/chronic fatigue

Emotional Health

- Low self-esteem
- Inability to care for yourself
- Feeling overly responsible for others, enmeshed in others' lives and energy
- Fearful, experiencing panic attacks
- Feeling weak or trapped
- Disempowered
- Taking the victim role, passive and blaming
- Overly aggressive
- Controlling, stubborn
- Exhibit bullying behaviors
- Overfunctioning and competitive

Finances

- Don't feel worthy to charge adequate prices or ask for a raise
- Lack self-discipline and follow through
- Don't know what career or path is right for you
- Don't receive the abundance of the universe

Love Life

- Don't feel worthy and spend time with toxic people
- Victim of "energy vampirism"
- Frequent communication difficulties
- Passive-aggressive
- Fight/conflict, engage in battle of wills
- Controlled or are controlling
- Lack of equality in relationships
- Too trusting, open, or loving with unsafe people
- Emotionally confused/confuse others
- Blaming, aggressive

Relationships with Friends and Family

- Frequent communication issues
- Controlled or are controlling
- Fight/conflict, engage in battle of wills
- Estranged from family
- Frightened of conflict, saying what you want
- Reluctance to be honest with people
- Lack of transparency, openness

Career and Creativity

- Lack clarity, direction; difficulty knowing what is right for you
- Self-absorbed, won't work as part of a team
- Lack self-discipline, motivation
- Lack self-esteem and confidence to share your creative ideas with others

Nourishing Chakra 3

Participating in the following activities or indulging these "likes" can help to enliven your third chakra:

- The color yellow
- Saying "no" if something isn't right for you
- The martial arts
- "Holding your center" when confronted with a differing opinion and responding only when you know your own truth
- Focus, persistence, and diligence
- Diplomacy and strength of character
- Acting like a "peaceful warrior"—someone who stands in a quiet place of power and strength

So what happened with Laura, Barbara, and Simone? I'm happy to report that the last I spoke with them, all three were doing much better.

Laura had cut back on her hours at the clinic and had taken on another acupuncturist as a business partner. With someone to share the workload, she felt much better about working fewer hours and taking time off for a much-needed vacation. She had also become more discriminating about who she dated, having realized that for years she'd chosen men based on the subconscious perception that they needed her help. Now, she sought a balanced relationship instead of one based on saving her partner.

Barbara did go to get her hormones tested straight away, and the test confirmed that her hormonal levels were very imbalanced. In fact, I later spoke with the doctor myself, and he told me that Barbara's were the most imbalanced levels she'd ever seen! Barbara began a liver and pancreas detox program and kept up with the chakra cleansing and strengthening, and in six months her health had greatly improved, and so had her mood.

As for Simone, in a short space of time—and to her amazement—her boss began acting differently around her. Her boss now rarely yelled at Simone or criticized her, and when her boss was in one of her moods, Simone simply let her be and got on with her own day, not allowing herself to waste her precious time being angry or upset. Simone's stomach pains went away, she could sleep better, and she had worked out how to better balance her home and work life.

Now let's turn our attention to chakra 4.

CHAPTER 24

CHAKRA 4: LOVE

Chakra 4 is the fourth level of your energy anatomy. Also called the heart chakra (because of its location), it is one of the most, if not *the* most important of your chakras. It governs all your emotions, especially love.

Chakras 3 and 4 work together closely in several ways. In chakra 3, you learn what it means to have self-esteem and self-confidence, as well as discernment, and how to be a peaceful warrior—someone who stands quietly but powerfully in a place of strength. It is in chakra 4 that you learn to *deepen* your ability to be a peaceful warrior, as it generates compassion and empathy, and governs how you become a vehicle and vessel for love. The heart chakra is the source of unconditional love without judgment, while the solar plexus chakra applies discernment to where and how you channel that love.

Your fourth chakra is selfless in terms of loving others, but it's also focused on unconditional self-love. To truly love and accept others and be free of ego, you must truly love and accept yourself. Achieving this, you become a vehicle for great healing and transformation; when you let go of the sense of separateness created by the ego, you are free to connect to everyone and everything.

A balanced heart chakra also cleans your energy field of emotional negativity, so it's vital that this chakra works. Otherwise you become emotionally and psychically polluted.

Chakra 4 Basics

Names

Chakra 4 is also called the heart chakra.

Location

It is located in the area of the heart.

Areas of Body Governed

This chakra oversees the physical areas of the heart, blood, chest, hands and arms, lungs, and circulatory system.

Drive and Issues

Chakra 4 oversees all our emotions, especially the pursuit and expression of love. It is concerned with giving and receiving love to others and to yourself, as well as compassion, forgiveness, and acceptance.

An imbalanced or weak heart chakra can affect your life in many ways. To see examples of these effects, let's look at case studies of some of my clients who have had challenges with chakra 4.

Case Studies

Anna

> *My first impression of Anna is so clear and sad, it makes my heart ache. I'm speaking to her on the phone, and as I tell her what she can expect from our session, I'm distracted by an image that's coming to me so strongly it's difficult to concentrate on what I'm saying to her.*

I see Anna, who looks to be in her thirties, wearing a simple, faded dress with her straight brown hair tied back in a loose ponytail at the nape of her neck. She sits at a window, looking out on the world. Outside is a beautiful garden bursting with flowers, and there are animals playing and children laughing. Suddenly Anna calls out to the children, "Here I am! Can I come play with you?" But she yells through the glass and the children can't hear her.

I watch as Anna searches the room, looking for a way out, but she can't find one. Finally, she gives up. She slumps to the floor, covers her face with her hands, and begins to cry.

I take a deep breath, trying to maintain my composure, but the vision of Anna is so terribly sad it's difficult to hold back tears. "Anna," I say, "I can see in your energy field that you had dreams for your life that haven't come true. As a result, you've shut down your heart to try to protect yourself from getting hurt again."

Anna begins to cry. "I don't have anyone in my life," she says. "I'm all alone, but I'm afraid to reach out to anyone."

"You're suffering from a broken heart chakra," I continue, "and because you've shut down your heart, you've blocked the flow of love into your life. In fact, you've shut it down so thoroughly that you've blocked the flow of everything good into your life. That's why you're struggling with money."

"I don't know what to do," she sobs. "I don't even know how to connect with people anymore; the thought of it is terrifying and exhausting."

I know Anna has been trying to heal, but her repeated failures have only made her shut down more. She was referred to me by her psychologist, who feared she was no longer making progress with Anna.

"Well, Anna, I have some good news for you. I'm not going to tell you to go out and talk to people."

The telephone line is quiet for a moment. "You're not?" she finally says, sounding slightly suspicious.

"Instead, we're going to work on healing your heart chakra. Then it won't be such a struggle to try and interact with people."

"But . . . I'm scared," she says.

"I understand," I reply, "because your third chakra is also very weak. Chakra 3 is critical to being able to love openly because it's the chakra that protects your heart. If your third chakra isn't working, your heart can't open safely. In fact, your first and second chakras could also use some support, but don't worry—we'll address all of them. Once energy flows freely through your chakras, you'll feel safer, more grounded, more confident, and more willing to let people in again. Once we get the love moving into your life again, Anna, all sorts of good things will start to flow to you. How does that sound?"

"Still scary," Anna says, "but also really good."

Luke

When Luke walks into the room, suddenly things feel stuffy. For a moment, I wonder if I'm coming down with something, because out of nowhere I feel too warm and as if I'm having trouble breathing. A few moments later, I understand why.

As Luke settles into the chair, I start to receive images and information from his energy field. He certainly seems likable enough, and he's young, handsome, and well groomed with his natty V-neck sweater and designer jeans. But I can see in his energy that he's having trouble with his relationships, and that the women in his past have found him needy and suffocating. No wonder I feel this way!

I take a sip of water to help shake the feeling, then explain to Luke how the session will go. "I can't wait!" he smiles, "I'll be so happy if you can help me."

"For starters," I say, "you feel you're having trouble meeting the right woman. You've already had lots of relationships, but none of them have gone the way you'd hoped, so you've recently given up."

"That's right," he says, shaking his head wistfully, "relationships just don't seem to work for me."

"Your past hurts have caused a blockage in your heart chakra—you're afraid to love again because you're afraid to get hurt, and that's creating a self-fulfilling prophecy. I can see that you're very resilient—you've 'toughened up' to deal with these hurts. But that toughness has also numbed you and has made it difficult for that love energy to move easily through your life."

"Yes, that makes sense. But . . . I don't know, I don't want to be rude . . . That doesn't sound that complicated. I mean, I think I could have figured it out on my own." Luke looks slightly tense as he anticipates my reaction.

I smile. "Well, yes, perhaps you could have . . . But there's more I want to tell you."

"Yes?!" he says, leaning forward, and I can't help but smile at his wide-eyed anticipation.

"Your second chakra is showing me a blockage there, as well. It's to do with your mother." His smile fades and he looks slightly deflated, but he says nothing. I can see that Luke's mother passed away when he was only eleven years old. The event was so tragic for him that it stunted his emotional development. He still harbors feelings of abandonment, especially because when she died, he was moving into puberty—a time of enormous change. He couldn't experience the normal developmental milestone of transitioning from emotional dependence on his mother to independence. I tell him all this, then add, "Because of this unresolved transition, you've been looking for your mother in your romantic relationships."

I give him a moment to take that in, then I ask him questions about his previous relationships to try and help him see this pattern: Were they mature women, older than you? Were they compassionate women who looked after you? Did you want to move in with them or have them move in with you very soon into the relationship? Were you emotionally dependent upon them, and did you expect them to solve your problems for you and protect you?

"I'm seeing it now," Luke says. "So many things are starting to make sense all of a sudden. I really have been looking for my mum all this time, and that's what's made my relationships fail." Then he gives a sharp laugh. "When my last girlfriend broke up with me, she even said, 'I'm not your mother!' I accused her of being dramatic, but she was right."

"And how has your sex life been?" I ask, catching him off guard.

"Great . . . at first. Then after a couple of weeks, things always seem to fizzle out. It felt like my girlfriends weren't attracted to me anymore."

"Well, I can tell you that no woman thinks it's sexy to feel like her partner's mother."

He smiles and nods, then asks, "But what can I do about this? How do I resolve this mother issue I have?"

"It might seem counterintuitive," I say, "but we're not going to worry about your mother issue—that is, we're not going to focus on your past experiences. Instead, we're going to focus on healing your chakras so they draw energy into your life to support healthier relationships and help you feel that independence you've been seeking. Once that happens, you'll find yourself relating differently to women."

"Thank God!" Luke says and leans back in the chair, obviously relieved.

Jane

Jane is exhausted, and I can see it in every aspect of her energy field. By outward appearances, though, she's got everything together. She's a middle-aged woman, well dressed, with her hair and makeup done beautifully. She sits down, smiling, with her legs crossed and hands folded, and I'm struck by the sharp contrast between her physical presentation and what I see in her chakras.

I give Jane my usual introductory speech, then begin to scan her energy field more deeply. Right away I see that her first and *second chakras are pale and severely depleted, and across her fourth chakra is a giant auric tear.*

"You work as a caregiver," I say.

"Yes, at the nursing home," she says.

"You're very good at it, but you're giving too much of yourself. That's why you're exhausted. Your lower chakras are completely drained, and there's nothing left for you."

Jane's smile begins to fade as her eyes tear up. "It's true; I am exhausted." She takes a moment to collect herself before continuing. "I just care about my patients so much. Sometimes I stay past my shift. I can't help it—I'm the only 'family' some of them have." She pulls out a tissue and dabs at her eyes.

"I understand," I say, "but you're so depleted you're start- ing to get sick. Jane, you have 'healer syndrome.' You are a powerful healer, yet you're helping people by giving them your own energy. That is a big no-no." I smile, and Jane smiles back in such a way that I know she knows what I'm talking about. "Healers need to channel the abundant energy of the universe," I continue, "not give to others from their personal supply. That energy is meant for you, to keep you going and healthy. Does that make sense?"

"Yes," she replies, again dabbing her tired eyes with the tissue.

"Healers have big hearts and want to help people, but you have to be wise about how you're doing it, and how much you're doing it."

"But how can I say 'no' to someone who needs me?" she says, and I can see in her energy field just what a truly caring person Jane is.

"There is no shame in saying 'no,' and protecting yourself, Jane. I know it's hard, but you've got to show some discernment about how much of yourself you give. You need boundaries."

Jane nods. "And I think you need a break from your work," I add. "A long one."

"I feel guilty saying this, but sometimes I think about retiring."

"Yes," I say, "I would seriously consider it. Energetically, you can't take it anymore. I know you love your job and you've helped a lot of people, but you've given enough. Once you recover, there are other ways you can help people—ways that are safer for you. In the meantime, I'm going to show you how to get your energy back and build up those boundaries!"

Chakra 4 Self-Assessment

To get an idea of how fit and healthy your fourth chakra is, ask yourself the following questions:

- Do I practice self-love?
- Do I feel connected to others?
- Am I free from past hurts? Have I let go of feelings of betrayal, disappointment, or bitterness?
- Can I forgive and accept myself and others?
- Can I be generous and joyous?
- Can I enjoy other people for who they are, or do I always find fault in others?
- Do I have heartfelt, intimate, thriving, supportive relationships in my life?
- Have I found what I love and am passionate about?
- Can I give and receive physical affection, such as hugs?
- Can I love unconditionally, without strings attached?
- Does the Law of Attraction work for me? Can I draw into my life what (and who) I love?
- Do I have a healthy heart, chest, lungs, and circulatory system?

If you answered "no" to a few of these questions, you have some challenges with your fourth chakra. If you answered "no" to many of them, you probably have a significant blockage.

Chakra 4 Out of Balance

If your fourth chakra is not working properly, you may have challenges with your physical or emotional health, finances, love life, relationships with family and friends, or your career and creativity. Remember, an imbalance in one chakra will likely affect the energy flow to the chakras above and below it. For example, if you have a weak or blocked chakra 4, you may experience one or more of the problems related to chakras 1 through 3 as well.

The following are some challenges you will experience if your fourth chakra is imbalanced.

Physical Health

- Heart issues, such as high blood pressure, heart murmur, heart disease, or circulation problems
- Chest problems, such as pneumonia, lung cancer, or asthma
- Breast cancer or other issues affecting the breasts
- Allergies
- Chest, shoulder, diaphragm, upper back, or arm pain

Emotional Health

- Emotionally closed down
- Isolated/withdrawn and lonely, brooding
- Highly judgmental, critical
- Depression, lack of joy/lightness
- Fear/lack of intimate relationships, unable to trust
- Secretly yearn to be loved and get affection
- Unwillingness to forgive and move on
- Grief, bitterness, regret, rage
- Focused on trying to find love externally
- Clingy, needy
- Demanding, attached
- Codependent, martyr

- Sense of self/identity is role-related: "the wife," "the mother," "the husband"
- Obsession with being a "good and giving" person

Finances

- Aren't making money doing what you love
- Lack of generosity, compassion, and genuine love and concern
- Can't maximize the Law of Attraction
- Inability to give and receive money joyfully

Love Life

- Can't have flourishing relationships
- Unrealistic expectations, high standards, pressure for your partner to be perfect
- Often feel hurt, disappointed, or betrayed
- Can't accept another person fully, or forgive
- Hypercritical, building resentments and bitterness
- Have toxic relationships
- Look externally to find the love you don't have for yourself
- Need other people to behave in certain ways to make you feel loved

Relationships with Friends and Family

- Similar issues as with romantic relationships
- Unrealistic expectations, high standards, pressure for your family to be perfect
- Often feel hurt, disappointed, or betrayed
- Can't let another person be who they are

Career and Creativity

- Lack of connection with your work
- Lack of joy in your work
- Don't do what you love

Nourishing Chakra 4

Among the activities and indulgences your fourth chakra enjoys are:

- The color green
- Heartfelt hugs, talks, and movies
- Practicing forgiveness
- Practicing gratitude
- Letting go of old hurts
- Smiles, kind words, and compassion
- A daily visualization of everyone on the planet living in health, harmony, and plenty
- Telling your loved ones how much you love them
- Random acts of kindness and prayer
- Undertaking any activities that you love

Anna, Luke, and Jane all experienced significant improvements after learning how to work with their chakras and making some much-needed changes in their lives.

Together with her psychologist, I helped Anna begin to open up her heart. I showed her how to cleanse and strengthen her chakras, paying particular attention to her heart chakra, and her psychologist led her through a process where she released her old wounds and forgave others. Last time I spoke with Anna, she proudly told me that she had joined a choir and was working at a local charity. She was also planning to study psychology and had moved back to the country of her birth.

Luke was so excited to get working on his chakras that I knew he'd have a quick turnaround. And he did. When I spoke to him several months later, he felt more confident about himself, in general, and had just started to date again after taking some time off to work on himself.

When I spoke to Jane to see how she was doing, I found that she had in fact retired. She felt more energized and was enjoying spending time rediscovering the things she loved, like gardening and decorating her house. She'd even joined a card club, gathering with neighbors every week to play bridge.

Now let's turn our attention to your fifth chakra.

CHAPTER 25

CHAKRA 5: EXPRESSION

CHAKRA 5 IS THE fifth level of your energy anatomy. Also called the throat chakra, it oversees your communication, and it's from here that you express yourself authentically, individually, and creatively.

Your fifth chakra is about honest communication and being able to communicate your needs and desires. When your fifth chakra is strong and balanced, you can express yourself truthfully and lovingly. A balanced chakra 5 also allows expression of spirituality and creativity, and helps you remain open-minded, keeping you from holding so strongly to your beliefs that you're closed to change.

This chakra also governs your will. In chakra 3, you develop your sense of willpower, such as sticking to a diet or standing up for your beliefs. Chakra 5, however, is about surrendering your personal will to divine will. When you are guided by your soul's will, you invite a higher consciousness to enter your psyche which empowers you to speak "your truth" and enact meaningful change in the world.

Chakra 5 Basics

Names

Chakra 5 is also called the throat chakra.

Location

It is located in the area of the throat.

Areas of Body Governed

This chakra oversees the physical areas of the throat, neck, jaw, teeth, thyroid glands, and vocal cords.

Drive and Issues

Chakra 5 governs your drive to express yourself authentically and originally. It oversees your self-determination, will, and ability to speak your truth.

Throat chakra issues can affect your life in many ways. To see examples of these effects, let's look at some clients I've worked with who have had challenges with their fifth chakra.

Case Studies

Paul

> *"You're depressed because you hate your job," I tell Paul. "And I'm not surprised, because I can see that you're clearly in the wrong field. What is it that you do for a living?"*
>
> *"IT," he replies flatly. We're speaking on the phone, but while I can't "see" Paul, I have a strong visual impression of him and it is not of him sitting in front of a computer. Rather, it is of him performing. His career is a mismatch for him!*
>
> *"I'm sorry," I say, "It's just that I can see you in front of people as an entertainer. I can also clearly see that you're a painter, and a quite gifted one. IT is just so wrong for you, like a polar bear sitting on the beach trying to get a tan!"*

Paul begins to laugh, seeing the absurdity of the situation.

"You've got massive blockages in your third and fifth chakras, Paul. They've gone on strike."

"On strike?" he laughs. Paul is a good sport. I realize I'm putting a lot out there, but his bubbly personality and openness are helping him take it all in his stride.

"Yes. Your third chakra defends what you believe in, and because you don't really believe in anything you're doing with your work, your third chakra has 'retired' as a result. Your fifth chakra has to do with your creative expression, which there's no opportunity for in your job, so it's also taken early retirement."

Paul sighs. "I started doing IT because I'm good at it and I needed a regular paycheck. I was only going to do it for a few years so I could save some money to pursue my true loves— painting, writing, and performing. That was ten years ago."

"Yes, and now you've got a house with a mortgage and lots of other debt, leaving you with no way to finance your dreams. You're also afraid that if you follow your heart, you'll lose the love and respect of your parents, who are proud of their 'reliable' son and his 'reliable' job. Paul, you've never even told them what you really want to do!"

"I know!" he says with such good humor that we both laugh.

"It's all okay. I'm going to show you how to get your chakras working so you can finally pursue the work you love."

I explain the chakra cleansing and mindfulness exercises that Paul can do to get his chakras strong and revitalized. As we're about to end the session, Paul interrupts me.

"Can I ask one more question?" he says sheepishly.

"Of course," I say.

"I don't know how to tell my girlfriend I want to end our relationship. Do you have any advice?"

"Girlfriend?" I ask, and I'm driven to an uncharacteristic fit of laughter. Paul's second chakra clearly shows me that he's homosexual.

Paul laughs too, as I tell him what I see.

"Well, I guess I have some other things to work on too," he says, and I know by his good-natured and open-minded disposition that he's going to be just fine.

Lisa

In this day and age, many people are waking up to the fact that they're in a job they dislike and which isn't aligned with them. Sometimes, however, people are convinced they should be in this career that's not right for them. This is the case with Lisa.

As soon as I hear Lisa on the phone, I know she's experienced significant disappointment and despair. Her voice is thick with bitterness and her energy field shows me she's been carrying a heavy burden of sadness for many years.

"Lisa, I'm reading your energy field and I see in your fifth chakra that you have been gifted with an exceptional singing voice, but that this gift is also a source of despair for you. You've always wanted to become a professional singer, but haven't been able to achieve your dream."

Lisa begins to cry. "Yes," she confirms.

"Early in your career you started having problems with your voice," I continue. "Sore throats, infections, strained vocal cords . . . You went to a number of specialists and no one could figure out why this kept happening to you."

"Yes," Lisa sniffs. "I had to cancel so many singing jobs that I was labeled 'unreliable,' and no one wanted to book me anymore. My career ended before it even began."

"And all this time you've felt like you lost out on your true calling."

"Yes," she says again, and the anguish in her voice is heartbreaking.

I can see forty-five years of accumulated despair and bitterness in Lisa's chakras. But I see something else, as well. "Lisa, you have an incredible teacher energy. Do you teach singing?"

"It pays the bills," she says sourly. "It's pathetic, isn't it? Here I am teaching other people how to fulfill my dream."

"Here's the thing, Lisa," I say, "I know how badly you wanted to be a singer, but you truly are a gifted teacher. Your lack of recognition of this gift, and of the positive impact you have on your students' lives, is robbing you of the joy it could bring you."

"But I was supposed to be a famous singer," she protests, "not some teacher!"

"Maybe that's not true," I counter. "Maybe you are where you are supposed to be. What if all the time you spent training to be a singer was actually training you to be what you were intended to become all along—an extremely talented singing teacher? Sometimes it's not our circumstances that present problems in our lives, but rather our beliefs about them." I say this not only to challenge Lisa, but also because it's what I genuinely see in her energy field. Her teacher energy is far stronger than her singer and performer energy. Sadly, she is so blinded by her bitterness at the loss of her singing career that she can't see the impact she makes as a teacher.

"Doesn't your heart fill with pride at hearing your students sing a song you taught them how to sing?" I ask. "Don't you love helping your students become great singers?"

"No," she says flatly. "Watching other people receive praise for their singing just drives the knife of loss deeper into my heart. It should be me out there. People should be looking at me and applauding me for my amazing voice."

I see that Lisa's fifth chakra blockage is causing her physical discomfort in addition to her emotional baggage. Not only is she lonely and isolated, but she also has chronic neck and shoulder pain.

I tell her this and explain that she can release her feelings of bitterness and heal from her physical pain if she commits to cleansing her chakras, with a special focus on chakra 5.

"Maybe it's just too late for me," she says.

"Just give it a try," I reply, and though she agrees to work on her chakras, as I hang up the phone, I am saddened and skeptical about whether she really will.

Suzie

"So what can you tell me?" Suzie says, settling into the chair and looking at me expectantly. She's wearing a perfectly tailored pantsuit and designer heels, but what stands out most about her appearance is her bright red lipstick. And what stands out most in her energy field are significant blockages in her third and fifth chakras.

After I go over the formalities about how the session will go, I start right in with what I see in her energy field. "You're having trouble meeting the right man."

"You can say that again," she says, rolling her eyes. "Every guy I meet turns out to be a jerk. But I guess I shouldn't be surprised—it takes a strong man to be with a strong woman."

"'Strong' is one word for it, but I'm seeing something else," I say. "You've got blockages in your third and fifth chakras, and I'm seeing that you can be quite argumentative. You tend to be very fixed in your beliefs about what's right and wrong, and you aren't a good listener."

"Sure, I know what's right and wrong," she says. "It's my job to teach others what's right and wrong. Really, they should thank me."

"I'm seeing that you also like to be the 'boss' in your relationships."

"Like my mother used to say: It's my way or the highway. She didn't raise me to be a pushover. She said, 'Suzie, you've got to stand up for yourself, otherwise you'll find yourself scurrying to have dinner on the table every night for some man you can barely stand.' There's no way that's going to happen to me."

In reality, most of the men Suzie has dated aren't jerks at all, but rather nice guys who simply get fed up with her nastiness disguised as assertiveness and her unwillingness to listen or compromise.

"Suzie," I say, "a healthy sense of self-esteem isn't about dominating others or making them bend to your will. It isn't about trying to make others believe what we believe. Rather, a person

with healthy self-esteem feels so secure within themselves that they are happy to let others simply be."

Suzie looks at me skeptically, but remains uncharacteristically quiet.

"I'm not telling you that you should be meek; it's good to know your mind. But imposing your will on others is really damaging your relationships. Are you open to trying something different?"

Suzie crosses her arms and sits for a minute. Finally, she nods. "All right," she says.

I'm not sure whether Suzie will follow my advice or whether her overenergized fifth chakra will draw her back to her old ways, but I teach her the chakra cleansing practice and hope for the best.

Allyson

I'm sitting in front of my computer, watching as a woman in her early thirties appears via Skype. "Hi, Allyson," I say. "Are you ready for your session?"

"I'm so excited," she says, clapping her hands together. "Let's do it!"

As I'm explaining to Allyson how the session will go, I'm already getting impressions about her, and I can see right away that she's recently launched a career as a life coach and intuitive. I see that she speaks to most of her clients via web calls like this one.

"How's your coaching going?" I ask her. In reality, I can see how it's going—slow. But I'm interested to hear what Allyson has on her mind, because I also see in her energy field that what she thinks is the problem actually isn't.

"Wow, you can see that I'm a coach? That's amazing!" Allyson flashes a wide smile, but she's not nearly as confident as it implies.

"Yes, you started recently after finishing an online course."

"That's right! I took time off work when my daughter was born and realized I didn't want to go back. One of my friends is

a life coach and an intuitive, and she told me I should take this course her coach offers to figure out what I want to do. Turns out I'm meant to be a life coach too!"

"So you invested in headshots and a website and all your materials, but you're having trouble getting your business going," I say. "And you've spent a lot of money on this course and on getting your 'branding' in order, but you're not sure where to go from here."

"Amazing," she says. "That's right. I just feel like there must be something blocking me from getting myself out there, you know? I've been reading about chakras and I think my throat chakra is weak or spinning backwards or something, otherwise I wouldn't be having problems getting myself noticed. What do you see?"

"I think one of your main challenges is time," I say, prompting a quizzical expression from Allyson.

"You mean I'm not spending enough time developing my business?" she asks. "I know my branding needs more work, but I'm doing a business booster seminar next week and—"

"That's not exactly what I mean," I interrupt. "From what I see, you've set off on this path of being a coach and an intuitive without any real experience. I can see that your natural intuitive abilities aren't very developed, and you haven't yet had the life or career experience to become a coach. In fact, I'm seeing that coaching is not a good choice for you. I do see some degree of imbalance in your fifth chakra, but what it's showing me is that you haven't yet surrendered to divine will; to the higher purpose of your life. You decided to become a coach because the opportunity presented itself and this school provided 'a path to success.' But coaching is not in line with your energy."

Allyson's gone pale and I feel badly for her, but I wouldn't be doing her any favors by hiding the truth. "What is in line with my energy?" she asks.

"I see you've got very strong creative energy, and you're very good at writing and art. At one point, you briefly considered

writing down and illustrating the stories you make up for your daughter, but you pushed it aside as unrealistic."

"It's amazing that you can see that! That's true!" she says.

"Yes, and I also see that being a children's book author and illustrator is something that appeals to you; it's definitely in line with your energy. Much more than being a life coach."

"I was so sure about this coach thing, but when you put it that way, I guess if I really listen to myself, you're right. In truth, I don't like working as a coach much. I did it because I thought it would be a good way to make money and be at home with my daughter."

"I understand, Allyson, and please know you haven't done anything wrong. What we need to do now is get your chakras balanced so you're better able to develop and listen to your own intuition," I say. "Your intuition was trying to give you that message in the first place. That's why you know that what I'm telling you is true."

"My husband's going to be upset. I just spent all that money on coaching."

"I understand, but it's not a loss. You can use all the tools you learned to become a coach to get started with this other venture. In fact, you could become so successful that maybe one day you'll start a side business coaching other book writers and illustrators. When you truly surrender your personal will to your soul's will, things have an interesting way of coming together."

Allyson gives a nervous smile. "Look," I say, "I understand that making money is a real concern. If you can go back to your old job, it could support you while you follow your creative path. And I have a hunch, call it a psychic one, that you can easily get your old job back."

"Well," she says, "I did like that job. It's just that . . . Well, I thought it would be an easier schedule and I could make a lot more money being a coach. But, now that you mention it, I really don't love talking to all these people about their problems and

struggles. I thought maybe it was because I'm not good at it yet, but I always get nervous for the calls, and I don't know what to say. Do you honestly think I should give children's books a go?"

"If it resonates with you, which it seems to, then yes. Just start slow, then you won't be putting so much pressure on yourself to succeed immediately. It should be something you enjoy!"

"You know, as you're saying this, I feel all lit up—like something in me is coming alive for the first time!" Allyson's smile is back, and this time it's genuine.

Chakra 5 Self-Assessment

To get an idea of how fit and healthy your fifth chakra is, ask yourself the following questions:

- Do I openly and honestly communicate how I feel/believe?
- Do I speak up if I feel mistreated?
- Do I try to clear things up if I've been misunderstood or have misunderstood a situation?
- Do I express and act upon my creative ideas and inspirations?
- Do I listen to other people, do other people feel heard by me, and do I allow others to have their own point of view?
- Am I open to all points of view and willing to grow and be challenged about what I believe?
- Am I respectful of other people's authentic self-expression?
- Can I objectively examine my own beliefs and acknowledge that I'm not always right?
- Do I have an outlet to express my authentic and individual self?
- Do I creatively express myself and "sing my own soul song"?
- Am I free of neck, throat, jaw, teeth, and/or thyroid problems?

If you answered "no" to a few of these questions, you have some challenges with your fifth chakra. If you answered "no" to many of them, you probably have a significant blockage.

Chakra 5 Out of Balance

If your fifth chakra is not working properly, you may have challenges with your physical or emotional health, finances, love life, relationships with family and friends, or your career and creativity. Remember that an imbalance in one chakra will likely affect the energy flow to the chakras above and below it. So if you have a weak or blocked chakra 5 you may experience one or more of the problems related to chakras 1 through 4 too.

The following are some challenges you will experience if your fifth chakra is imbalanced.

Physical Health

- Neck, jaw, teeth, or tongue problems or disease (such as cancer)
- Sore throats, losing your voice, a weak voice, or other vocal problems
- Thyroid/hormonal problems
- Gum problems, mouth ulcers
- Chronic cough
- Swollen glands, laryngitis, tonsillitis

Emotional Health

- Shy, nervous, won't speak up, overly introverted
- Fear of public speaking and of being seen and heard
- Soft/weak voice
- "Ghost-like" energy or demeanor
- Speaking difficulties, such as stuttering and pronunciation problems
- Brash, loud, aggressive, overly extroverted, and attention-seeking
- Gossiping, talking too much, and can't listen
- Dishonest, "telling tales"
- Lack of will and decisiveness, not clear in your choices/actions
- Critical, judgmental, envious

Finances

- Don't have a job/career that fits your unique expression
- Crave to do/be what you love
- Difficulties getting what you want, aren't seen and/or heard
- Can't work as a team with others
- Can't put your unique stamp on things
- Can't tell the world what you want to say

Love Life

- Communication issues including misunderstandings and frustrations
- Feel rejected and alienated
- Struggle to have a love relationship where your partner accepts who you are and what you want to do in the world

Relationships with Friends and Family

- Similar issues as with romantic relationships
- Communication issues including misunderstandings, frustrations
- Feel rejected and alienated

Career and Creativity

- Communication issues
- Fear of speaking out, public speaking, honest and open conversations
- Writer's block
- Difficulty expressing your creativity
- Fear of expressing your individual self

Nourishing Chakra 5

Among the activities and experiences your fifth chakra likes are:

- The color blue
- Singing
- Public speaking

- Writing, acting, and performing
- Speaking your truth
- Great discussions with interesting and like-minded people
- Any activity in which you feel you are expressing yourself

You likely will not be surprised to learn that among Paul, Lisa, Suzie, and Allyson, there were mixed results.

Paul did well sticking to his chakra cleansing routine and when I spoke to him several months after his session, while he was still working in IT, he was painting again. In fact, he had even sold two of his paintings and was paying down his debt, as well as devising an exit strategy from his job. He was also doing some deep exploration into his sexuality, allowing himself to acknowledge feelings he'd long suppressed.

Sadly, when I spoke to Lisa, she was still in the same lonely and bitter space as before. She admitted to having tried the chakra cleanse once or twice, but said that she didn't see how it could possibly help her.

Suzie surprised me. When I spoke with her she said she'd been working consistently to balance her chakras. She reported that she felt more calm overall, and had begun to see how her previous aggressiveness had hurt many of her relationships. She was even thinking about taking her mother to a meditation class with her!

When I spoke to Allyson nearly a year after our web session, she was perkier than ever. She had returned to her old job and had taken to the idea of children's books with gusto, writing down all her favorite stories. She planned to illustrate a mockup of one of these stories for an upcoming conference where she'd have a chance to show it to some agents.

Now let's turn our attention to your sixth chakra.

CHAPTER 26

CHAKRA 6: INTUITION

Chakra 6 is the sixth level of your energy anatomy. Also known as the third eye chakra, this is where you encounter your higher mind. Chakra 6 is located above and between your eyebrows, in the middle of your forehead.

In working on your fifth chakra, you began learning to express yourself originally and authentically, and to surrender your personal will, allowing yourself to hear the guidance of a higher consciousness. In working on chakra 6, you explore this higher consciousness further, expanding your awareness to what lies beyond the earth plane.

Chakra 6 rules your spirituality as well as psychic abilities, mediumship, and intuition. This is the chakra to focus on when you seek to develop these aspects of your life, including "opening the third eye."

Your sixth chakra is about transcendence, or going truly "above and beyond" by opening yourself to real wisdom—the balance of imagination and intellect. An open and healthy sixth chakra allows a balance to be struck between the right (feminine/creative/imaginative) and left (masculine/organizational/intellect-based) sides of the brain. Author and intuitive Doreen

Virtue describes the right brain as the artist and seer—the visionary dreamer—and the left brain as the manager—the artist's caretaker, loving the artist's dreams and visions, and supporting her work. When your sixth chakra is strong and healthy, both of these sides of your brain work in partnership together. Then you can dream big things into being!

Chakra 6 Basics

Names
Chakra 6 is also called the third eye chakra.

Location
It is located above and between the eyebrows.

Areas of Body Governed
This chakra oversees the physical areas of the head, including the brain (the hypothalamus, pituitary gland, and pituitary nerve plexus), ears, and eyes.

Drive and Issues
Chakra 6 governs your ability to transcend this earth plane and to access wisdom.

Most people are weak in their sixth chakra, and this imbalance can play out in a variety of ways. Let's look at some clients I've worked with who have had blockages and other imbalances in chakra 6.

Case Studies

Celia
> *Celia practically floats into the room. She's dressed all in white, with a long, sheer white top, billowy white pants, and white sandals. She has the most serene expression on her face and rather than sit down, she sweeps towards me.*

"My friend, it is so good to see you again," she says. "The angels tell me we have known each other during several lifetimes. They told me to come see you and that you will tell me something life changing." She pulls me into a big hug and I hug her back.

She's a lovely woman. However, I can see clearly that she and I have not met before in this or any other lifetime. I don't want to start the session in a way that could come across as unkind, so instead of telling her this, I smile and kindly ask her to take a seat.

As I look at Celia's energy field, I'm struck by the massive imbalance between her higher and lower chakras. "Right away, I'm seeing that chakras 6 and 7 are engorged, while your lower chakras, especially 1 through 3, are quite weak. I see you spend a lot of time in meditation, and you work as an intuitive," I say.

I can see in her energy field and just from looking at her that Celia is barely here. I almost feel like I need to tie a tether to her before she floats away! Lately I have seen this more often. Many people are taking an increased interest in consciousness and spirituality, which is wonderful, but often they don't know about the importance of strong lower chakras. Without their strength, you can't awaken the higher chakras.

"Your lower chakras are showing me a disconnectedness from your body," I say. "You're spending a lot of time and energy focusing on transcendence and listening to your guides, but what you're hearing as guidance isn't always accurate." Finally her gauzy demeanor shifts.

"But I hear them clearly," she says, obviously surprised by what I've said.

"I can see that you are more intuitive than most," I reassure her, "yet what you perceive isn't always clear; the messages are sometimes garbled. This is due to an imbalance between the feminine and masculine sides of your brain—you're almost entirely in the feminine. It's the balance between feminine and masculine that increases intuitive abilities."

184

Celia smiles and her eyes again soften and mist over. "It is the divine feminine working through me. The sisterhood is rising," she declares.

"Yes," I say, "the vibration of the earth plane is shifting dramatically at this time. Yet the feminine and masculine energies are of equal importance; their polarity is necessary for balance. In your case, your inability to engage your left brain is why you're struggling to take your business where you want it to go. You're praying for success and meditating on it, sage-smudging your home and workspace and doing cleanses, but you're not being as practical as you need to be to make your dreams a reality. You must also take time to devise and implement a plan to make it all happen."

"Hmm," she says, contemplating what I've said.

"Also, it's important to understand that our guides and angels don't tell us what to do—that's not their role," I explain. "They may help us to see various elements of a situation, but they don't have an agenda of what choices are 'right' or 'wrong' for us. They support free will; you must make your own choices. Their real purpose is to help us learn from and integrate the lessons we encounter as a result of those choices."

"Then who would you say is giving me this guidance?" she asks.

"It could be your ego . . . Sometimes what we think we hear as guidance is actually our ego encouraging us to do something in its interests."

"Hmm," she says again, nodding, taking it all in.

"Strengthening your lower chakras and working on that left-right brain balance will support your intuitive capabilities and help you distinguish your intuition from your ego," I say. "And speaking of strengthening the lower chakras, you would also benefit from exercise," I continue. "And you need to get off your meditation cushion and get outside and interact with nature," I say, smiling. Celia laughs and smiles back. "This will help you ground into your body and strengthen your lower *chakras. You need to be in touch with the earth and feel the joy and delight of this earthly existence instead of trying to 'bliss out' all the time."*

"Hmm," she says again. "I hear what you're saying, and I'm willing to explore it."

"Good," I say, and I go over with her how to balance her chakras.

Jacob

Frankly, I'm surprised Jacob has come to see me. As he sits before me in his button-down shirt, casual blue jeans, and loafers, he seems relaxed and friendly, yet I can see in his energy field that he is highly skeptical of me. In fact, he thinks the entire field of medical intuition sounds like a bunch of woo-woo garbage.

"I understand how you feel," I tell Jacob after I give him my introductory speech. "I'm skeptical about many psychics and intuitives as well."

He raises his eyebrows and I smile. "I can see it in your energy field," I say. "I also see that you're here because your girlfriend told you to come." Jacob looks slightly uneasy as he uncrosses then re-crosses his legs.

"I think it's healthy to be skeptical. That's one reason I didn't want you to tell me anything before I read your energy field—so you can have confidence that what I tell you is what I see. Now let's get started and you can make up your mind for yourself."

Jacob gives a nod and leans back into the chair.

"I see you've been having migraines for a long time now," I begin. "Since you were a child, in fact. That's going on thirty years. You used to get them only once in a while, but now you get them more frequently and it affects your work." Jacob stares at me, poker faced, and I continue. "You've also started having anxiety attacks in the last few months, and the interferences this is creating in your work is causing you particular embarrassment."

I pause, and though I'm not looking for confirmation—I can see all this in his energy field—Jacob does offer a small nod.

"I know you've been to a number of specialists, trying medications and even some alternative therapies, and nothing has helped. And I can see why. Now, stick with me, because I know how this is going to sound to you . . ." I tell him about the chakra system, explaining that chakras are energy vortexes that govern various areas of our lives, including our physical and emotional well-being. "You've got a large blockage in your sixth chakra, and that's what's causing your headaches and anxiety." As I anticipated, Jacob sighs and gives me a "you've got to be kidding" look.

I smile. "I understand this doesn't fit with how you see the world. You're analytical. You want facts and proof, but this is also binding up your throat and heart chakras. You are trying to tightly control your life and exert your will in it rather than listening to divine will, and you are not communicating your feelings and letting love flow freely in your life. This in turn is causing problems in your relationship with your girlfriend. You don't allow yourself to love or express yourself openly. She feels you are withholding. You also have a wonderfully creative aspect, yet you don't let yourself explore it because you don't value it. I see you used to love putting on plays as a child."

Now I've struck a chord. "How do you know that? My girlfriend doesn't even know that."

"Like I said, it's here in your energy field . . . Jacob, you've got to learn to embrace your intuitive and creative side—that's what's bringing on these headaches and anxiety attacks. You're actually highly intuitive, but you suppress it. When you were a child, you used to see and feel all kinds of things about people, but when you told your parents, you were scolded. They looked at you as if you were strange, and that hurt so much you shut that part of yourself down. Most of us start shutting down our natural intuitive abilities in childhood because adults discourage this kind of thing. In

187

*your case, you became so judgmental of creative and vision-
ary types because of the judgment placed on you that you
sought the opposite path and went into a field where you
could be surrounded by the certainty of numbers."*

*Jacob is speechless for several minutes. I know I've given
him a lot to process, so I allow him space to sit with what I've
said.*

*"My girlfriend says I act like a robot sometimes, but . . ."
he pauses. "I have feelings, I just . . . I don't know how to
express them."*

*"I understand. You've numbed yourself to a lot of what you
felt as a child, and it's difficult to undo that. But it's possible. It
will take work, but you can learn to open those parts of yourself again in a way that feels safe. All your chakras could use
some love and attention, Jacob. Are you willing to put your
skepticism aside for a bit and try?"*

"Will this make my headaches go away?" he asks.

*"It may take time, but yes, I believe it will, if you meditate
and dedicate yourself to a regular chakra balancing practice."*

*"Ugh." Jacob rolls his eyes. "My girlfriend won't let me hear
the end of it; she's been trying to get me to try meditation for
years," he says, but his tone is soft.*

*"This is the thing, Jacob. You shut yourself down because
you're such a sensitive person, but this has led to you functioning only in your left brain—the analytical side. The chakra
work and meditation will help you create a healthy balance
between left and right, bringing in more of that creative and
emotional side, and making a safe space for those aspects of
yourself you've been hiding."*

*"All right," he says, "I'll give it a try, but only because I feel
like I can trust you."*

"See?" I say, "you're already starting to listen to your intuition!"

Arthur

Arthur is an adorable older gentleman who has come to me because his wife was thrilled with the work she and I had done together. He's been doing my chakra cleanse and meditating, and we've done work with the White Light during a previous session, but he's contacted me saying he still feels "absolutely nothing."

At first I'm surprised; some people don't feel the effects of the chakra balancing and White Light immediately. After a few weeks, however, Arthur tells me things haven't improved, so we've set up a telephone call to get to the bottom of things.

I can't help but smile at this sweet man; I get such a clear psychic impression of his appearance, with his downy white hair and glowing eyes. He is a deeply kind person, with a delightful enthusiasm about becoming more spiritually aware.

When I look at Arthur's energy field, I see that his sixth chakra is tiny. "Arthur," I say, "it looks like your sixth chakra is sleeping!"

"Well how do we wake it up?" he says, nearly shouting, and we both laugh.

"We just need to do some focused training to help enliven it, then it can channel energy." I assure him that in no time at all he'll be able to experience the White Light, as well as start to get intuitive hunches.

"Great! Then maybe I'll start playing the lottery!" he jokes.

We laugh again. "The sixth chakra opens you up to the world beyond that which you knew previously existed," I continue. "After this, your energy will begin to move to the seventh chakra and here, you'll begin to experience the bliss of knowing you are one with all that is."

"All right," Arthur says, rubbing his hands together expectantly. "Let's get started!"

Lara

Lara comes to me after having attended one of my lectures at a spirituality conference. She sits cross-legged in the chair opposite me. She's a pleasant young woman with dark, braided hair, wearing a peasant blouse and jeans. What stands out most about her appearance, however, are the brightly colored and sparkling temporary tattoos of ornate symbols that adorn her chest and arms.

So far in the session, I've read her energy field and provided her with some advice for balancing her underactive first and second chakras.

"Now I'll answer any questions you have," I say.

"Here's the thing," she says, leaning forward in the chair. "Ever since I saw you at the conference, I've known that I want to be psychic! I just know 'the seer' is one of my archetypes." *Her eyes are dancing as she speaks.* "I want to have visions and be able to read people's energy fields too."

I smile and nod. Over the years, many people have asked me how they can become psychic or "like me." I tell Lara what I've told them.

"I think it's wonderful that you want to develop your psychic abilities, but I feel I must caution you. Being extremely psychic and empathic is more complicated than it appears, and more labor-intensive," I say. "It's a lot to manage. Even with the years of work I've done on my chakras to help balance my abilities and keep healthy boundaries, it's still a work in progress. It's also important to understand that each of us is unique. It's not possible for you or anyone else to be just like me or any other psychic or intuitive."

Lara's expression falls slightly.

"However," I say quickly, "that doesn't mean you can't develop some kind of psychic or empathic abilities. Just keep in mind that there are many different kinds of sensing. Clairvoyance, or 'clear seeing,' is only one. When you develop your abilities, you could be clairaudient or clairsentient, or a combination."

"Okay!" She brightens up again. "How do I do it?"

"It takes time to develop these abilities," I say. "You have to build yourself up to it. A sudden massive psychic opening would throw you into an imbalance and could even be dangerous."

I explain the chakra balance and meditation techniques. "If you do these regularly and get your lower chakras energized, when you're ready, you can start channeling White Light to boost all your chakras, including 6 and 7. Over time—and it may take years—you'll likely notice an increase in your psychic abilities."

"Cool!" Lara says, grinning.

Chakra 6 Self-Assessment

To get an idea of how fit and healthy your sixth chakra is, ask yourself the following questions:

- Am I intuitive, and do I follow intuitive hunches?
- Do I use my intellect as well as my intuition? Am I balanced between my left and right brain?
- Can I visualize? Can I envision my ideal life?
- Do I use my imagination? Do I dream, daydream, or see images and stories in my mind?
- Am I aware of my negative programming, of how the visionary side of me has been discouraged?
- Do I have a high degree of self-awareness?
- Have I had psychic/intuitive experiences? Have I had visions, premonitions, or feelings (including sensory experiences) about something that have proved to be accurate?
- Am I aware of other beings, such as angels and spirit helpers? Can I communicate with these beings and receive guidance?
- Am I free from headaches, migraines, nightmares, and brain, eye, or ear problems?

If you answered "no" to a few of these questions, you have some challenges with your sixth chakra. If you answered "no" to many of them, you probably have a significant blockage.

Chakra 6 Out of Balance

If your sixth chakra is not working properly, you may have problems with your physical or emotional health, finances, love life, relationships with family and friends, or your career and creativity. Again, remember that an imbalance in one chakra will likely affect the energy flow to the chakras above and below it. So if you have a weak or blocked chakra 6 you may experience one or more of the problems related to chakras 1 through 5 as well.

You might experience some of the following challenges if your sixth chakra is imbalanced.

Physical Health

- Sinus, nasal problems
- Eye problems
- Deafness
- Seizures
- Learning difficulties
- Headaches, migraines
- Hallucinations
- Brain tumors
- Stroke
- Neurological disturbances

Emotional Health

- Lack wisdom, self-perception
- Lack "vision," can't see possibilities
- Can't focus, concentrate, visualize, imagine
- Can't be intuitive, see/hear/feel communicate with energy/ spiritual worlds
- Can't remember your dreams
- Limited thinking, can't reprogram yourself
- Left and right brain hemispheres aren't balanced
- Deluded, hallucinations
- "All up in your head," not grounded in reality
- Superhero complex, nightmares, lucid dreaming

Finances

- Lack insight about what is blocking your financial flow
- Lack insight about how to make money
- Won't dare step into the unlimited possibilities and create what you desire
- Can't focus and concentrate

Love Life

- Close-minded
- Live in a fantasy world, not grounded
- Not able to, or resist self-evaluation
- Feelings of being inadequate
- Don't learn from your mistakes
- Lack vision, scope for your relationship

Relationships with Friends and Family

- Similar problems as with love life
- Can't understand people/social cues

Career and Creativity

- Lack vision
- Lack perspective
- Can't take career or creativity to great heights
- Poor memory
- Struggle with focus

Nourishing Chakra 6

In addition to the Chakra Cleanse Meditation (see Chapter 30), among the things your sixth chakra likes are:

- The color indigo
- Meditation
- Visualization
- Brainstorming and goal setting
- Mastermind groups

- Consciously dreaming your ideal life
- Any activities that inspire you to stretch yourself and be great

What about Celia, Jacob, Arthur, and Lara?

When I spoke with Celia several months later, I was happy to hear she'd taken what I said to heart. In addition to doing the chakra balancing, she had started a tai chi practice, which helped her feel more grounded in her body and got her outdoors more often. She still had work to do, but she had definitely made progress. She had also stopped asking her angels for advice on all her decisions and had learned instead to use the increased clarity of her intuition to guide her.

Jacob initially had trouble giving the chakra balancing and meditation a go; he had to work to get beyond his skepticism. But he eventually tried it and after several weeks, his migraines and anxiety attacks did begin to abate. He was also slowly opening up to the idea of revisiting aspects of himself such as the deeply caring and intuitive nature he'd suppressed since childhood.

To Arthur's excitement, it only took a couple of sessions for his sixth chakra to respond. Now he and his wife could both talk about what they experienced when they meditated and worked with the White Light.

Five months after her session, Lara approached me after another lecture when I was chatting with members of the audience. To her credit, she'd persisted with the Chakra Cleanse Meditation and had been channeling White Light regularly. She told me that while she hadn't developed the ability to have visions about the future as she'd wished, she had started to sense things about people and situations, and was delighted that, increasingly, the things she sensed were confirmed to be true. "I'm doing it!" She smiled and threw her arms around me, giving me an enthusiastic hug.

Now let's turn our attention to your seventh chakra.

194

CHAPTER 27

CHAKRA 7: ENLIGHTENMENT

CHAKRA 7 IS THE seventh level of your energy anatomy. Also called the crown chakra, chakra 7 is located at the top of the head. This is the chakra where you experience enlightenment.

In chakras 5 and 6, you begin the process of surrendering to the divine. This process is fully realized in chakra 7.

By truly merging with divinity, we experience oneness with all that is. When you "let go and let God," you commit an act of radical transformative power; you allow divinity to express itself through you. You then start to live your life based on this alignment with your higher path or calling.

Your seventh chakra enables you to feel true interconnectedness and enlightenment. Experiencing this enables you to trust in the universe. When you stop believing in the idea of your separateness, which is a creation of the ego, you lose your fear. Instead, you trust and know that you are one with all that is.

Chakra 7 Basics

Names

Chakra 7 is also called the crown chakra.

Location

It is located on the top of the head.

Areas of Body Governed

This chakra oversees the physical areas of the upper brain and nervous system.

Drive and Issues

Chakra 7 governs your ability to feel a sense of oneness with the universe and surrender to divinity.

Just as most people are weak in their sixth chakra, most also have challenges with chakra 7. I've worked with many clients who have had blockages and other imbalances in their seventh chakra. Let's look at a few of them.

Case Studies

Terry

Before we even begin our session, I can see that Terry feels like an outsider; as if she's unseen by God or somehow outside the realm of the divine. We're Skyping, and as she sits there in a cozy sweater in front of a roaring fire, I can't help but see the sadness in her energy field.

"You carry a deep sense of loneliness because you feel you've been trying to make a connection with God or the universe, but you don't feel anyone's speaking back to you. You want desperately to feel that peace and connectedness, but you're struggling to get there," I say. "You've read lots of books about spirituality, and you even attend a consciousness-raising group, but the

problem is that you're trying to understand God and divinity through your mind. There's very much an experiential as well as emotional component to opening yourself to divine connection. You have to 'feel' God. That's how you can know God."

"That's what they told me in the group," she says. "But how do I do that?"

"By doing things such as meditating and allowing yourself to connect deeply with nature; things that evoke the experience of 'feeling' God," I say. "And by letting it happen in God's time. You can't rush these things."

I go on. "Your lower chakras are very weak, so you're having trouble passing energy up through them to your higher chakras. Strengthening the lower chakras supports this passage of energy. When energy flows properly to the higher chakras you're then capable of having that experience of connecting to the divine. I can't emphasize this enough—it's critical to work from the bottom up to create balance and open the path to connectedness."

Terry nods and chews her lower lip as she contemplates what I've said.

"I also see you're having issues with your back and digestive system," I say, "and balancing the lower chakras should help sort out these problems as well."

"Oh well, that's good news," Terry says, offering a slight smile.

I see that Terry is afraid: She wants to believe what I'm saying, yet she has struggled with this for so long that she wonders if she's capable of doing what I suggest. I explain the chakra balancing and mindfulness practices to her and try to reassure her that she's not beyond hope. Far from it! She's a warm, kind person; she needs to start trusting herself, strengthening her lower chakras, and allowing herself to be open to the experience of oneness.

197

Samuel/Adam

Samuel contacted me because he is deeply concerned about his son, Adam, and he asks if I can read his son's energy field through him. I tell him I can, but will do so only if his son grants me permission, and if Samuel agrees not to tell me beforehand why he's worried about his son.

Adam consents, so Samuel and I set up the call. I get a strong psychic image of Samuel as a gray-haired and balding man with a kind face. His brow is furrowed with worry, and for good reason. I can see through him that something is very wrong with Adam's energy field!

Right away I see that there is almost no energy in Adam's lowest three chakras, and chakras 6 and 7 look enormous and distorted. They appear blown out, with the lower chakras buckling under the weight of the massive, overfilled higher chakras. Adam is completely ungrounded and has lost touch with reality.

What I see shocks me, and I gasp. "What happened to him?" It's so concerning to me that I go against my rule of receiving information from the client in advance. In all the energy fields I've ever read, I have never before seen this degree of imbalance.

Samuel tells me that it started when his son began attending a meditation and psychic development group. One evening after the group, Adam came home talking about all the "different lights and auras" he could see around people. The next morning, he wouldn't get out of bed. Since then, he has suffered from frequent panic attacks, migraines, and nightmares.

I ask Samuel what type of meditation practices his son has done, but he's not sure. All he knows is that Adam had talked about how his teacher could make people psychic.

The pieces of the puzzle quickly fall into place for me. Adam's teacher had taught Adam how to raise his energy quickly into chakras 6 and 7 so that he could become psychic, and I tell Samuel this. "Adam's five lower chakras were not yet strong enough. His energy field couldn't deal with the amount of energy surging into his higher chakras, so Adam suffered a 'blowout,' which has made him unstable."

Samuel sounds both horrified and heartbroken. "Can you help him?" he asks, his voice filled with desperation.

I know that chakra balancing will help Adam tremendously, because what happened to him reminds me of what I experienced when I was exorcised. I experienced a massive auric tear and chakric imbalance as a result, though fortunately it did not make me unstable to the extent Adam experienced.

"Adam has suffered some psychic damage," I say, "but it is possible to correct it." I explain the chakra balancing technique to Samuel. "Do you think you can teach him how to do this, and monitor and gently remind him to keep doing it?" I ask.

Samuel agrees. "Yes, anything to help him. His mother and I are worried sick."

"Just have Adam keep with the program. You should see a turnaround before long," I reassure him.

Jerome

Jerome is a metalworker, and as he sits in front of me in his plaid shirt and jeans, slouched and looking bored, I know he would probably rather be anywhere but here. I can see that he's here because his wife has sent him.

I explain to Jerome how the session will work, and he simply shrugs.

When I look at Jerome's energy field, what stands out are very underactive chakras 6 and 7, and this is causing chronic insomnia. "I see you have trouble sleeping, and this has been a problem for you for years," I say.

Jerome stares at me.

"You're also feeling stiff and sore, making it difficult to do your job as it's so physical," I continue. "I can see you eat quite a lot of meat. Among other effects, this raises the acid level in the body, which is one reason you feel so stiff. Your body's energy system doesn't cope well with a high meat intake, nor does it

respond well to caffeine, sugar, or alcohol or other drugs. Many people are also sensitive to grains."

Jerome continues to stare, and I can't help but think that his wife probably has her hands full if she's trying to change his diet. I continue with the reading, telling Jerome various other physical and emotional challenges. Finally, I explain the chakra system and how these physical and emotional issues link to challenges in his energy system.

"Your seventh chakra is concerned with your spirituality," I explain to the expressionless Jerome, "but beyond this, when chakra 7 is open and energy can move through it easily, your brain waves are nourished. This has a positive impact on your sleep. Your weak seventh chakra is why you have insomnia; your brain waves aren't being nourished."

Jerome crosses his arms in front of his chest.

"Now that I've read your energy field," I say, "do you have any questions?"

"No," he says, then looks at the clock, and back at me.

I explain to Jerome how he can balance his chakras. At the end of the session, he's perfectly polite; he stands and shakes my hand and thanks me for my time. I tell Jerome I'll send him an audio recording of the session in case he wants to listen again to what I've told him. He shrugs and walks out.

Chakra 7 Self-Assessment

For an idea of how fit and healthy your seventh chakra is, ask yourself the following questions:

- Have I glimpsed enlightenment, the state of totality, bliss, and oneness with all that is?
- Do I know I am consciousness, above and beyond the mind and its polarities?
- Do I feel deeply connected to God, the universe, and divinity?
- Can I sit quietly without the need to think or do something? Can I simply be?

- Is my energy mostly rooted in the present moment? Can I meditate easily?
- Do I have an inkling of my soul's purpose?

If you answered "no" to a few of these questions, you have some challenges with your seventh chakra. If you answered "no" to many of them (as most people do), you probably have a significant blockage.

Chakra 7 Out of Balance

If your seventh chakra is not working properly, you may have problems with your physical or emotional health, finances, love life, relationships with family and friends, or your career and creativity. And remember that an imbalance in one chakra will likely affect the energy flow to the chakras above and below it. So if you have a weak or blocked chakra 7 you may experience one or more of the problems related to chakras 1 through 6 as well.

The following are challenges you could experience if your seventh chakra is imbalanced.

Physical Health
- Migraines, headaches
- Brain problems, such as a tumor or aneurysm
- Scalp, upper head issues
- Vertigo
- Hypersensitive in the extreme
- Chronic tiredness
- Hopelessness, depression

Emotional Health
- Lack faith, trust, aren't "spiritual"
- Can't still the mind or be still
- Lack purpose, orientation, don't know what you are here to do

- Delusions of grandeur, hallucinations, no grasp on reality
- Confusion, escapism

Finances

- Lacking in faith and trust; living in fear
- Always hurrying to get somewhere or stressed about completing tasks
- Haven't begun to understand your life purpose, which has a dampening effect on your career

Love Life

- Can't see that we are all one and interconnected and can't connect with others
- Lack a humanitarian spirit

Relationships with Friends and Family

- Similar problems as with love life
- Can't see that we are all one and interconnected, and can't connect with others
- Lack a humanitarian spirit

Career and Creativity

- Creative blocks
- Lack of understanding that you have a life purpose, or what that purpose is

Nourishing Chakra 7

The following are things your seventh chakra likes:

- The color violet
- Meditation, meditation, and more meditation!
- Periods of stillness and reflection
- Books about saints, yogis, and the great women and men of the world

What about Terry, Samuel's son Adam, and Jerome?

When I checked in with Terry, right away I could tell she had more joy in her life. She confirmed that she wasn't feeling so despondent and that she'd started meditating regularly and working on her chakras. While she hadn't yet had the dramatic enlightened moment she was hoping for (I reassured her that everyone experiences things differently), she was starting to have glimmers of something that felt like oneness.

When I spoke to Samuel again, his energy field showed a different man; he was much happier, and so was his son! He said that just a few weeks after starting the chakra balancing exercises, Adam began to make a steady turnaround, and now he was back to his old, cheery self.

Several weeks after my session with Jerome, his wife called to tell me that one day while Jerome was at work, she and their children had listened to the recording I'd sent him of our session. She said they laughed for hours afterwards because my description of him and his behavior had been so accurate, despite him being so noncommittal. The session details also helped her finally understand some of the core reasons for Jerome's behavior. Unfortunately, Jerome refused to do the chakra balancing or listen to the session again, but his wife said she would keep encouraging him.

Now let's look at your full energetic system and how the chakras work together.

CHAPTER 28

THE CHAKRA SYSTEM

You now have a basic understanding of chakras 1 through 7; the aspects of your life and body they govern, as well as the imbalances and problems blocked chakras cause. However, in order to change your energy and change your life, it is important to also understand how these chakras work as a system.

Heal Your Life: Your Lower Five Chakras

During this time of the great cosmic shift, we're being called to radically change and heal our lives, but to do this (and for us to embrace the new spiritual way of life and live its magic), we need to heal our past. Only when our five lower chakras (chakras 1 through 5) are strong and free of blockages and stagnation can we do this—heal our shadow and embrace our light.

Before this cosmic shift, we had much more time to spiritually evolve. We gradually worked our way up the ladder of spiritual ascension, taking many years and many lives to rise . . . The process was slow but steady.

Now, the process has accelerated, and although we're able to ascend much more quickly, it is also happening less steadily. Think of it as taking a ride on a speedboat instead of a cruise ship. You will get there faster, but the ride likely will be bumpy.

We're in a faster world, trying to work out how to navigate our way through it—how to make the ride less bumpy. We wonder *where we are* and *why* everything feels so unstable and temporal. We yearn for stability, structure, and clarity. We yearn for support, and for someone (or something) to show us how to make our way through these changing times and rise up.

The White Light is the answer.

The White Light is the frequency of our time. It's the ultimate energy stabilizer and vibration raiser. And when we open our five lower chakras, then use the White Light to cleanse, balance, and strengthen them, we are:

- Healing our lives and creating flow
- Creating a strong platform and funnel for the energy to rise
- Staying grounded, secure, and strong, and enabling ourselves to create heaven on earth

I describe the White Light in more detail in the next chapter. First though, it's important to understand that to ascend (move to a more spiritual life), you need your earth-life to work; this means getting your five lower chakras healthy and strong.

If you live in survival mode and struggle because of weak or blocked lower chakras, you won't have the time or resources to pursue your spiritual talents or soul purpose. Think about it: If you live from paycheck to paycheck, or suffer from a health condition, or don't have help and support in your life, you'll find it difficult to pursue your talents or passions.

For example, imagine that you know your life's purpose is to work as a healer and intuitive. You're passionate about this, and want to start straight away. You receive the intuitive guidance to open a healing center where you can offer your services to many people. But to do this, you must have strong lower chakras.

Without the help of chakra 1, you won't easily find the right space for your healing center. Being stuck in survival mode, you'll have trouble transitioning from your current job to your work as a healer and intuitive because you won't have enough money, energy, or support to invest in your new business.

Without the help of chakra 2, you'll lack passion for your work. Passion magnetizes and draws the right people and circumstances to us. Passion also creates beauty, and to have a successful healing center, you'll want it to be beautiful and inviting.

Without the help of chakra 3, you'll lack clear boundaries. This affects how you conduct yourself as a healer as well as how you manage your finances. You also won't have good self-esteem, and the key to being a successful healer and intuitive is having a strong sense of self. You need to learn how to get out of your own way and be a conduit for the right information and healing energy.

Without the help of chakra 4, you won't let love into your life. Your clients won't get enough of your love and attention, and you'll also block them from giving you these things. If your soul's purpose is to express your spiritual talents and abilities by working as a healer and intuitive, you need to let your clients love you and give to you. Without this, you won't have a fulfilling and thriving practice.

Without the help of chakra 5, you won't be clearly seen and recognized for your unique talents. Many people nowadays feel called to work in the healing arts. For your uniqueness to be recognized and for people to be drawn to you and your particular way of healing and working, you need to have a strong chakra 5. Otherwise you'll be drowned out, lost in the sea of people offering similar things.

As you can see, without strong lower chakras, you simply can't manifest your dreams here on earth. Further, if your lower chakras are weak or blocked, energy isn't passed up into your higher chakras, which is where your spiritual evolution takes place.

Unlock Your Spiritual Talents and Abilities: Your Higher Chakras

When you cleanse, balance, and strengthen your lower chakras, you enable the energy to rise easily and steadily into your spiritual chakras: chakras 6 and 7.

Your third eye and crown chakras play an important role in the energetic upgrade because these are the chakras whose energy is suddenly being awakened in this time of massive change. During this shift, chakras 6 and 7 are either already receiving lots of energy, or are *wanting* to receive this energy so that you can awaken to the spiritual side of life.

As chakras 6 and 7 are activated, they also need to be purified. This means that you not only awaken your spiritual talents and abilities of intuition, psychic ability, mediumship, empathness, and so on, you also cleanse and heal any persecution about your spiritual talents and abilities that you suffered in past lives. To best live the spiritual side of life, you need to heal the shadow and pain you experienced previously.

When chakras 6 and 7 come alive and are energized, you simultaneously unlock and remember your spiritual talents and abilities, as well as heal your past karma about them. Also, energy flowing through chakras 6 and 7 acts as a bridge to allow your energy to freely pass even higher—to your cosmic chakras—unlocking the path to understanding your soul's purpose.

Discover Your Soul's Purpose: Your Cosmic Chakras

In addition to chakras 1 through 7, you have five chakras that govern your soul's purpose. Chakras 8 through 12 are your cosmic chakras, completing your energetic system. With your five lower chakras healed and your two spiritual chakras activated and purified, your energy then naturally rises into chakra 8 and you begin to discover your soul's purpose for coming here in this lifetime.

This knowledge came to me during my enlightened moment. I saw that each one of us needs to develop our "vibrational muscles"; we need a strong energetic structure within our energy fields to lift us up into the very high vibration of chakra 8 and that of chakras 9, 10, 11, and 12.

While the vibrations of chakras 6 and 7 are higher than the vibrations of chakras 1 through 5, chakra 8 and your other four cosmic chakras vibrates at an even higher rate. This is why people can find these times of the great cosmic shift so destabilizing. We're shooting upwards into places and realms that are largely uncharted and unexplored. As our vibration rises into our higher chakras, we get closer to our soul's purpose, but further from the earth plane.

Once people learn that the key to discovering their soul's purpose is by *accessing* their cosmic chakras, they want to get there as quickly as possible. Practicing the Chakra Cleanse Meditation and channeling the White Light through the lower seven chakras is the way; it prepares you to take this journey into your cosmic chakras.

That said, by now you're probably eager to begin, so let's look at the tools you'll use to cleanse and balance your chakras, starting with the White Light.

CHAPTER 29

THE WHITE LIGHT

In the previous chapters, you've learned about the chakras and their importance. You've learned that cleansing and balancing our chakras is key: It enables us to live a fulfilled life, awaken our spiritual self, and begin to discover our soul purpose. The next step in our modern mystic journey: learning how to work with the White Light.

The White Light not only supports our work with the chakras, it also keeps us *grounded* during these times of the great cosmic shift. As the vibration is rapidly rising and the veil between the earth plane and the spirit realms is being lifted, people are being suddenly thrust into a higher and more spiritual way of life . . . For many, this feels turbulent and disorienting.

To thrive in these changing times, we must be grounded and strong *while* our energy shoots upwards into a higher way of life.

The White Light helps us with this.

One important thing to note (before we learn about the White Light): Until you have a personal experience of the White Light, it can be difficult to understand it. This is because its vibration is so much higher than human consciousness; it's pure light, and exists outside our human range of perception and comprehension. Trying to grasp its nature and functioning can be perplexing, but once you begin to experience the White Light for yourself, your understanding of this powerful force will expand exponentially.

So in this chapter, I'll do my best to explain what the White Light is, and how it's used in healing your chakras and raising your vibration.

A Transformative Force

The White Light gently yet powerfully heals *any* blockages in chakras 1 through 7, enabling you to quickly move up into your higher chakras. At the same time, the White Light supports you in keeping your feet on the ground.

You'll remember that during my enlightened moment I came to understand that the White Light is the *frequency* of our time. I learned that it isn't only the "great vibration raiser," it's also the "great stabilizing force." The White Light helps you create *heaven on earth* by bringing a heavenly energy down into your earthly life.

It is essential that you feel grounded, safe, and protected while you cleanse your chakras and shift into your more spiritual self; otherwise, life can feel turbulent, challenging, or out of control. The White Light's spiritual energy stabilizes you, keeping you in the here and now while your energy is rising into your higher chakras. This enables you to evolve rapidly, taking a quantum leap in your spiritual development without feeling as if your life has become chaotic.

That said, there will be challenging moments in your development; this is normal and natural. But working with the White Light will help you feel safe, protected, and cocooned.

You can also think of the White Light as the "ultimate harmonizer" because it brings everything into perfect balance. As you learn to use it, you will experience a profound sense of peace and harmony in your life as well.

At its essence, the White Light is alchemical; its energy transmutes that which is negative, dark, or blocked into that which is positive, light, and free-flowing. These transformational properties enable the White Light to balance and heal your energy system and remove blockages, and to transmute your shadow—your past and pain—from dark to light. And all of this brings greater peace into your life.

This is what the White Light *does*, but what exactly *is* the White Light?

What Is the White Light?

The White Light is what sages and ancient mystics called "the light of the universe." It is the highest frequency of all. When people who have had near-death experiences talk of "seeing the light," this is the light they speak of; it is the light we see at our moment of death (though that is not the only time we can see it).

During my enlightened moment, I experienced the White Light as the highest vibration in the spectrum of dark to light. When I arrived at the vibration of pure light, the light was so intense, so strong, that it blinded me, and I experienced the feeling of being "burst open." What I experienced at that moment was the power of unconditional love.

That's right—simply put, the White Light is *unconditional love*.

We commonly use the words "unconditional love" when referring to all kinds of human relationships, but most of us have not truly had the experience of being loved in this way. If you have known unconditional love, you'll already know the tremendous transformative power it holds. If you haven't, you will experience it by working with the White Light.

The incredible force that is unconditional love is spiritual, healing, supportive, loving, and grounding. It raises your vibration and fills you with light. And it's also a psychic force that opens you to your true self, giving you a deep sense of harmony, beauty, totality, and wholeness.

Also, the White Light *is* you.

The White Light is what you are at your core being; it is your soul. You are the vibration of pure light. This is who you are on the Other Side. When you work with the White Light and channel its beautiful and splendid energy into your energy field, you are connecting with your soul—with the highest form of your self.

Why Channel White Light?

A natural question many people have is: If I am already cleansing and balancing my chakras (as I'll show you how to do in the next chapter), why do I need to also work with the White Light?

When we start working with your chakras, you will begin with the chakra at the lowest point in your physical body—chakra 1. You then work up to chakra 2, and so on. This rising energy—called *chi*—brings you up into your spiritual chakras. But in addition to rising up into your spiritual self, you also need to be *grounded* here on earth, and this is the piece that many current spiritual practices are missing. They are concerned only with the rising energy. Yet, a downward flow of energy is also needed to balance you.

If you only worked with the rising energy—chakras 1 through 7—you would help your chakras heal, *but* become increasingly ungrounded as you moved up into your spiritual chakras. However, when you channel White Light down—chakra 7 through 1—you stay grounded and safe while you reach up and go beyond! (Remember what happened to Samuel's son, Adam, in Chapter 27? His vibration was raised too quickly, without any downward, grounding force.) So in addition to being a healing energy, the White Light is a critical balancing force.

A Shift in Perspective

Through my work with clients, I discovered that balancing your chakras and channeling White Light is the key to healing and strengthening your energy system. For more than a decade, I have seen thousands of people change their lives by *changing their energy* using these methods.

For most of us spiritual seekers, though, this way of thinking is a radical shift in perspective. We're often taught that to heal ourselves we should use our willpower, or that we must revisit events in our past. Or that if we say affirmations or chant mantras, this will transform our lives. While it's true that affirmations and mantras are powerful, changing our energy—changing our energy fields and chakras—is what is needed to truly heal us. When your energy changes, your negative thought patterns automatically change along with it!

Before my enlightened moment, I thought I needed to dig up my past to heal my life. I thought that by focusing upon and trying to fix my problems and those of others, I could heal myself. But I learned that focusing upon the past is mostly unnecessary (though sometimes understanding past-life hurts can bring clarity and acceptance). Rather than staying stuck in my shadows; I needed to step boldly into the light. I needed to make a radical shift and begin to identify with my light-filled self, and by doing this, the darkness in my life would fall away.

Moving away from needing to understand or fix my past in an attempt to change my life was a huge challenge. It also affected how I worked with others to help them heal their lives. My work as a medical intuitive consisted entirely of telling people what was wrong with them. My friends and colleagues were doctors, healthcare practitioners, and therapists, so they also believed that focusing on people's problems was the answer to addressing their problems. In many ways, stepping away from this line of thinking meant stepping away from my entire life.

Fortunately, I had Eckhart Tolle's *The Power of Now* to guide me, as well as my newly discovered work with the chakras and the White Light. Knowing the power of this new work—it was already creating amazing changes in my life—I knew I simply needed to keep going, and to figure out a way to share it with others.

Aligning with the light is a shift in perspective; it's a relinquishing of the need to delve into our past to heal our shadow.

Who we are in our highest form is unconditional love. We are whole, complete, and healed. We are already the light.

And when you make it a regular practice to work with your chakras and channel White Light—when the White Light starts to pour into your energy field and fill up your chakras—your life will soar!

Even knowing all this, you may still struggle to make this internal shift, and this is common. Here is an example of a client I worked with who had difficulty letting go of her emotional hold on her past pain.

Case Study

Karen

I'm speaking with Karen on the phone. I have a psychic image of her as an elderly and fragile woman of seventy-five years of age.

Karen has been cleansing her chakras for months and has experienced amazing shifts, but an old back-pain problem has flared up and she's struggling. We've already had two sessions about it, but Karen won't accept the pain so that she can move through it. She keeps asking me why it's happened and what else she needs to look at in her past.

"Karen, I have explained to you that trying to figure out why is exacerbating the problem!" I have to talk loudly so Karen can hear me. She's angry and shouting.

"Karen, calm down, please," I say. "You'll make your back pain worse."

"But there must be something more!" she insists. "Something else you aren't seeing!

"No, I've already told you what happened. Your father left when you were a small child, abandoning you and your mother, and this caused a 'wound' in your first chakra. That's why you've had lifelong problems with back pain. But you keep asking me for more."

"Yes, because there must be more! I wouldn't have suffered this dreadful back pain all my life otherwise. What else do you see?"

"There is nothing else apart from what I've already told you. And in fact, you didn't even need to know that your back pain stems from you feeling abandoned by your father."

"But why do you tell people where their problems come from then?" she presses. *"Why do you work as a medical intuitive?"*

"Because I want people to accept their pain so they can move through it. For most people, if I explain to them why they feel the way they do, why they have the problems they do, where it all stems from, they're usually much more able to accept it because they understand themselves better. You have to accept your pain to heal it. Acceptance is the first step," I explain.

"But I hate this back pain! I hate it! I've had it all my life and it doesn't go away. I hate this old pain!"

"This is exactly what I mean," I say to Karen. *"You hate your pain; you hate the way it's been in your life for a long time and you are angry that it has come back. So you aren't accepting it. You aren't allowing it to be here in the present moment. But worse than the physical pain is your emotional pain; your hatred of and your resistance of your back pain is making the pain so much worse."*

"But it really hurts!"

"I know," I say, *"but let me show you how to release the emotional pain and accept the physical pain. Because when you can do this, you allow light into your energy field and chakras, and can heal yourself."*

I tell Karen to take a few deep breaths and that when she's calm, to bring her awareness to the pain in her back.

"Now," I say, *"I want you to 'feel into' the area where it hurts."*

"That isn't hard to do!" she snaps. *"It hurts like hell."*

"Okay," I say, *"focus on how it 'hurts like hell,' and tell me what it feels like."*

"It feels bad and horrible and really annoying! I've had this problem for so long now! I just wish it would go away! I want—"

I interrupt her because she's losing focus again. "What you're telling me is the story of your back pain; you're telling me about its past and history. You're telling me how long you've had it and how you're tired of it and how you hate it. You're telling me about the emotional pain of it. But I want you to not think about the pain in your back, but instead to feel into it. How does the pain in your back feel? Feel into it and don't tell me the story of it."

"You don't know how much it hurts and how hard it's been living with this for almost seventy years!" Karen is now shouting so loud down the phone my ears are ringing.

"Yes, I do know," I say, "I know because I'm psychic and can feel your pain. But even if I weren't, you're not going to heal your back pain until you accept it. I want you to feel into your back pain and tell me how it feels," I say again. "Don't think about it now. Feel it."

Karen huffs and sighs and says she thinks the exercise is silly. But she's willing to give it a try later that afternoon. I put down the phone, relieved both that she will try again and that my eardrums can have a rest.

I speak to Karen again the next day. She is apologetic and meek.

"I'm sorry I shouted at you and I told you the exercise was silly. I wasn't very nice yesterday."

"That's no problem, Karen. I know you are suffering and in a lot of pain."

"Well actually . . ." she says, "I'm no longer in a lot of pain. A lot of my pain went away yesterday."

"How?" I ask.

"I did the exercise you recommended. After we got off the phone I sat down on the couch and tried to focus on the feeling *of pain in my body without attaching the past and the story to it, and remarkably, today I feel much better."*

"I think we need to give it more time to assess if a healing has started," I say. "How about every time you have a back flare-up, you practice feeling the physical pain of it and not attaching any negative emotions and story to it, and then call me again in three months and tell me how you get along?"

"Will do," she says.

Three months later, Karen contacts me again.

"My back pain is definitely better," she says. "I've had a few flare-ups but instead of getting angry about it and attaching a 'story' to it, I've instead just focused on the physical pain, the physical discomfort. And you know what? When I do that, I realize my back actually doesn't hurt that much. Sure, there is discomfort and soreness, but my emotional pain about it was exacerbating the problem. And not only that, I've also realized when I get angry or frustrated about something it causes my back pain. Can this be the case?"

"Sure," I say. "When you get upset, you put stress on your body and this can cause your back problems to flare up. So it's a catch-22—they get worse when you get angry about them, and when they happen you get angry. The lesson in this?"

"Not getting so angry!" Karen laughs.

"Exactly!" I laugh back.

"But I have another problem now," Karen says.

"What's that?" I ask.

"Every time I do the chakra cleanse and then channel White Light, I start to cry. I'm not crying because I'm in pain, I'm crying because I'm free of pain! When I channel the White Light down into my body through my chakra 7, and when it comes pouring into my lower chakras, into my back and pelvis area, I'm so overwhelmed with love and gratitude that this area feels free and open and painless that I sob."

"Ha!" I say. "Yes, it was the same for me! I cried for three months straight when I first started working with the White

Light. This is what happens when you begin to heal your shadow and move from dark to light. You become filled with light and love!"

What Can the White Light Do?

The White Light can do anything. That's not an exaggeration. Over the years, I've witnessed thousands of healings and miracles.

The White Light is a spiritual energy, which can:

- Cleanse and strengthen all your chakras
- Clear your home and your workspace of negativity
- Unlock your natural healing abilities
- Unlock your inherent psychic abilities
- Connect you with your soul
- Show you how to live a life of authenticity
- Help you discover and live your life's purpose

The White Light can also be used to heal or change any physical condition or problem in your life, such as:

- Headaches
- Backaches
- Poor digestion
- Bad skin
- Insomnia
- Fatigue
- Weight gain
- Letting go of habits that are bad for you
- Attracting the perfect solution for your problems
- Igniting your creativity
- Finding your dream job
- Finding your ideal life partner
- Creating harmony in your home life

At this point in my work, I not only teach people how to channel White Light for themselves—as I'll explain how to do in the next chapter—I also help them receive White Light.

One way I do this is by offering a free weekly White Light healing. (More details about these healings appear in Appendix C.) Every week, I send White Light to hundreds of people all over the world. The many testimonials and thank-yous that come back to us in return are deeply humbling and gratifying to read.

The White Light Angels

The White Light Angels are evolved beings who work and live in the vibratory level of the White Light. Their job is to help our energy fields and chakras assimilate the healing power of the White Light. They help us cleanse and strengthen our chakras and reprogram our subconscious minds so we can heal from past hurts.

Whenever I send White Light to people or channel it for myself, or when I watch another person channel it, the White Light Angels are always there, busily and eagerly helping the person open up and heal. Watching thousands of the White Light Angels descend and flock to the sides of the people receiving the free weekly White Light healings is a wonder to behold!

I first encountered the White Light Angels during my childhood. Though I saw and sensed them, it wasn't until my enlightened moment that I realized they were *beings* of the White Light.

In time, as you cleanse your chakras and work with the White Light, you too may see the White Light Angels. But rest assured that even if you can't see them, these gentle, humble beings are always there, helping, supporting, and loving you!

It is important to understand that the White Light Angels are not your spirit guides or helpers. Your spirit guides are your "personal helpers." They look after your spiritual evolution by answering your questions and helping you integrate lessons and gain insights about your life experiences. Your spirit guides take an interest in the day-to-day running of your life.

The White Light Angels, however, do not interact with you in this way. Their only purpose is to help you assimilate the White Light, so if you encounter them, do not be discouraged when they don't respond to your questions. They wish only to do their jobs, which is to help provide you with the healing power of unconditional love.

By now, I'm sure you're excited to start channeling White Light! But before you can do this, you need to cleanse and open your lower chakras. In the next chapter, I'll explain how to do this.

CHAPTER 30

CHAKRA BALANCING AND WHITE LIGHT CHANNELING

NOW THAT YOU'VE READ about the chakras and the White Light, it's time to start working with them! In this chapter, I'll explain my Chakra Cleansing Meditation—a proven meditation I developed to heal, cleanse, and strengthen your chakras as well as channel White Light.

Chakra Balancing

I mentioned this previously but it warrants repetition: It's essential that you cleanse your chakras *before* you attempt to channel the White Light. Both the earth-to-heaven energy and heaven-to-earth energy flow systems are needed to cleanse your chakras properly: The energy must flow cleanly upward, opening chakras 1 through 7, so that chakra 7 *can* be opened and the White Light can flow down. Without an open and strong chakra 7, you can't channel the White Light and receive its healing, grounding energy.

The Chakra Cleanse Meditation presented in this chapter heals your chakras and your life by strengthening your lower five chakras (1 through 5). It also activates and purifies your spiritual chakras (6 and 7), and prepares you for the journey into your five cosmic chakras (8 through 12). That's it—one meditation, done consistently, does all of this.

This meditation is tested and proven—a method I spent years developing (and adjusting). It's based upon what I could see in the energy fields of people doing it. As a result, I am fully confident that if you do this meditation on a regular basis, you will see positive changes in your life.

Ideally, you would do this chakra cleanse every day, but if you are new to meditation, aim to do this two to three times a week. Even if you do it only a few times a week, within months, you'll have already healed many parts of your life. Some people see major changes after just a few weeks.

How Does the Chakra Cleanse Work?

The Chakra Cleanse Meditation works in the following way: First, through the meditation, you enliven and open each of your lower chakras, starting with chakra 1 and going up to chakra 7. Second, you "ignite the energy" of your five higher cosmic chakras by channeling the White Light down from your cosmic chakras into chakra 7, and on through to chakra 1.

To enliven and open each of the lower chakras, the meditation guides you to focus on the *point*—the physical location—of the chakra. First you focus on chakra 1, then 2, and so on. Then, once chakra 7 is open, the meditation guides you in allowing the White Light to flow downward. It's really that easy. Our energy system is designed in such a way that by just focusing on the physical point of the chakra, it opens, energizes, and balances itself!

Getting Started with Chakra Cleansing

Before you get started with cleansing and balancing your chakras, there are a few important things to note:

The Chakra Cleanse Meditation takes approximately thirty minutes to complete, and it's important to do the entire meditation. You need to properly cleanse and balance all twelve chakras as well as channel White Light for the meditation to be fully effective.

I realize that thirty minutes might sound like a long time if you're new to meditation. Please don't panic! If you can only meditate for ten minutes a day at first, that's great—do that! Ten minutes a day of meditation and working with your chakras is a great start. Soon, you'll find it easy to stay restful and focused, and before you know it, you'll be meditating for thirty minutes, properly cleansing and balancing all your chakras.

Also, do the meditation in a place where you can relax and not be disturbed. This may sound obvious, but in our culture of busyness and multitasking, it's important to mention. Don't try to do it while checking messages on your phone, driving your car, or answering your kids' questions.

It's up to you as to when you do the meditation; there is no optimal time of day. Some prefer to make it part of their morning routine. Others practice later at night when everyone else has gone to bed. Some even do it on a lunch break. The most important thing is to find the time when you will most likely sit down and do it.

Another important point has to do with how you work with the chakras. Focusing on the point of each chakra is the primary practice, but as you read through the script for the meditation, you'll notice that I also mention the color of each chakra. The most powerful way of opening and cleansing the chakras is to hold your awareness on each chakra point. So if you have trouble visualizing the chakra colors—many people do, though others find it can assist this process—simply skip this part of the meditation. You don't need to visualize the chakra colors for the meditation to be effective.

People often ask me if they need to visualize the chakras spinning, or opening up, or being filled with the White Light in order for the meditation to work properly, and the answer is "no." If this naturally occurs while you hold your awareness on the chakra point, that's fine. Let it happen and flow with it. But don't worry about visualizing anything beyond the point of each chakra. Once you bring your awareness to each chakra point and the chakras open themselves, you'll then be able to channel the White Light easily and effectively.

Every time you make contact with the White Light, it will come into your energy field through chakra 12. It then will go down into chakra 11, 10, 9, 8, 7 . . . right down into chakra 1, and then into the earth. However, while you receive the White Light through chakra 12, you don't visualize that chakra. Although the White Light enters your energy field at the chakra 12 level, you are not able or ready yet to work with this chakra.

The vibration of chakra 12 is extremely high; so high, in fact, that only a handful of people on the planet have an open and activated chakra 12. For the rest of us, we channel the White Light through the highest chakra we can work with at the time. For you, right now, that is *chakra 7*.

The Chakra Cleanse Meditation

Without further ado, here is the Chakra Cleanse Meditation. Note that this is the full transcript of the professionally recorded guided meditation available from my website (please also note that in the transcript where I count from one to ten for each chakra point, you'll need to do this for yourself as you follow along). To purchase the Chakra Cleanse Meditation (from my online shop, where it's titled "The Guided Chakra Cleanse Meditation for Busy People"), visit:

www.belindadavidson.com/store/

Begin now, by allowing your body to relax.

Breathe in . . . and out . . .

Breathe in . . . and out . . .

Take a deep breath in . . . and gently breathe out the tension in your body . . .

Breathe in . . . and out . . . and relax your muscles totally, allowing your breath to flow gently and softly out your nose.

Take a deep breath in, breathing in relaxation . . . and release the breath, breathing out any remaining tension.

Draw your awareness now to your lower abdomen and pelvic region. This is where your first chakra is located. The color of this chakra is red.

You begin to cleanse your first chakra by holding your focus on your lower abdomen and pelvis area.

As you breathe in and out, smoothly and softly, hold your point of focus on the first chakra.

As I begin to count from one to ten, you will continue to hold your focus on the area of your lower abdomen and pelvis . . . one, two, three, four, five, you hold your focus steady on the point of the first chakra while I continue to count, six, seven, eight, nine, and ten.

Now, visualize the color red, red like a red rose, or a strawberry or a raspberry. Imagine the color red beginning to flow into your first chakra.

With every in-breath, visualize the color red flowing into and filling up your first chakra . . . and with every out-breath, allow yourself to let go.

Breathe in, and as you do, you see red flowing in and filling up your first chakra . . . and as you breathe out, allow yourself to let go . . .

Draw your awareness now to just below your navel. This is where your second chakra is located. The color of this chakra is orange.

225

You begin to cleanse your second chakra by holding your focus on the area just below your navel.

As you breathe in and out, smoothly and softly, hold your point of focus on the second chakra.

As I begin to count from one to ten, you will continue to hold your focus on the area just below your navel . . . one, two, three, four, five, you hold your focus steady on the point of the second chakra while I continue to count, six, seven, eight, nine, and ten.

Now, visualize the color orange, orange like the setting sun or perhaps of an orange.

With every in-breath, visualize the color orange flowing into and filling up your second chakra . . . and with every out-breath allow yourself to let go.

Breathe in, and as you do, you see orange flowing in and filling up your second chakra . . . and as you breathe out, allow yourself to let go . . .

Draw your awareness now to your stomach and solar plexus area. This is where your third chakra is located. The color of this chakra is yellow.

You begin to cleanse your third chakra by holding your focus on your stomach area.

As you breathe in and out, smoothly and softly, hold your point of focus on the third chakra.

As I begin to count from one to ten, you will continue to hold your focus on the area of your stomach and solar plexus . . . one, two, three, four, five, you hold your focus steady on the point of the third chakra while I continue to count, six, seven, eight, nine, and ten.

Now, visualize the color yellow, yellow like the sun or a sunflower.

With every in-breath, visualize the color yellow flowing into and filling up your third chakra . . . and with every out-breath allow yourself to let go.

Breathe in, and as you do, you see yellow flowing in and filling up your third chakra . . . and as you breathe out, allow yourself to let go . . .

Draw your awareness now to your heart region. This is where your fourth chakra is located. The color of this chakra is green.

You begin to cleanse your fourth chakra by holding your focus on the area of your heart.

As you breathe in and out, smoothly and softly, hold your point of focus on the fourth chakra.

As I begin to count from one to ten, you will continue to hold your focus on the area of your heart region . . . one, two, three, four, five, you hold your focus steady on the point of the fourth chakra while I continue to count, six, seven, eight, nine, and ten.

Now, visualize the color green, green like rolling hills, or trees in a forest.

With every in-breath, visualize the color green flowing into and filling up your fourth chakra . . . and with every out-breath allow yourself to let go.

Breathe in, and as you do, you see green flowing in and filling up your fourth chakra . . . and as you breathe out, allow yourself to let go . . .

Draw your awareness now to your throat. This is where your fifth chakra is located. The color of this chakra is blue.

You begin to cleanse your fifth chakra by holding your focus on the area of your throat.

As you breathe in and out, smoothly and softly, hold your point of focus on the fifth chakra.

As I begin to count from one to ten, you will continue to hold your focus on your throat . . . one, two, three, four, five, you hold your focus steady on the point of the fifth chakra while I continue to count, six, seven, eight, nine, and ten.

Now, visualize the color blue, blue like the sky, or the ocean.

With every in-breath, visualize the color blue flowing into and filling up your fifth chakra . . . and with every out-breath allow yourself to let go.

Breathe in, and as you do, you see blue flowing in and filling up your fifth chakra . . . and as you breathe out, allow yourself to let go . . .

Draw your awareness now to your third eye. Your third eye is located in the middle of your forehead, directly above the top of your nose. This is where your sixth chakra is located. The color of this chakra is indigo.

You begin to cleanse your sixth chakra by holding your focus on your third eye.

As you breathe in and out, smoothly and softly, hold your point of focus on the sixth chakra.

As I begin to count from one to ten, you will continue to hold your focus on the area of your third eye . . . one, two, three, four, five, you hold your focus steady on the point of the sixth chakra while I continue to count, six, seven, eight, nine, and ten.

Now, visualize the color indigo. Indigo is a dark blue purplish color. Indigo is the color of a clear night sky.

Imagine the color indigo beginning to flow into your sixth chakra.

With every in-breath, visualize indigo flowing into and filling up your sixth chakra . . . and with every out-breath allow yourself to let go.

Breathe in, and as you do, you see indigo flowing in and filling up your sixth chakra . . . and as you breathe out, allow yourself to let go . . .

Draw your awareness now to the top of your head. This is where your seventh chakra is located. The color of this chakra is violet.

You begin to cleanse your seventh chakra by holding your focus on the top of your head.

As you breathe in and out, smoothly and softly, hold your point of focus on the seventh chakra.

As I begin to count from one to ten, you will continue to hold your focus on the area of the top of your head . . . one, two, three, four, five, you hold your focus steady on the point of the seventh chakra while I continue to count, six, seven, eight, nine, and ten.

Now, visualize the color violet, violet like lavender or grapes.

With every in-breath, visualize the color violet flowing into and filling up your seventh chakra . . . and with every out-breath allow yourself to let go.

Breathe in, and as you do, you see violet flowing in and filling up your seventh chakra . . . and as you breathe out, allow yourself to let go . . .

Your awareness now moves to the area above your head, above where your seventh chakra is located. Chakras 8, 9, 10, 11, and 12 are located above the head and they ascend, starting at chakra 8 and ending with chakra 12, into the heavens.

Breathe in and out.

. . . and now, breathe in again . . . and out.

Draw your awareness again to above the top of your head, and hold your awareness there while I count . . . one, two, three, four, five, you hold your focus steady on the area of the higher five chakras while I continue to count, six, seven, eight, nine, and ten.

Now, visualize a White Light. The whitest and most brilliant White Light that you can possibly imagine. Hold this image in your mind's eye for a few moments . . .

Now, visualize a funnel sitting on the top of your head . . . Now visualize the White Light pouring into this funnel. Hold this image in your mind's eye for a few moments, and remember to keep breathing deeply, gently, and evenly while you do this.

Now, you can see White Light pouring into your body through the funnel on the top of your head. You can feel the White Light filling up each of your chakras as it descends towards your feet.

You can feel the White Light pouring into your seventh chakra . . . and now into your sixth chakra.

Breathe in and out . . . and you now feel the White Light pouring into your fifth chakra . . . and it's now moving down past your throat into your heart, filling up your heart chakra with White Light.

Breathe in and out . . . you now feel the White Light moving down from your heart into your solar plexus, filling up your solar plexus with White Light.

Breathe in and out . . . and as you do, feel the White Light moving down from your solar plexus into your belly and abdomen, filling it up with White Light.

Now the energy is moving down to your pelvis and lower abdomen, filling them up too . . .

Breathe in and out . . . and now you feel the White Light moving down both of your legs, over your hips, over your knees, over your ankles, over your feet and down into the earth. You can see the White Light going deep, down into the earth, grounding you with the earth.

All of your twelve chakras are now completely cleansed and balanced. Well done.

White Light Channeling

Working with the White Light is always done best in *conjunction* with the Chakra Cleanse Meditation. However, when you make the chakra cleansing a regular or daily habit, you can eventually channel White Light on its own.

In the next chapter, we'll explore this, as well as advanced methods of working with the White Light.

CHAPTER 31

ADVANCED WHITE LIGHT TECHNIQUES

YOU NOW KNOW THAT once your lower chakras are open and enlivened, practicing White Light channeling will boost your chakra work, as well as raise your vibration, keep it raised, and help you thrive in these changing times. But there is even more you can do with the White Light.

Through the School of the Modern Mystic®, an online school I created in 2013 (see Appendix C), I teach students how to use the White Light to do some incredible things, from instantly removing blockages, to manifesting their hearts' desires, to becoming psychic and powerful. In my courses, we also do deep dives into the chakras, spending many months working on chakras 1 through 7. Then, we move on to the advanced practices . . .

When your chakras are ready, and you've been practicing the Chakra Cleanse Meditation and White Light channeling for some time, you too can do advanced practices like White Light zapping, which you'll learn now.

What Is White Light Zapping?

One of my favorite ways to use the White Light is to channel it when I'm tired, drained, or find myself in a low-vibration space. I call this method White Light zapping, because you are "zapping" yourself with White Light to quickly raise your vibration and boost your energy field and chakras. It's a great technique to use to feel invigorated, clear, or more protected, and it can be practiced almost anywhere at any time (while you wait to collect your children from school, in the dentist's office, in the supermarket, and so on). White Light zap when you're tired and struggling to get through the day, when you're surrounded by negative people, and in life situations such as when your children are sick, or you're having one of those difficult work conversations.

With practice, you'll be able to, within only a couple of minutes, White Light zap and completely change your energy and that of others around you. You'll become a powerful modern mystic and White Light worker, and will transform dark into light wherever you go!

Note: This only works if you've been dedicated to a regular practice of the Chakra Cleanse Meditation and have successfully begun to channel the White Light as a part of that practice.

How to White Light Zap

Step 1: Make sure chakra 7 is open and ready to receive White Light.

Bring your awareness to the point of chakra 7, on the top of your head, and hold your awareness there, preparing it to receive the White Light.

Step 2: Wait for the "signal" that chakra 7 is open and ready to receive White Light.

When you bring your awareness to chakra 7 and continue to hold it there, you will start to feel the chakra open up. This is your signal that you can now channel White Light. This signal, or the feeling of an open chakra 7, is different for every person, but commonly consists of:

- Warmth
- A sense of expansion
- Seeing the chakra color (vivid violet)
- A feeling of vibration
- A feeling of pulsation
- An increased vibrancy

Although it is different for each person, I've come to learn that the most reliable signal for an open chakra is simply that the person intuits that the chakra is open. Generally, most people can detect if a chakra is open because it feels "expansive," and that a chakra is closed because it feels "constricted." (Tip: If you still aren't sure, try to "feel into" your seventh chakra. Generally, most people can detect if a chakra is open or closed. If it's open, the chakra feels "expansive"; if it's closed, the chakra feels "constricted." Ask yourself: How does my seventh chakra feel?)

Step 3: Bring the White Light into your energy field and "pulse" it through.

Being able to quickly and easily draw the White Light into your energy field and move it throughout and down your chakras is called "pulsing." Once you feel your chakra 7 is open and ready to receive White Light, it's time to draw it into your energy field. You'll do this by following the White Light meditation below, which you will recognize as the White Light channeling section of the Chakra Cleanse Meditation.

Visualize a White Light. The whitest and most brilliant White Light that you can possibly imagine. Hold this image in your mind's eye for a few moments . . .

Now, visualize a funnel sitting on the top of your head . . . visualize the White Light pouring into this funnel. Hold this image in your mind's eye for a few moments, and remember to keep breathing deeply, gently, and evenly while you do this.

Now, you can see White Light pouring into your body through the funnel on the top of your head. You can feel the White Light filling up each of your chakras as it descends towards your feet.

You can feel the White Light pouring into your seventh chakra . . . and now into your sixth chakra.

Breathe in and out . . . and you now feel the White Light pouring into your fifth chakra . . . and it's now moving down past your throat into your heart, filling up your heart chakra with White Light.

Breathe in and out . . . you now feel the White Light moving down from your heart into your solar plexus, filling up your solar plexus with White Light.

Breathe in and out . . . and as you do, feel the White Light moving down from your solar plexus into your belly and abdomen, filling it up with White Light.

Now the energy is moving down to your pelvis and lower abdomen, filling them up too . . .

Breathe in and out . . . and now you feel the White Light moving down both of your legs, over your hips, over your knees, over your ankles, over your feet, and down into the earth. You can see the White Light going deep, down into the earth, grounding you with the earth.

In time, you can make this process of White Light zapping happen almost instantaneously. As soon as you bring your awareness to chakra 7, it will open (step 1), you'll receive the White Light (step 2), and you'll quickly and easily draw it into your energy field and pulse it down through your chakras (step 3).

When you can properly pulse the White Light through your body, it will feel like a wave, ripple, or a current of energy moving from your head down to your feet. Usually when you first begin White Light channeling, the White Light moving through your body feels like a slow wave of energy, but the more proficient you get, the quicker the pulses or currents will become. Soon the slow wave becomes a quick current, and when you are very good at it, the wave moves through your body like a pleasant electrical zap.

Learning how to channel White Light and White Light zap will happen for you, but for most people, it takes time before they feel the White Light pulsing throughout their entire body. If the White Light does not pulse down into and throughout your chakras, you're not yet successfully channeling it. That's no problem: Simply stay at step 2, and remain there until you receive the signal that chakra 7 is open. Then, move on to step 3 and visualize White Light coming down into chakra 7, and pulsating down into each of your chakras.

Keep doing the Chakra Cleanse Meditation and practicing White Light channeling and zapping, and soon you too will feel the ripples of love, healing, and light throughout your energy field and body.

In the next chapter, I'll discuss the final spiritual tool to help you raise your vibration and heal your life—mindfulness.

CHAPTER 32

MINDFULNESS

THE THIRD AND FINAL practice I recommend, in addition to chakra cleansing and channeling White Light, is mindfulness. Mindfulness (or presence, as it's also called) is the practice of being fully aligned with the present moment. It is the practice of being *in the now*. You endeavor to always have your attention in the here and now, and when your attention leaves the present—when you begin to rehash the past or worry about the future—you purposefully bring your attention back to the present. Mindfulness is being open to the light: When we're distracted or our thoughts run wild, our energy loses its potency and it's impossible to channel White Light.

When we practice mindfulness, our thoughts and energy are more focused because we are in the present, making us transparent to the light and to the true essence of our nature. This happened to me in my enlightened moment—I opened myself up to the light; the experiences I had took place because I had been practicing presence, and like Eckhart Tolle says in *The Power of Now,* I then learned, "... that the light is not separate from who we are but constitutes our very essence."

Through practicing presence, I had rapidly raised my vibrations and strengthened my chakras. This allowed me to have my enlightened moment. Since then, I have not only been dedicated to working on my chakras and with the White Light, I have also been dedicated to the study of Eckhart Tolle's teachings and the practice of mindfulness. In this chapter, I'll discuss mindfulness in general and give you some practices. (But I also recommend Eckhart Tolle's books for his in-depth examinations of the power of mindfulness. See Appendix C.)

Mindfulness and the Light

Your ego (shadow; the pain of your past) can only "live on" in you if you focus on it. And if you focus on it, it only grows in strength. By healing your chakras and working with the White Light, you heal the pain of your past by clearing the blockages of the negative and self-depleting thoughts and belief systems stored within your chakras. You bring light into your energy field, and as a result, your shadow heals and your ego diminishes.

To support this process of healing your shadow, you must seek to continually bring your attention to the present moment and not return to thinking about your past. You need to learn how to stop thinking about your problems (past and future)—how to mentally let go of them. (Remember Karen from Chapter 29?)

In my enlightened moment, I learned that we have a choice whether to align with the dark or the light. But because most of us have inherited negative and self-depleting ways of thinking—we're conditioned to focus on the negative—we don't realize we habitually choose to align with the dark.

When we raise our vibrations through chakra cleansing, channeling White Light, and practicing mindfulness, we begin to return to our natural state of light-ness. Practicing mindfulness helps us change our energy and align with the light. For most of us, though, this process takes time because we weren't taught (or brought up) to behave this way—as if we are the light.

After we have cleansed our chakras and worked with the White Light, we need to learn to keep our energy fields clean—pure, strong, and resilient— using mindfulness so the blockages can't take hold again. This is the key to rapid healing and trans-formation, and for me, it was the missing piece in the puzzle of my health crisis.

Case Study

Belinda

> *For years, I was plagued with horrible stomach and digestive problems. After I started working on my chakras and channel-ing the White Light, my health improved greatly, overall. Yet my digestive issues persisted.*
>
> *I was trapped in a negative pattern. I thought obsessively about what I ate, wondering which foods might make me sick. I would want to go out and be social, but would worry about getting ill on the bus and not being able to get off in time and find a bathroom.*
>
> *I was a prisoner of my fears. I would do the chakra cleanse, but then would quickly start thinking about my digestive issues again. It wouldn't be long before thoughts like, "Oh, I just wish these stomach problems would disappear forever," would invade my mind.*
>
> *I had spent years being scared about my health, but my worry had only exacerbated the problem because it lowered my vibration, allowing the illness to persist. Although I was healing my health problems by pouring White Light into my energy field and chakras, I wasn't allowing it to penetrate deep into me and bring about a permanent healing because I was thinking the thoughts of a sick and fearful person. I was stop-ping the light from doing its job. I had to train myself to not dwell on or worry about my health.*
>
> *This wasn't easy, but once I realized I was "standing in the way of the White Light," I trained my brain—rewired it—to focus on the present moment and be in the now. This stopped me from focusing on the past and how often and how long I'd had this problem. And it stopped me from worrying about the*

future and fearing how to handle or cope with the problem if it happened again. With these changes, I was able to completely heal my digestive problems!

Practicing presence had other amazing benefits. It made me centered; I could now think clearly and make good decisions and I could focus more and for longer periods of time. Mindfulness also connected me to my body; I began to enjoy dancing and sport and feeling the joy of being "in my body." It connected me to nature, as well. I began to enjoy nature much more and started to feel deeply connected to it. It cleared space in my mind. I began to be more peaceful and rested as I was no longer bombarded by noisy and unnecessary thoughts. It made me more creative as well, and I began to pursue soul-aligned creative projects.

As you can see, the practice of mindfulness adds a needed boost to your spiritual efforts. Without mindfulness—without bringing your energy into present time—it's difficult to create full, lasting health.

How to Practice Mindfulness and Stay Open to the Light

After practicing mindfulness for almost ten years and helping other people to do the same, I've accumulated a list of my favorite ways to get present and stay open to the light. These mental trainings will help you keep your vibration raised throughout the day. Quick and easy to do, they only require one thing of you: that you do them!

Being in the Body

Being in your body is the quickest and easiest way to get present. To do this, simply draw your awareness to a certain area (or areas) of your body and "feel into" them—use your consciousness to "touch" that point. When you do this, you quickly draw your attention to the now and stop the torrent of thoughts in your mind.

This is also a helpful technique when you try to meditate but find yourself distracted by your thoughts. If that happens, practice being in your body. When your mind focuses on something, when you draw your awareness to the present moment by feeling an area of your body, your mind calms and the thoughts and worries fade to the background. It's as if now that your mind has something to focus on, like a dog chewing a bone, it becomes preoccupied with this and calms down.

Eckhart Tolle also advocates a "being in the body" practice as a powerful way to get present. He recommends that you begin with either feeling the flow of air in and out of your lungs when you breathe, or focusing on a body part (a hand, or foot, or your chest) and feeling the life-energy inside it.

Simply focus all your attention on feeling your breathing or your hand or your foot or your chest. As soon as you do this, you'll notice that the chaos of thoughts in your mind begins to calm. Another way to do this is during physical activity of some sort. As you walk, dance, jog, cycle . . . focus on your physical body. Rather than mentally reviewing your to-do list or replaying that conversation you just had, be in your body—feel your legs walking, your arms moving, your heart pumping, and yourself breathing.

When you first practice these "being in the body" techniques, you'll most likely fluctuate between being mindful and being consumed again by your thoughts. Most of us struggle with this at first, but in time you'll find that you can hold your attention in your body for longer and longer periods of time. Eventually, you'll develop the habit of having some of your awareness *always* in your body. Being in your body will become your full-time modus operandi! And when you can do this, you will always be powerfully connected to the present, and the work that you've done with your chakras and the White Light won't be undone by your thoughts.

Oh, Yeah. There's That Thought Again!

This practice involves recognizing repetitive and destructive thoughts so that we can choose to let them go. Mindfulness teaches us to observe our thoughts, and we can then choose *not* to believe those thoughts or take them too seriously. Many teachers of the practice of mindfulness point out that the thoughts that go through our minds are mostly our imagination at work, or simply irrational, or negative, or all three. Therefore, it makes no sense to pay much attention to them.

The Happiness Trap by Russ Harris (my second favorite book about mindfulness) shows us techniques to observe our thoughts and "defuse" the negativity and power of them. One way to do this is to observe the thought and comment upon it.

For example, if the negative thought, "I'm overweight and unattractive," pops up in your mind, mentally step back from it. Emotionally distance yourself. Then observe, "Oh yeah. There's that thought again!" When you do this, you defuse the power of the thought by creating distance between it and yourself. You don't immediately accept it as truth; the distance allows you to question its validity.

This technique is best used with persistent negative thoughts not easily defused by the "being in the body" practice—those deeply negative, deeply ingrained thoughts that we tend to whole-heartedly believe without question. They are those thoughts which we have been thinking (and believing) for a long time and have, through the Law of Attraction, also self-created as a reality in our experience of life.

These thoughts are often the ones that we secretly (and shamefully) believe about ourselves. Ones like: *There is something wrong with me. There is something bad about me. I'm worthless and a disgrace. I'm disgusting and useless. I'm a fraud.* These are the thoughts we are ashamed to admit to other people but secretly believe or fear that other people think about us anyway.

My own secret shameful thought was that I was bad. After being exorcised when I was a child, I couldn't look at myself in the mirror. I couldn't look into my own eyes because I was scared (and convinced) that if I did this, I would see the eyes of evil, of demons, staring back at me. So the secret thought I carried around with me (and wholeheartedly believed) was that I was inherently bad. This thought not only plagued me, it also manifested itself in various ways—I had adults, clergymen, and therapists tell me that they feared I was bad and that something was wrong with me. It took time and effort to defuse the power of this destructive thought, but I did it and so can you.

Drop It Like a Hot Potato

When you begin to practice being in the body and observing your thoughts, you quickly notice that many of your thoughts are of an attacking nature. That is, they are attacks on other people, on the state of the world, on the present moment, upon yourself, and so on.

A method that can help you "drop" these deeply negative thought patterns is something I call "drop it like a hot potato." After practice with basic mindfulness techniques (such as being in the body and observing your thoughts), you'll find that you can take a leap and can completely drop a negative thought or mood.

These attacking thoughts are the result of an overactive ego and something most of us experience from time to time. The ego believes it can get what it wants by fighting against or trying to manipulate reality. When it doesn't like something, it thinks it can change it by "throwing daggers" at that person or situation. But this attacking mentality only lowers your vibration. And it doesn't heal or change things. Instead, these negative thoughts create resistance and blockages.

To truly heal or change something, you need to let life flow. Make sure you aren't offering life any resistance or negativity;

let perceived problems and obstacles *flow through you*. If you allow these things to just keep moving, your lack of resistance allows them to be transmuted into love and light.

I discovered the "drop it like a hot potato" method when my daughter, Sarah, was two months old. One night I had mastitis and I couldn't get Sarah to feed properly. I'd spent most of the night trying to settle her and was exhausted. Sarah had always been difficult to settle; she was a poor feeder and sleeper, and I usually got up to tend to her five or six times a night.

Like all mothers of newborn babies, I was sleep deprived and exhausted, and now with the mastitis, I couldn't get Sarah to feed to relieve the pressure! I crawled up the stairs and fell into the shower, then lay on the shower floor and wept. My breasts felt like they were filled with concrete, my back was aching badly, and I had terrible pains running up and down my legs.

I was miserable, and my mind was racing: *How can I go on like this? I'm exhausted! This is dreadful! When will this ever end?*

At that moment, I loathed motherhood and breastfeeding, and I loathed my life because I was so exhausted.

Then my thoughts turned into self-attack: *You're a bad mother! You can't breastfeed your daughter properly and you can't get her to sleep! You're doing it all wrong! Poor Sarah having a mother like you! You're terrible!*

On and on went the thoughts, attacking me and telling me how dreadful I was. Then suddenly, in one crystal-clear moment, I found myself observing my thoughts. I saw that I was viciously attacking myself, and that by doing so, I was making the situation *much* worse. I was already feeling low. Why kick myself while I was down?

As soon as I saw the absurdity of it, I decided not to believe these thoughts. I decided then and there to "drop it." So I visualized bundling all my negative thoughts and emotions into my hand and dropping this bundle like a hot potato. I resolved to let it go once and for all and to not allow the negativity to come back.

As soon as I did this, incredibly, my mind was clear and free.

I stepped out of the shower and went back to bed. My breasts still hurt, and so did my legs and back, but internally I was peaceful, and because of this I quickly fell peacefully asleep, sleeping soundly (for a few hours, until Sarah woke me again).

You too can drop your negative thoughts by practicing visualizing them all going into a bundle and then dropping the bundle like a hot potato. This technique does take practice, but when you master it, you will experience instant relief and calm. Plus you'll also keep your energy field clean and open to the light.

Focus on One Thing at a Time

The art of presence, of mindfulness, is being in the now, of staying deeply anchored to the present moment. And when we become good at being in the body, observing our thoughts, and dropping negative thoughts like hot potatoes, we suddenly find we have more mental space. When this happens, we become much more peaceful, settled, and creative.

One way to create more mental space is to focus on one thing at a time. This may seem unfashionable in our age of multitasking, but dealing with one task at a time allows you to bring your full energy to that task. It's impossible to achieve true "flow"— that satisfying and productive space where everything feels like it's coming together perfectly—if our attention is split among multiple thoughts and tasks. And when you are in flow, you imbue whatever it is you're focused on with love and light.

Put another way, having a clear mind—without the constant bombardment of internal chatter, commentary, negativity, images, urges, and resistance—fosters creativity. It frees us from excess mental activity and overstimulation, and we're then able to channel our creativity into useful and productive ventures.

When you have mental space, you are more receptive to your creative ideas, and when your mind isn't full and you're open to the light, you will also clearly know *what* creative ideas are soul-aligned and which ones are ego-driven. You can differentiate between the soul-aligned ones that bring you love, comfort, peace, and prosperity, and the ego-driven ones that bring you strife, chaos, conflict, and struggle. When you have mental space, you can clearly see and act upon the intuitive guidance of your soul.

When your energy is focused and strong like a laser beam, you pour power into your projects, services, and offerings. But when your energy is scattered, when you multitask or don't focus on the task at hand, it's weak and diluted. It's not high vibrational; you aren't open to the light and channeling it.

Get into the habit of doing one thing at a time and focusing your full attention on your task at hand. This will not only keep *you* high-vibe, it will also infuse *everything you do* with the highest vibration, so you will literally spread light wherever you go.

Lose Yourself to the Moment

Losing yourself to the moment goes hand in hand with focusing on one thing at a time. When you've lost yourself in the moment, you allow yourself to become fully enveloped by what is happening, whether it is working on a complex project or observing a field of flowers. You allow your senses to receive every piece of input available about whatever it is you are focused on.

When your focus is narrowed, you begin to be more in the now. When that happens, you'll notice that you think less, which means you will have fewer thoughts, commentary, and judgments about the world. You'll also notice that you think less about yourself and your problems.

This doesn't mean you're less engaged in life. Quite the contrary! It means you no longer fight life—resist its ups and downs—but instead let it flow through you. You roll with it, and in doing so, choose to stay permanently open to the light.

When we think about ourselves or the world constantly, when we constantly comment, analyze, and judge the world around us, we separate ourselves from it. The mind creates a "smoke screen" between us and the world and we feel outside of it and separate. But we aren't.

Our energy fields connect to the greater energy field of the universe. At an energetic level, we are made up of the same stuff as other humans, animals, and plants. We are not separate from the universe. We are one with it. Any thoughts we have of separateness are simply an illusion perpetuated by the ego.

When we practice mindfulness and are in the now, the beauty of life begins to open up to us. We begin to be able to see the *light* within the world—within ourselves, others, and nature.

When we were children, we saw the light in the world. We saw joy and beauty around us. Think back to when you were a child and the way you could lose yourself to the moment. How you could play all day in a tree or at the park with your friends or at the beach with your siblings. Think about how tall and magnificent and green the trees looked. How huge and blue and glassy the ocean seemed. Remember how amazing it was to stare up at the sky and watch clouds pass overhead, and how incredible it felt to do cartwheels on the grass or flips and turns and somersaults on your bed.

When we were young, we could lose ourselves to the magic of the moment because it was light-infused. We could see the light in it! When you become more mindful and present, your mind empties itself and clears, and then you too will return to the state of wonder and joy you experienced when you were a child. Then you will feel and know it to be true that every moment is sacred, and light-filled, and God-like.

Death Meditation

It may seem like a complete turnabout to go from talking about life being filled with vibrancy and love to encouraging you to meditate on your death, but this technique can truly make your life richer and more light-infused. Meditating upon the transience of your life and of your human body and of your possessions powerfully brings you into the present moment. Imagining yourself (and everything you have, own, or love) dissolving into *nothingness*, draws you *closer* to those things in your life that matter, and it moves you away from those things that don't.

When I meditate on my own death (which I do frequently), it brings me nearer to my soul—to that part of me that is eternal, infinite, and immortal. For me, it's a powerful way to clear out the thoughts, worries, or life issues that, in the grander scheme of things, simply don't matter. Meditating on my own death helps keep me focused on what's *important* in my life, giving me permission to let go of what isn't.

I also meditate on my own death to remind myself to have no regrets. Over the years, I've spoken to hundreds of spirits—deceased people who have left the earth plane and found the light—and from them I've only ever heard one regret. There is only one thing they wish they'd done differently:

They regret wasting their life waiting for it to begin.

When I ask spirits what they'd do if they could live their lives over, they always say: *Live it! I wouldn't have sweated the small stuff! I wouldn't have worried so much, struggled so much, or wasted so much time! I would have lived and loved with reckless abandon! I would have followed my heart and loved everything and everyone! I wouldn't have waited for life to happen to me; I would have lived it!*

Don't waste your life or have regrets. Take heed of the advice of spirits: Live and love with reckless abandon!

The Death Meditation, as well as the other mindfulness practices shared in this chapter, will keep your energy field clean, your vibration high, and your chakras fit and healthy. It will help you be present and enjoy life.

At the end of the day, that's what we're here for!

CONCLUSION

My dear fellow modern mystic,

We've reached the end of our journey together for now. It's my sincerest wish that my story, along with the information and tools I've provided here, will serve you for a long time to come!

Remember: The key to thriving in these changing times is to change your energy. This is the path of the modern mystic and spiritual seeker. It is what will change your life and help you discover your soul purpose.

This is the way to the light.

As you continue with this work and raise your vibration, you'll likely experience new challenges, but also new triumphs and successes. Just stay committed to the spiritual tools I've outlined in this book and you will keep moving forward, developing your intuitive, modern-mystic, and psychic abilities, along with the other skills that will help you navigate the rising vibration.

In White Light + Love,
Belinda

APPENDIX A

CHAKRA CHART

Chakra	Color/ Vibration	Location	Areas of the Body Governed	Drive	Issues	Likes
Chakra 1 (base chakra, root chakra): Chapter 21	Red	Perineum and between the feet	Spinal column, legs, feet, hips, lower part of the large intestine (colon)	To ensure one's survival and make sure we have everything we need here on earth	Grounding, survival, belonging, the body	The color red, nature (hugging trees), grounding (walks in nature, hiking, gardening), all forms of movement including exercise and sport, environments in which you feel good and at home
Chakra 2 (sacral chakra): Chapter 22	Orange	Just below the navel	Lower abdomen, pelvis, reproductive system, kidneys, bladder, upper part of the large intestine (colon)	Pursuit of individuation and pleasure	Individuation, magnetism, sexuality, pleasure, creative expression	The color orange, beautiful environments (art galleries, botanical gardens, old Gothic churches), massages, hugs, lovemaking, romance, gorgeous sunsets, losing yourself in the beauty of the present moment, dancing naked, anything you find delightful

Chakra	Color/ Vibration	Location	Areas of the Body Governed	Drive	Issues	Likes
Chakra 3 (solar plexus chakra): Chapter 23	Yellow	Stomach region	Stomach, liver, gall-bladder, digestive system, spleen	Personal power and boundaries	Self-esteem, self-empowerment, will, ambition	The color yellow, saying "no" if something isn't right for you, martial arts, holding your center when confronted and knowing your truth, focus, persistence, diligence, diplomacy, strength of character, acting like a "peaceful warrior"
Chakra 4 (heart chakra): Chapter 24	Green	Heart region	Heart, blood, chest, hands and arms, lungs, circulatory system	Pursuit and expression of love	Self-love, giving and receiving love, compassion, forgiveness and acceptance	The color green; anything heart-felt (hugs, talks, movies); smiles; kind words; forgiveness; letting go of old hurts; compassion; visualizing people living in health, harmony and plenty; telling others how much you love them; random acts of kindness and prayer; undertaking any activities you love

Chakra Chart

Chakra	Color/ Vibration	Location	Areas of the Body Governed	Drive	Issues	Likes
Chakra 5 (throat chakra): Chapter 25	Blue	Throat region	Throat, neck, jaw, teeth, thyroid glands, vocal cords	Authentic and original expression, self-determination and will, speaking one's truth	Ability to express needs and desires, open and honest communication, creativity, surrendering personal will to divine will	The color blue, singing, public speaking, writing, acting, performing, speaking your truth, interesting discussions with like-minded people, any activity in which you express yourself
Chakra 6 (third eye chakra): Chapter 26	Indigo	Above and between the eyebrows	Head, brain (hypo-thalamus, pituitary gland, pitu-itary nerve plexus), ears, eyes	Transcendence (to go "above and beyond")	Wisdom (the balance of imagination and intellect), intuition and clairvoyance, creating our own reality	The color indigo, meditation, visualization, brainstorming and goal setting, consciously dreaming your perfect life, mas-termind groups, any activity that inspires you to stretch yourself and be great
Chakra 7 (crown chakra): Chapter 27	Violet	Top of the head	Upper brain and nervous system	Oneness, surrendering to divinity	Enlightenment and soul purpose	The color violet; meditation, meditation, meditation!; stillness and reflection; books about saints, yogis, and great men and women of the world
Chakras 8 through 12 (cosmic chakras or soul purpose chakras): Chapter 28	Their colors are outside the range of our percep-tion	Above chakra 7, one on top of the other, ascend-ing into the sky	None	Knowing yourself to be a cosmic being of light	Discovering your true soul's purpose	White Light channeling

Q & A

As I travel the world sharing my story and teaching people how to work with their chakras, the White Light, and mindfulness, there are questions I'm asked again and again. In this section, I've included transcripts of the most frequently asked questions along with my answers, divided by topic area.

Some questions and answers repeat what you'll have already read in this book. I include them here because in some cases, I use different language in my responses, which may help give you another perspective. In other cases, the information is so important and I'm asked about it so often, that it's worth repeating.

I hope this section will help expand your understanding of how you can change your energy and change your life.

In White Light + Love,
Belinda

About Chakra Cleansing and Meditation

Q. *Your Chakra Cleanse Meditation lasts for half an hour but I don't have that long in the mornings. Can I just do ten minutes of it, and will I still get results if I do this?*

A. I would challenge the assumption that you only have ten minutes for meditation. Let's be clear—you have as long as you want for meditation. You could get up earlier to meditate, you could go to bed later, you could spend less time on eating, working, watching television, showering, and so on . . . So when you say you only have ten minutes for meditation, what you are really saying is that's all you can do at the moment. And that is perfectly fine.

To properly cleanse and balance all your chakras, as well as bring the White Light down into your energy field, you do need at least thirty minutes. However, doing ten minutes of meditation every day is better than not meditating at all. And if that is what you can handle right now, it's a great start.

In time try to increase this to thirty minutes. Then you can rest assured that every day all your chakras are getting exactly what they need to function properly.

Q. *I've been doing the Chakra Cleanse Meditation for five months now and I love it. It has certainly brought me more peace and purpose! My life has become calmer, my health has improved, I feel much clearer, and my marriage problems have sorted themselves out. But I'm still struggling with focus . . . When I bring my awareness to each one of my chakra points, my awareness jumps away. I can only manage to hold my awareness on each one of the chakra points for a short period of time before thoughts come rushing in. I find this frustrating and it makes me feel like I'll never be able to chakra cleanse properly. What can I do?*

A. It's perfectly normal and natural that you can't focus on each chakra point without thoughts coming into your mind . . . Even those of us who have been meditating for a long time have this problem. But rest assured that you are chakra cleansing properly. Otherwise you wouldn't have had these shifts in your life.

When your awareness jumps away from the chakra point and you find yourself thinking or lost in thought again, simply and calmly bring your awareness back to the chakra point. And if it jumps away again, simply and calmly bring your awareness back to the chakra point. Just keep coming back to focusing on the chakra point. Don't get frustrated; just refocus. You'll find that you still may go back and forth between focus and thought for some time. However, your brain will become trained to always come back and focus on the chakra points. So eventually you will find yourself more and more able to focus with less and less stress.

Q. *I can't visualize the colors of the chakras properly. Is this a problem?*

A. No, it isn't. Being able to visualize the colors of the lower seven chakras (the colors of the five higher chakras are beyond our range of perception) is secondary to the practice of holding your awareness on each one of the chakra points. To cleanse, balance, and strengthen your chakras, you need to hold your awareness on each one of the chakra points. When you do this, you "fuel" the chakra, giving it energy, attention, and love, and then it can open up and draw in the light. So this is the primary practice and what you need to do to get the chakras to heal themselves.

However, visualizing the colors of each one of the chakras does benefit this process, and many people love to visualize color (I added visualizing chakra colors to the meditation because people asked for it). But don't worry if you struggle to visualize color. Focus instead on bringing your awareness to each chakra point and holding it there.

Q. *My lower chakras are weak. When I do the Chakra Cleanse Meditation I find it hard to hold my focus on my base, sacral, and solar plexus chakras. I can't feel or sense these chakras properly. Does this mean they are weak? I can feel my heart, throat, and third eye chakras more strongly, but my lower ones seem "nonexistent."*

A. Yes, this is a sign that these chakras are weak. When a chakra is weak, many people have the experience that they can't feel it. It seems to not be there.

257

But we can also experience weak chakras as stagnant, sad, or flat, or tight and constricted. When you begin to cleanse your chakras regularly, you'll grow in awareness and can begin to sense and know the state of your chakras. This is the beginning of you developing your skills as a medical intuitive!

So keep it up. Just keep working on your chakras (paying particular attention to your lower ones) and soon you'll sense them growing and becoming stronger and more resilient.

Q. *When I do your guided Chakra Cleanse Meditation, I find myself wanting to spend more time on each chakra. Though your voice is already guiding me on to the next chakra, I intuitively feel I want to stay at the chakra I'm working on. Can I do this?*

A. Yes, of course, and this is what you should do! My guided chakra cleanse was designed as a beginner's tool—a way to have guidance and support when you first learn to work with your chakras. In time you should try to cleanse and balance them yourself because, as you've already found, each of your chakras has different needs.

You'll find that your stronger chakras need less attention and that your weaker ones need more. Cleanse and balance your chakras at your own pace, simply moving up to the next chakra and beginning to work with it when you intuitively sense or feel that the chakra you are working on is "done" and the next one is ready to go.

Q. *Thank you for the extra tips for strengthening weak chakras. These have been really helpful because I have a very weak chakra 1 and chakra 3. I do the Chakra Cleanse Meditation every day and I also make sure I do good things for my base and solar plexus, like getting out into nature and "standing my ground." But would you recommend that I focus on strengthening one chakra at a time, or do them together?*

A. I recommend that you begin with your base chakra and focus your attention on strengthening it, and then when that is strong, that you then focus on your solar plexus chakra. It's always best to work from the bottom up—to get your base chakra fit first. Your base chakra is the platform, the springboard of your life and spiritual development, and if it's not working properly this impacts all your chakras.

In my online School of the Modern Mystic® (see Appendix C for more information), we undertake a powerful three-month chakric journey where we quickly heal and strengthen each of our seven chakras. We start with the base chakra and work our way up. We do this because we want our energetic foundation, the base chakra, to be strong and fit and able to funnel the energy up into our higher chakras and down into the earth.

Q. *I've been doing the Chakra Cleanse Meditation for three weeks now and I still can't feel my chakras. Does that mean that they are all weak? Or does it mean that I haven't yet developed the intuitive skill to sense them?*

A. If you can't feel *any* of your chakras, it's most likely that you haven't yet developed the intuitive skill to sense them. This will develop in time, so please don't worry about it. But it is important to know that sensing the state of your chakras—whether they are strong or weak—is not a prerequisite for the chakra cleanse. You don't need to know the state of your chakras in order to heal them.

The most important thing is to work on your chakras and get into a regular habit of chakra cleansing. The rest flows from this.

Q. *How long do I need to work on my chakras before I get results?*

A. That depends entirely on you and how often you do the Chakra Cleanse Meditation, and if you complete the meditation or not.

If you do the entire Chakra Cleanse Meditation two to three times a week for six weeks, you will see changes in your life. You will become calmer, clearer, healthier, more focused, and aware. But the key to success is sticking with it and making chakra cleansing a regular, lifelong habit.

Q. *How can I help my children with their chakras? Can they do the Chakra Cleanse Meditation?*

A. Yes, they can, and many children do. There are children as young as seven who use the Chakra Cleanse Meditation! But for younger children or other children who struggle to do this, you can best help them by helping yourself. The more you work on your chakras, the stronger your chakras become, which in turns helps and supports your child and their chakras. Until the age of seven, children are energetically attached and connected to us; they protect their energy fields through ours.

What you can also do, and many parents do this, is put your child/children on my weekly White Light healing list (see Appendix C). That way they can receive White Light every week, and this helps them with their chakras and spiritual development.

Q. *Should I stop taking my medication and work on my chakras instead?*

A. No, you shouldn't. You should chakra cleanse *in tandem* with taking your medication, and when your health begins to improve, you should speak with your doctor or healthcare practitioner about the next steps.

Q. *Can I chakra cleanse when I'm pregnant?*

A. Absolutely. What a wonderful way to support yourself and your baby during this precious time!

When you work on your chakras, you balance yourself and create a strong and luminous energy field. This not only helps you through your pregnancy and birth, it also gives your baby energy and light. I can't think of a more wonderful way to look after your child while it's in utero.

About White Light

Q. *When I chakra cleanse and channel the White Light I fall asleep. This also happens when I receive White Light from you on Monday evenings. Why is this happening? Am I doing something wrong?*

A. This happens to many people when they first start out. It happened to me too! I would become so drowsy I could no longer keep my eyes open and I'd fall asleep.

When you do the Chakra Cleanse Meditation, you are rapidly opening up and healing your chakras. They are being activated, you are channeling a high spiritual energy into them (the White Light), and you are healing your deepest blockages. This is a big job; it can be taxing and make us want to sleep.

Many of us feel sleepy because our shadow (or ego) is resisting the work. It is creating subconscious blockages (drowsiness, sleepiness) to stop us from doing the work. Your ego benefits from you *not* meditating. When you have blockages in your chakras and aren't connected to the present moment, the ego runs the show. Your shadow is in charge, so to speak, and resists you when you begin to heal the shadow and bring light into your energy field. And you can become sleepy or drowsy . . .

To prevent this, make sure you sit or stand to do the Chakra Cleanse Meditation. If you lie down, you'll likely fall asleep. And when you're asleep, you can't cleanse and balance your chakras!

Q. *I can do the Chakra Cleanse Meditation and bring the White Light down afterwards. So, I can channel the White Light easily after I've just cleansed and balanced my chakras, but doing it on its own, doing it without chakra cleansing beforehand, is much more difficult. I follow the three steps: focusing on chakra 7, waiting for chakra 7 to open, and then pulsing it through, but the flow of the White Light is weak. It is much weaker than when I receive your Monday White Light healings or when I've chakra cleansed beforehand.*

A. It is easier, at first, to channel White Light *after* you've cleansed and balanced your chakras because you have just prepared your chakras for it. They are ready and open. But when you White Light channel or White Light zap without having cleansed and balanced your chakras beforehand, you do it without any preparation. Still, it is important to be able to do these techniques because channeling White Light is a powerful way to rapidly raise your vibration.

Try it when you're on the bus going to work, or on your lunch break, or when you suddenly feel tired and need a pick-me-up, or have just had a draining conversation with your mother-in-law or boss, or you need to quickly bring light into your energy field and "lighten up." Find a quiet place (maybe the bathroom, if you are at work) and follow the three steps to channel White Light. This will probably be more difficult when you first start because you haven't prepared your chakras for it beforehand, but this is a great and powerful tool to know.

I White Light zap all the time. I practice this whenever I need a boost: if I'm tired, or on an airplane surrounded by anxious and noisy passengers, or sitting next to someone who is unwell, or I need to quickly summon energy and push through a project.

Q. *When I follow the three steps to channeling White Light, I can feel it moving down into my head and neck and throat but it stops at my chest. Why is this? Why is it stopping at my chest? Does this mean I'm not yet properly channeling the White Light?*

A. The White Light is stopping at your chest because there is a blockage in your heart chakra. This blockage stops the White Light from flowing down into the lower half of your body. The more you use the Chakra Cleanse Meditation, the more you will heal your blockages in your chakras, so make sure to keep up this practice.

It is true that we are properly channeling White Light only when we can feel the flow (or pulsation of it) throughout our entire body—from our heads down into our feet—but for most people it takes time before this happens. So keep going!

Q. *Why do we channel the White Light down into our energy fields? Why don't we channel it from the ground up?*

A. The natural flow of the White Light is from heaven to earth. There are two energy flow systems in the body: earth-to-heaven and heaven-to-earth. When we start at the base chakra and work our way up, we foster the earth-to-heaven energy flow system; and when we work with the White Light, starting at the crown chakra and working our way down, we work with the heaven-to-earth energy flow system.

For years I tested different types of chakra cleansing meditations, and found that when we do both—chakra cleanse and White Light channel—we quickly and powerfully heal our chakras. These are the fastest and easiest ways to raise our vibration.

Q. *I've heard other people talk about the twelve-chakra energy system. But they talk about it in a different way than you do. Why are there different interpretations of it, and how can I know who is right?*

A. I don't know why there are different interpretations of the twelve chakras, and I find this situation unfortunate, as it creates confusion. It would be so much easier if we all perceived the same thing.

The way I see the chakras—starting from the base chakra and ending at chakra 12, with each chakra on top of the other, ascending into the heavens—is the way I've always psychically perceived them. Since I was a child I've seen the chakras this way. (Obviously back then I didn't know they were called chakras, but I always saw them this way.)

Around the year 2000, I started to become aware of the five higher chakras. I could see five higher chakras in people's energy fields. I then began to study them and "download" the information within. At the time I had never heard anyone else talk about twelve chakras, including the five higher ones. I began calling them the five higher cosmic chakras, and since my enlightened moment in 2007, I have spent many, many hours traveling into these chakras and sharing with people what I've experienced.

I can't answer your question about how to know who is right and who isn't. The only guidance I can give you is to follow what you *feel* is right; what feels like your truth.

Q. *How is the White Light different from Reiki or other types of energy healing systems?*

A. I have not studied other types of energy healing systems. When I was nineteen, I learned the basics of Reiki from a friend, but I haven't learned any other type of energy healing, so unfortunately I can't comment on that.

Q. *I want to connect to the White Light Angels and ask them for help and guidance. How can I do this?*

A. The White Light Angels are not your guides or spirit helpers; you can't connect to them and ask them for guidance. The White Light Angels are the helpers of the White Light, so when you work with the White Light, they are there helping you open up to receive it.

When you become attuned to the White Light and have worked with it for some time, you may become aware of the White Light

Angels working on your energy field, but they won't give you guidance or advice. This is not their cosmic purpose.

Q. *What is the White Light? Is it God or the universe, or it is an energy form? I find it hard to understand what the White Light is.*

A. Don't feel bad about not understanding what the White Light is. I have been working with the White Light every day (mostly more than once a day) since 2007, and I'm still learning about what it is. It's hard to grasp the power and vastness of this ray of pure and divine light!

I believe this description comes closest: The White Light is universal, unconditional love. It's the purest ray of love and light.

Q. *Can I channel White Light for other people? Can I channel it into myself and then send it to others?*

A. No, this isn't how we send White Light to other people. We don't channel it into ourselves and then send it to others.

The best way to help others is to empower them to learn how to do it for themselves: Encourage your friends, family, or clients to learn how to do the Chakra Cleanse Meditation and White Light channeling themselves. This way you don't have the stress, strain, and responsibility of trying to do it for them.

When I send White Light to people, I don't channel it through my body to send it to them. Instead, I support people by helping them raise their vibration so that they can connect to the White Light themselves. The White Light doesn't come through me. It's simply me helping them reach the vibration where they can effectively receive the White Light and its healing powers.

But if you want to send White Light to a child, or sick or elderly person who is unable (or incapable) of learning how to work with the chakra and the White Light, you can put them on my weekly White Light healing list (see Appendix C).

Q. *I feel confused because different people advocate different ways to raise your vibration, create health and wealth, and discover your life purpose. There is so much information out there about all this, so many self-help books and ways to God that I feel overwhelmed. I don't know what to do or who to trust!*

A. Yes, I understand how confusing this can be. I recommend the spiritual tools that I do because: A, it happened to me in my enlightened moment; B, they healed my own life; and C, when I shared them with others it healed their lives too.

For me, these tools are the *quickest* way I know to raise your vibration and change your energy and your life. But there are many paths to God; we each need to find our own. And you can do this by turning within, getting quiet, and asking yourself if this resonates with you as truth.

About Mindfulness

Q. *The technique of being in the body is amazing. It quickly brings me back to the present moment and I notice how my mind clears and I'm anchored and joyful in the here and now. I love it! What I also find is that I feel much more protected! It's difficult to describe, but it feels like my energy feels much more "within" me. I find that when I'm in the body—when I'm focusing on a part of my body, my hands or feet or entire energy field—and interact with people I don't seem to pick up their negative emotions or feelings. Is this really the case? Does being in the body protect your energy?*

A. Yes. When you are within your own energy and are firmly anchored in the now, you are vibrating at a high level. Your vibe is raised, and this acts as a natural protection. Eckhart Tolle says, "If the master is not present in the house, all kinds of shady characters will take up residence there." Nothing else can enter because you are fully occupying your own energy field.

But there is something else you can do to protect your energy even more: shielding. You can create a powerful shield around your energy field that keeps your energy strong and resilient so that nothing of a lower vibration can get in.

Here are the steps:

Bring your awareness to your solar plexus chakra.

Your solar plexus chakra is your inner warrior; it's the body-guard of your energy field, and its job is to make sure your energy isn't being compromised. When you feel tired or drained or feel that something is taking your energy, simply bring your awareness to your solar plexus chakra. This instantly activates (engages) your energy field shield, and you are protected.

Place your hand or keep your awareness on your solar plexus chakra for the duration of the tiring or draining activity.

We live in a modern world in which we need to interact with other people and noise and ego. But instead of fearing this or running from it, we can hold our ground and continue to interact. If you feel drained by your boss or coworkers or children, you can't simply run away. But when you learn to shield, you learn that you don't need to run: You can continue to interact with them and *also* be protected. Shielding is a pow-erful way to protect your energy. Just through the simple tech-nique of bringing your awareness to your solar plexus chakra and engaging it, I've witnessed many incredible transforma-tions: marriages being healed and restored, unsettled children becoming quieter and peaceful, people healing their anxiety and panic disorder, etc.

Q. *How is the ego different from the shadow? Or is it the same thing?*

A. Your ego is your shadow. It's the dark shadow cast by the light of your soul. I sometimes use the word "ego" to describe our past and our pain and suffering, but mostly I use the word "shadow." The two are interchangeable.

Q. *In your medical intuition sessions you tell people all about what is wrong with them. You tell them about their past lives and childhood, so you talk about what happened in their past and how it's affected them. But it's my understanding that mindfulness teaches to let go of the past and focus our attention fully in the present moment. I've also heard you say that you don't need to know what is wrong with you for you to heal your life. Can you please explain this contradiction?*

A. It is true that you don't need to know what is wrong with you or what happened to you in the past for you to heal your life. Many people spend a lot of time analyzing and digging up the past in the hope that they will discover something that will take away their problems of the present. But this approach is futile. It's through raising our vibration and embracing the light within ourselves that we heal our life. And those things about ourselves or our past that we need to know (because they aid our spiritual growth), we'll know . . . Aligning ourselves with the light will make us aware of them; and the rest will simply be healed.

I told people in my medical intuition sessions about their past-life patterns and childhood hurts (I'm using the past tense because I don't give these sessions anymore), because I found that it enabled them to *deeply* accept their shadow.

When I told them the reasons *why* they were feeling a certain way, or why they'd become a certain way, or why they were afraid of or drawn to certain things, it helped them make sense of themselves and their lives. It gave them an "aha" moment. They were then more easily able to accept themselves, and acceptance is the first step to healing: Accept what is and then you can radically shift it.

Q. *I love your favorite ways of being mindful. I love being in my body, observing my thoughts, focusing on one thing at time, losing myself to the moment, and dropping it like a hot potato . . . they make me feel clean and clear. But I don't like the thought of focusing on my own death. This seems negative and macabre, and I don't want to do it.*

A. Have you tried it yet? Have you tried focusing on your own death and imagining yourself dissolving into nothingness? Perhaps the thought of it makes you fearful, but when you do it you will find it liberating and peaceful.

But if you do try it and find that it doesn't bring you peace; if it doesn't help you clear out what *doesn't* matter so that you clearly see what *does*, then don't pursue it. I do think, though, that focusing on one's death is a radical and transformative way to peace.

Q. *Practicing mindfulness has made me feel depressed. Since practicing your favorite ways to be mindful, I've become aware of how often I'm lost in thought and how rarely, if ever, I'm present. It's also made me realize that I've wasted so much of my life . . . I'm sixty-five years old, and have spent most of my life worrying, criticizing, blaming, stressing, and striving . . . I'm grateful that I'm aware of this now and can enjoy my remaining years on earth, but I seem to be going through a grieving process of sorts. I seem to be grieving the years that I've wasted. Could this be the case? Can you shed some light on this for me?*

A. When I started practicing presence and began to embrace my inner light (and move away from the dark), I too went through a grieving process. I was twenty-eight at the time, so for me it wasn't about having wasted my life, it was more feeling that the dreams I'd had since I was a child were being shattered.

When I began working daily with my chakras and the White Light, I clearly saw that I had been creating castles in the sky. I saw how I'd spent a lot of my time hoping and wishing for a better future, mentally mapping out my future successes and joy and happiness. I wasn't experiencing happiness in the present moment. I was waiting for happiness and fame and fortune to find me.

When I realized I wasn't experiencing joy now and was waiting for it to happen someday—I needed to destroy my castles in the sky. I needed to stop daydreaming and wishing and hoping, and I needed to ground my energy in the here and now. This was a painful process because it felt like I was killing my dreams and aspirations. Of course, I wasn't. I was simply letting go of projecting into the future and waiting to be happy . . . but at the time it felt like I was abandoning my dreams.

What is amazing about all of it, though, is that nowadays I'm living those dreams! What I wanted and wished for came about! But not through wishing and mentally projecting myself into the future: rather it came from the work with the chakras, the White Light, and practicing mindfulness.

With this work, it's not unusual to experience somewhat of a grief process as things in your life shift and you make choices about what's most important to you, then, let go of the rest. Keep going with the techniques and as things begin to align, your mood will lighten.

Q. *Since practicing mindfulness I've had deeply negative thoughts about myself; about how much I dislike, or even hate, myself. Why is this happening?*

A. It's most likely that you were having these negative thoughts *before* you began practicing mindfulness, but now that you're being in your body and observing your thoughts, you've become aware of this inside you. This was probably always going on inside you, but now, for the first time, you are aware of the level of negativity within your energy field.

Don't be alarmed by these thoughts. They are simply thoughts and don't hold power over you if you learn how to disengage from them. Use the technique of "Oh yeah, there's that thought again!" to defuse them. And keep chakra cleansing and working with the White Light. You are healing deeply ingrained patterns of self-hate that not only belong to you as a person, but to most of the human race. You are doing important and sacred work not only for yourself, but for all of humanity. Keep going!

Q. *I find it exhausting to always observe my thoughts and bring my attention back to the present moment. It feels like every day is a tug of war. I lose myself to my thoughts, then I notice that I'm not present, so I bring my awareness back to the present moment by feeling into my body. This works for a short time but then I lose myself to my thoughts again, and have to repeat the whole cycle . . . This is frustrating and tiring. Is there an easier way?*

A. After my enlightened moment I went through a similar process. I could be present for a short period of time and then thoughts would rush in and I would be lost in my head again . . . It *did* feel like a tug of war, and the practice of constantly observing my thoughts made me feel like the "thought police." I wondered if I'd ever be able to hold presence for longer than a few moments. But that time in my spiritual development was an important one. I was creating the brain habit of being mindful, and every time I caught myself being out of the body and not present, I had the opportunity to change it.

I was forming the neural pathways of presence. I was developing the habit of being in the here and now. And all this work paid off because I developed the subconscious habit of, as Eckhart Tolle calls it, "returning to presence." So automatically now in my life, without having to think about it, when I lose the present moment and get lost in thought, I find myself being brought back to the now. My brain has been trained to detect that I've drifted off . . . and then it brings me back to the present moment.

Q. *I love the method of dropping it like a hot potato and find that it often works, but sometimes it doesn't. I visualize dropping it all, but then sometimes the negative thoughts come straight back again! Am I doing something wrong?*

A. Dropping it like a hot potato is an advanced practice of mindfulness. It takes mental resolve to drop something fully and wholly and not to allow yourself to think about it anymore. You need to be determined not to let the thoughts come back in.

The next time you practice this, affirm that you are dropping these thoughts once and for all and that you won't allow them, no matter what, to come back in. After you've dropped the thoughts like a hot potato, make sure you are being in your body. When you're anchored in the present moment, your chakras are open and working properly and your energy field is strong and luminous. Negativity can then no longer find its way in.

Q. *You often talk about Eckhart Tolle and his book,* The Power of Now. *Do you see him as your teacher?*

A. *The Power of Now* is the most powerful book I've ever read. It is also the highest vibrational book I've ever read. It has changed my life in so many amazing and profound ways, and continues to do so. I read passages from *The Power of Now* (or *Stillness Speaks*, another book by Eckhart Tolle) almost every day and often refer to it as "my bible." *The Power of Now* has a permanent place on my bedside table, regardless of whether I'm home or traveling. So yes, I do see Eckhart Tolle as my teacher. He is my earth teacher; my teacher in human form on earth. The White Light is my cosmic teacher.

About Being Intuitive and Empathic

Q. *I could completely relate to your story about being an empath. I am sensitive too, and pick up other people's feelings and thoughts. I feel drained and pulled down by other people. How can I protect myself?*

A. Previously I talked about the method of shielding, of protecting your energy field by engaging your solar plexus chakra. This is the quickest and easiest way to protect your energy. Of course, keeping your vibrations raised by doing the Chakra Cleanse Meditation also protects your energy, but the most important thing to do is *not* to worry about protecting your energy field.

When we worry if our energy is being protected or not, we become fearful. Fear makes our chakras constrict, and this stops chi and light from flowing into our energy field, making us less resilient and strong. The best way to protect our energy is to *not* be afraid.

It is a popular belief in the self-help and spiritual movement that to protect ourselves, we need to "disconnect." We're encouraged to visualize ourselves "cutting cords" that are connecting us to others or to visualize ourselves in a protective bubble or to close down some of our chakras or pray for protection. All this is detrimental and unnecessary, and usually carries with it a vibration of fear. (The fear-based thought of: I need to protect myself against others because they could harm me.)

If fear is the motivating force of *why* you are protecting yourself, it doesn't matter what technique you apply, you will simply attract more fear. (More people will steal your energy or you will become more fearful of people stealing your energy.) The most powerful way to protect your energy field is by being powerful! It's by raising your vibration by looking after your chakras, White Light zapping, and shielding. This way you become a *conduit* of love and light. You not only become luminous and immune to the negative psychic energy of others, you also act as a catalytic force. The White Light flows through you and into the lives of others.

Don't shut down and be fearful. Open up and spread the light!

Q. *In your story you talk about discovering that you are different things: a psychic, an empath, a sensitive, a medium, a ghost whisperer, a shadow hunter, and a truth-teller. Can you please explain what these different things mean?*

A. A psychic is a clairvoyant, someone who has "clear vision." We perceive and interpret energy and information through receiving visions and images through our mind's eye.

An empath is clairsentient, someone who has "clear feeling." We perceive and interpret energy and information through receiving feelings and emotions. Oftentimes we know how other people feel by feeling it in our own bodies. (Clairsentience is sometimes referred to as clairempathy.)

A sensitive refers to someone who is sensitive to the psychic and spirit realms and can detect and often interpret their meanings. A sensitive person is mostly clairsentient (clairempathic) and can be some or all the following: clairvoyant, clairaudient ("clear hearing"—perceives and interprets energy and information through hearing); clairscent ("clear scent"—perceives and interprets energy and information via smell); clairtangency ("clear touching"—perceives and interprets energy and information through touching); and clairgustance ("clear tasting"—perceives energy and information through psychically "tasting").

I have very heightened senses and have the ability to see, feel, hear, touch, and taste energy and information, but I predominately use clairvoyance and clairaudience.

A medium is someone with the ability—through any of the "clair senses" mentioned above—to connect to and communicate with spirits; with people who had lived on earth and are now back home on the Other Side.

A ghost whisperer is someone who has the ability—through any of the "clair senses" mentioned above—to connect to and communicate with ghosts; with people who have lived on earth and are still stuck or trapped on the earth plane.

"Shadow hunter" is a term I created to describe the new type of mystic and light worker who is incarnating on earth now. It is a mystic and light worker who works for the light in the realms of the dark. It's a light worker who isn't afraid of the shadow or the shadowlands; it's one that joyfully *hunts* the shadow to alchemize it and transform it into light. Though, until shadow hunters realize they are a shadow hunter and so are naturally attuned to the dark, they're often afraid of their abilities . . . But their gifts are powerful and most needed.

A truth-teller is someone who can see through the layers and masks of the ego to what lies beneath. Truth-tellers want to get to the heart and soul of things; they want to understand and illuminate the truth. They feel called to bust myths and challenge clichés and generalizations. They don't feel comfortable living within the status quo.

Q. *How can I become more psychic? I want to be more clairvoyant. I already sense things, so I'm clairsentient, but I want to see much more.*

A. Many people ask me how to become more clairvoyant. Like you, they want to have visions and see images and symbols in their mind's eye because they believe that clairvoyance is the "true" and "right" measure of a psychic or sensitive person. But you can be psychic and not be clairvoyant. I know—this is a contradiction in terms. Being clairvoyant means clear sight, and clear sight means being psychic, but when some people say, "I'm psychic," what they really mean is, "I'm intuitive." Nowadays the words "psychic," "sensitive," and "intuitive" are interchangeable.

Still, many people want to be able to "see." They want to have visions and images in their mind's eye, but clairvoyance, for many people, is not the most accurate or reliable clair sense. People who are clairvoyant also tend to rely on clairaudience as well as clairsentience to know how to interpret the energy and information they receive.

It is my experience that the most accurate sense is clairsentience. And it's also my experience that the most accurate and gifted intuitives are the ones who use clairsentience as well as some or *all* of the clair senses to derive their information. If you want to become an excellent psychic and intuitive, train your senses. Find out first which one (or ones) of your clair senses is dominant; when you receive "information" what form does it come in? Feeling, hearing, sight, and so on. Then train your secondary (weaker senses) to make them stronger. You can do this by spending a week at a time on each one of your secondary senses and exploring the world through them. For example, if clairaudience is a secondary sense, when you're out and about in the world or in meditation, focus only on what you can hear. Block out all the other senses and focus on hearing only. Next, do the same for clairgustance. When you're out and about or interacting with people or in meditation, try to "taste" how the world around you tastes. Of course, you aren't literally putting things into your mouth—you're psychically tasting the world around you . . . But you'll be surprised how much information you receive this way.

Often, to get an accurate understanding or diagnosis for a problem or ailment, I would use clairgustance (or clairscent). Then I could usually detect whether it was bacterial or fungal, etc., or what vitamins and minerals were lacking in someone's blood or body, etc.

Q. *It's my understanding that if our sixth chakra is open and working properly that we can all be intuitive. But I doubt if that is the case with me. I'm a Muggle (Harry Potter reference, meaning a non-magical/non-psychic person), and I never see or hear anything . . . I've been to numerous psychic development classes over the years, but nothing happens, ever. I'm always left feeling frustrated and sad because everyone else gets these amazing visions and receives these amazing messages, but it never happens for me. Are you sure that when I work on my lower chakras, enabling the energy to rise into my spiritual chakras, that I too will become intuitive?*

A. Yes, you will. When chakras 1 through 5 are strong enough and chi can easily flow into your chakras 6 and 7, you will become intuitive. This happens because you're energetically designed this way; to be "open" and sensitive. But when your spiritual chakras become activated, it doesn't necessarily mean you'll become clairvoyant. It does mean that one or some of your clair senses will become activated and that you too will be able to perceive and interpret energy and information.

However, many people that claim to be "Muggles" or "not psychic at all" often do sense things strongly. They are usually clairsentient, but because they don't realize this is an intuitive sense (and usually the most reliable), they disregard it.

Yes, this is true! I do sense a lot but I thought that meant I wasn't open and intuitive. Now I know I am!

Yes, and if you want to develop your clair senses further, train them (in the way I mentioned before). And you never know—your clair senses of clairvoyance and clairaudience may develop and you'll be able to see visions and hear messages.

Q. *Can you tell me more about how drugs can open you up and make you more psychic? You had a scary experience with acid, but I know people who have done ayahuasca and it really helped them become more psychic. Do you think taking drugs would help me?*

A. I think one needs to be cautious about taking drugs for this reason. Personally, I don't think it's necessary for most people. You are energetically designed to be intuitive, so all you need to do is get chakras 1 through 5 fit and healthy and then your spiritual chakras will naturally (and gently) open up. I also know many people (and have worked with many people) who have taken drugs or plant medicines to open up and it has had negative consequences. It has opened them up too quickly and they couldn't handle it or have experienced psychic blowout because of it. However, under the right circumstances—with the right person or shaman or guide—it can be helpful.

You mean like the story of Adam (Samuel's son), who raised his energy too quickly into his chakras 6 and 7 and became unstable?

Yes. Adam's energy field became severely imbalanced because his lower chakras weren't strong enough to hold the amount of energy being poured into his higher chakras . . . Although his case is extreme—most people don't suddenly become unstable— it often happens that people feel they can't cope. They feel ungrounded, detached from reality, and too "plugged in"; they can't handle their newfound abilities.

It is much easier and safer to follow the route nature intended for us: cleansing and strengthening our lower chakras so that the energy can *naturally* rise into the higher chakras.

Q. *You mention that there is a correlation between sudden hormonal changes and a spike in psychic/intuitive abilities. Can you speak more about this?*

A. Studies in psychic and supernatural phenomena have shown that there is a marked increase in poltergeist and spirit activity in homes or areas when a child who is intuitively gifted goes through puberty. For some reason this seems to "charge" or strengthen the abilities and powers of both the intuitive and spirit. Why this is, I don't know. When I went through puberty, my psychic sense suddenly become much stronger, almost overnight.

Women have told me the same about menopause: They suddenly find themselves much more open and intuitive.

Q. *Are you psychic about yourself? Can you look inside yourself and see what health problems you have? Can you do this with your own family?*

A. Yes and no. Mostly, I'm not psychic about my own self because I'm not objective about myself. I have fears and hopes and dreams, and this makes me "attached" . . . And when we're attached, our judgment is cloudy and we don't see things the way they *really* are. Through the practices of chakras, White Light, and mindfulness, though, I've become more objective. And because of this, I'm more detached. So, yes, I do see things and know things about myself and my family that one would call "psychic knowings."

Q. *I feel scared about opening up to my psychic and intuitive sensibilities. How can I make sure I don't see ghosts or become a shadow hunter like you? I want to see angels and auras but I don't want to see bad things or pick up bad energies.*

A. You can't have one without the other. You can't choose what you wish to see and don't wish to see. It doesn't work like that.

When you open up your spiritual chakras, you begin to see the world as it *really* is; how it's made up of light and dark. You also begin to see the many levels of vibration within our world, as well as the spirit beings and entities that inhabit them. Opening your spiritual chakras means expanding your limited perception so that you can see the truth: Here on earth and in the spirit realms there are higher and lower vibrations. *As above, so below.*

However, you can protect yourself from having your energy drained or brought down by lesser-evolved beings and ghosts by having a strong and luminous energy field. You'll remember from my story this was the way the ghost hauntings (as well as my being an oversensitive empath) stopped. I still saw ghosts (because ghosts are real), but they didn't affect me anymore. Don't be afraid of what you see. They are there anyway, so why fear them?

About Shadow Hunters and Ghosts

Q. *I would love to learn more about your experience of discovering that you are a shadow hunter and that shadow hunters are the new breed of mystic and light worker. This is the first time I've heard of this and it's fascinating!*

A. In my enlightened moment I saw that there was a new type of mystic and light worker now incarnating on earth; a light worker with a shadow-hunting, shadow-working skillset. Because the vibration of the planet is rapidly rising, more darkness than ever before is rising to the surface and it's the job of the shadow-working mystics and light workers to find the shadow (hunt it out) and help alchemize and transmute it. I wasn't given the words "shadow hunter" or "shadow worker" in my enlightened moment. I just called them this because these words best described what I saw.

My next book—book two in the Shadow Series—will deal with shadow hunting and shadow working, and in it you'll learn how to work for the light in the shadows.

Q. *You say that when you went into the cave, it felt as if you were about to do shadow work. And then you stepped onto the twelve spiritual lines and started freeing your soul fragments. Is this what you mean by shadow work, and is freeing our soul fragments something we also learn in your second book?*

A. Freeing your soul fragments is only one part of what you'll learn in the next book. There are other processes as well. Among other things, you'll take a journey into the shadowlands to heal your spiritual persecutions and to embrace your shadow-hunting, shadow-working nature.

Q. *You say you've come to accept that you are a shadow worker and that you are more attuned to the dark than the light, but what does this mean? That you see dark and depressing things all the time? If so, how do you cope?*

A. When I understood that I'm a shadow-hunting type mystic and light worker, it was hugely liberating! For a long time I'd experienced "spiritual shame." In spiritual groups and circles I was the one who saw the dark and what was wrong with people and the world, and I was often labeled "negative" and "serious." Compared to other light workers, I seemed dark and pensive. They were light and cheery and saw angels and unicorns and fairies, but I saw ghosts and poltergeists and problems in people's energy fields . . . It even happened to me once that someone told me that they didn't think I was a light worker but a dark worker! Of course, she was right. But at the time it was painful because I was afraid that there was something wrong with me. When I realized it was a *gift* to be naturally attuned to the dark, and that it was the way in which I do my light work, I no longer felt bad about myself.

Q. *When you talk about the ghosts I feel incredibly sad. I've never thought about the fact that they were once people and that they could have been someone I knew and loved . . . This is heartbreaking! It also makes me sad that we are taught to fear ghosts. They are portrayed in Hollywood films to be malevolent and destructive; you mostly don't see them as being lonely or frightened. But my question is, shouldn't we be afraid of ghosts? You had some terrible experiences with them. Shouldn't we be wary of them too? Or can we talk to them and try to help them? I must admit I'm still afraid of them and don't want to start suddenly seeing them like you do.*

A. The ghosts you see in the Hollywood films are mostly polter-geists. Angry and malevolent poltergeists only make up a fraction of the ghost population. Also, I was born a ghost whisperer and very psychic (too psychic), so what happened to me in my childhood was unusual. Although many children *do* see ghosts, most of them don't get harassed by them the way I did.

Even so, it's important to know that ghosts are needy, like anyone who is suffering and trapped and lonely. Because of this, trying to communicate with ghosts and help them can be exhausting; and if you're an empath type, you may pick up their feelings and emotions of deep suffering and this isn't a pleasant experience. One needs to learn how to deal with ghosts. Without this, the experience can be unsettling; and that is also why people are afraid of ghosts, because they have had an encounter with them and intuitively picked up the suffering of the ghost, and it was frightening.

Therefore, the best way to help ghosts is by creating your own luminous and powerful energy. When the light shines through you, it shines to them. So instead of trying to speak to or engage with ghosts, simply work on your own chakras.

You can also put your resident ghost on my weekly White Light healing list (see Appendix C). Every week I send thousands of people *and* ghosts White Light!

Q. *I see ghosts but I'm afraid. I saw them when I was a child and it was terrifying. It has taken me many years to be able to sleep at night without having the light on. Now I know that they are people who are suffering, people who can't find the light, I feel bad for them. I want to help but I'm so afraid.*

A. I understand your fear of ghosts. I have met very few people who aren't afraid of ghosts, and that's because ghosts (or the idea of ghosts) drives right to the heart of our core fears of vulnerability and safety. Most people see ghosts when they are in bed at night. This isn't because ghosts come prowling after us then—ghosts are always there, night and day—but in the night-time when it's dark, we have less stimulus and mental activity and are naturally more attuned to the subconscious and psychic part of ourselves. And this enables us to see and sense more . . . Many of us also had scary experiences when we were children and we either didn't tell anyone about it because we were afraid they'd think we were crazy, or we *did* tell someone about it and they told us we were making it up. So speaking about ghosts and the paranormal triggers deep fears in most people, and often-times people aren't willing to look at these fears and overcome them. They would rather pretend ghosts don't exist or hope that they don't see them.

But ghosts exist, and our fear and rejection of them *only* per-petuates the cycle. The more we fear death and ghosts, the less we're able to help people find the light after death.

Yet, as I said previously, I don't recommend that you work with ghosts directly. Don't try to communicate with them or engage them in discussion. Work on your own energy field and put them on the weekly White Light healing list. Many people do this and I've already helped them and their resident ghosts this way.

Q. *My son says that he sees things at night in his bedroom. He says there are shadows and dark things floating above him or hovering near the ceiling. He often comes into our bedroom at night but my husband doesn't like it. He says that he needs to learn to sleep in his own bedroom. But after hearing your story, I'm worried now that he might be seeing ghosts. What should I do?*

A. Many children see ghosts, so he may be seeing them. But it doesn't matter whether they are *really* there or if he is *creating* them to be there. Children have vivid imaginations, and I've experienced it many times with my daughter that when she'll watch a movie or read a book—about dinosaurs or witches or monsters—she'll tell me she is scared of seeing these things in her room or that she *is* seeing these things in her room. Of course that is her imagination, but then there are times when they *are* seeing something—dark shapes or figures of spirits or animals, and so on. In both cases, though, you respond in the same manner: You listen to your child so that they feel seen and heard, and you make sure you aren't, through your own fear, making them feel afraid. The most important thing is to validate your child's experience by making them feel safe, and the second most important thing is to raise your own vibrations to overcome your own fear.

Simply ask your child to describe to you what they are seeing and then tell them to close their eyes and visualize White Light in their energy field and chakras and around them. And then, channel White Light into your own energy field and chakras. Create your own luminosity! Until children are about seven or eight years old, they protect their own energy field *through* yours, so understand that the stronger you are energetically, the more they will not only be protected but also feel safe and secure. This is key.

Also, put your child on the free weekly White Light healing list (see Appendix C). This sends the ghosts over to the light and helps you and your child feel safe and protected.

Q. *Your experience of being exorcised was chilling. My question is how do you feel about the Christian church now? And do you believe that people can get possessed and need to be exorcised?*

A. I have no resentments or anger towards the pastor or the Christian church. Being exorcised was the most traumatic and terrifying experience I've had, but nowadays I see it as my greatest gift. People often say they find my approach to spirituality, the paranormal, and life in general *fearless and brave*, but when you've experienced what I have, when you've learned that our fear of things only increases fear in our lives, you learn to face your fears head on and overcome them.

I've lived too much of my life in fear. I want to stay free of it.

Yes, people can get possessed. This is not something that most people want to hear; most people want me to tell them that it's untrue and an urban legend, but unfortunately possession is real. However, it doesn't occur often, and when it does—when a ghost or entity fully takes over a person's psyche—the exorcism doesn't need to be as traumatic as they often are. The person conducting the exorcism shouldn't try to rip or pull ghosts out of people and then force them away. It can be done with gentleness and kindness, so that the ghost or entity possessing the person can find the light, and so that the one who was possessed doesn't have to undergo such a psychologically, psychically, and physically traumatic ordeal.

About Soul Purpose and Cosmic Chakras

Q. *You talk about chakras 8 through 12 being the gateway to understanding your soul's purpose. I'd like to access my soul's purpose. How can I do that?*

A. The first and most essential thing to do is to work on your lower chakras by doing the chakra balance meditation and channeling the White Light. You need them fit, clear, and strong so they can support your spiritual work. As you become more able to open and strengthen chakras 6 and 7 and as you continue to channel the White Light, you will naturally begin to be brought into chakra 8 (so that you can do shadow work), and then 9, and so on. But this process takes time.

If you commit to the work—cleanse your chakras, channel White Light, and be mindful—in time, it will happen! You can also sign up through my website for my weekly White Light healing list (see Appendix C) and ask for support as you do this work.

RESOURCES

Here are some additional resources I recommend and offer to support your spiritual practice and journey.

Books by Others

The Happiness Trap, Russ Harris
Anatomy of the Spirit, Caroline Myss
Why People Don't Heal and How They Can, Caroline Myss
The Power of Now, Eckhart Tolle
Stillness Speaks, Eckhart Tolle

My Resources

Free Weekly White Light Healings

Every Monday at 9 p.m., I send White Light to everyone who signs up for my free weekly White Light healing list. I've offered this service since 2008, and will continue to do so for the rest of my life. For more information and to sign up for these powerful healings, simply visit my website: www.belindadavidson.com.

Guided Chakra Cleanse for Busy People

Visit my online store, www.belindadavidson.com/store, to purchase the audio recording of my Chakra Cleanse Meditation (on my site it's called "The Guided Chakra Cleanse for Busy People"). Professionally recorded and set to a soundtrack of tranquil music, this meditation not only balances and cleanses your chakras, it also teaches you how to channel White Light for yourself.

White Light Stay at Home Retreat

Also available through my store: If you seek a more powerful experience with the White Light, I offer a White Light Stay at Home Retreat where over three days, I connect you to the White Light to help you clear blockages in your chakras and change your energy and change your life. More information on these powerful sessions is available on my website.

School of the Modern Mystic®

School of the Modern Mystic® is a unique and extensive online facility that teaches you how to create an exceptional life. Hundreds of people from all over the world experience the power of these trainings every year. In School of the Modern Mystic® you not only learn the chakric practices, White Light, and mindfulness (everything I learned in my enlightened moment), you also learn many advanced practices, like how to heal and manifest with the White Light and begin to work with your chakra 8.

If you want to learn how to change your energy; create perfect health, abundance, and magic; and discover what you were born to be—if you want to embrace your calling as a modern mystic—then School of the Modern Mystic® is for you! Learn more at www.schoolofthemodernmystic.com.

ACKNOWLEDGMENTS

MY HEARTFELT THANKS TO all who have supported and shared this journey with me: my friends and family (in this world and in the next); my amazing editor and friend, Kelly Madrone; my incredible copyeditor, Deb Baker; the White Light; and you, my treasured reader.

I thank you with all my heart chakra and send you White Light and love.

ABOUT THE AUTHOR

BELINDA DAVIDSON IS AN international speaker, author, and modern mystic. Her life purpose is to help people change their energy and heal their lives. She travels the world extensively, offering courses, workshops, and healings.

For almost twenty years, Belinda worked as a medical intuitive and coach. Among her clients were doctors, celebrities, CEOs, and well-known business leaders.

Belinda was born extrasensory and very psychic. "A curse in her childhood," she says. "A wonderful gift later in life."

Belinda is often described as a spiritual change agent and thought leader for her generation. But she feels most comfortable being described as a "modern mystic"—a modern-day woman with one foot in this world and one foot in another.

Made in the USA
Columbia, SC
03 November 2017